The Murray family,

The Imitation of Mary

Fr. [illegible]

Fr. Quan D. Tran, S.T.L.

The Imitation of Mary

Keys to Growth in Virtue and Grace

SOPHIA INSTITUTE PRESS
Manchester, New Hampshire

Cover design by LUCAS Art & Design, Jenison, MI.

Cover image: *The Virgin in Prayer*, ca. 1660 (COU65786), by Il Sassoferrato (Giovanni Battista Salvi) © Bridgeman Images.

Nihil Obstat: Reverend Father William B. Goldin, S.T.D.,
Censor Deputatus, May 8, 2020

Imprimatur: + The Most Reverend Kevin J. Vann, J.C.D., D.D.,
Bishop of Orange, May 13, 2020

Sophia Institute Press
Box 5284, Manchester, NH 03108
1-800-888-9344

www.SophiaInstitute.com

Library of Congress Cataloging-in-Publication Data

Names: Tran, Quan D., author.
Title: The imitation of Mary : keys to growth in virtue and grace / Fr. Quan D. Tran, S.T.L.
Description: Manchester, New Hampshire : Sophia Institute Press, 2020. | Includes bibliographical references. | Summary: "Examines twelve qualities of the Virgin Mary and explains how to emulate them"—Provided by publisher.
Identifiers: LCCN 2020029800 (print) | LCCN 2020029801 (ebook) | ISBN 9781644133293 (trade paperback) | ISBN 9781644133309 (ebook)
Subjects: LCSH: Mary, Blessed Virgin, Saint.
Classification: LCC BT603 .T73 2020 (print) | LCC BT603 (ebook) | DDC 232.91—dc23
LC record available at https://lccn.loc.gov/2020029800
LC ebook record available at https://lccn.loc.gov/2020029801

To Mary, our Mother and model

Contents

Foreword

In the Church of my formative years, signs of the life-giving, protective presence of Mary, the Mother of God, were everywhere, from the fifteen-decade rosary worn by my Dominican aunt and the Dominican sisters who taught me, to the solace that the Memorare afforded all of us in difficult moments, to the Blessed Mother's altar in our parish church where my mother would stop to light a candle and pray for us after every Mass. When I was an adult, my pilgrimages to Lourdes (especially the candlelit procession) and Guadalupe (where I had a profound experience of the Mother of God's presence) helped me to recover the sense of Mary's maternal love that somehow seemed to be waning in the Church and the world.

With his work *The Imitation of Mary: Keys to Growth in Virtue and Grace*, Fr. Quan Tran helps us to continue to experience the love of the Mother of God as an integral part of our lives. *The Imitation of Mary* is not just a devotional book to be read occasionally; indeed, Fr. Tran states that "the more we read and learn about and get to know Mary, the more we will fall in love with her." In addition, he refers to the role of Mary in his conversion and his daily life and explains how these experiences inspired him to preach and write about her. His reflections are not only a good summary of Catholic Marian theology; they are also a living testimony of how to walk hand in hand with Mary as a good disciple of Jesus Christ and to know that her exhortation "Do whatever He tells you" is not just a series of words on a page: it is an invitation for all of us to listen with our hearts to the Mother of God as she speaks to us each day of our lives!

+ The Most Reverend Kevin J. Vann, J.C.D., D.D.
Bishop, Diocese of Orange
August 8, 2020
Feast of St. Dominic

Acknowledgments

I am most grateful for all the prayers, support, and encouragement of so many parishioners, friends, and followers on social media. But I would like especially to acknowledge the contribution of the following people: Ellen Ha for her prayers, encouragement, and inspiration; Judy Bobier for her prayers, editing, and suggestions; Fr. Domenico Di Raimondo for his spiritual direction and guidance; Nancy Cesar for proofreading the manuscript; Fr. William Goldin for his theological and editorial suggestions; and the Carmelite Sisters of the Most Sacred Heart of Los Angeles for providing me a place to pray, write, and rest at their Sacred Heart Retreat House in Alhambra, California.

The Imitation of Mary

Introduction

The more we imitate Mary and respond positively to God's gifts, the more they will flourish.

And he came to her and said, "Hail, full of grace, the Lord is with you." (Luke 1:28).

Many people have asked me about the inspiration for my apostolate, Fullness of Grace, on which this book is based. I can point to three main ideas behind my work: first, many people do not fully understand the true meaning of supernatural grace and how it works. In order for grace to be effective, we must have a proper disposition and response to it. Second, by these dispositions and responses, we may *merit* an increase in grace. Third, God has given us a perfect model of these dispositions and responses in the Blessed Virgin Mary, our Mother. By imitating the qualities of the Blessed Virgin Mary, we may merit an overabundance of God's gifts.

The Imitation of Mary

Gifts Unclaimed

Many of us do not realize that we are missing out on many graces. In her *Diary*,[1] St. Faustina writes,

> Today I saw the Crucified Lord Jesus. Precious pearls and diamonds were pouring forth from the wound in His Heart. I saw how a multitude of souls was gathering these gifts, but there was one soul who was closest to His Heart and she, knowing the greatness of these gifts, was gathering them with liberality, not only for herself, but for others as well. The Savior said to me, Behold, the treasures of grace that flow down upon souls, but not all souls know how to take advantage of My generosity.[2]

1 In this book, private revelations are used uncritically; that is, they are accepted as true. But the faithful do not need to believe them. When the Church approves private revelations, she declares only that there is nothing in them contrary to matters of faith or morals, and that they may be read without danger or even with profit; no obligation is thereby imposed on the faithful to believe them. The *Catechism of the Catholic Church* states, "Throughout the ages, there have been so-called 'private' revelations, some of which have been recognized by the authority of the Church. They do not belong, however, to the deposit of faith. It is not their role to improve or complete Christ's definitive Revelation, but to help live more fully by it in a certain period of history. Guided by the Magisterium of the Church, the *sensus fidelium* knows how to discern and welcome in these revelations whatever constitutes an authentic call of Christ or his saints to the Church" (*Catechism*, no. 67, hereafter CCC). On the other hand, public revelation forms the deposit of faith entrusted to the apostles by Christ and handed down to the Church in the form of Sacred Scripture and Tradition. This kind of revelation ended with the death of the apostles, and must be believed by all the faithful.

2 Maria Faustina Kowalska, *Diary: Divine Mercy in My Soul*, 3rd rev. ed. (Stockbridge, MA: Marian Press, 2014), no. 1687.

The Lord wants to pour out torrents of graces upon us, but so many of us do not know how to receive all the gifts He wants to give. Only a few, those who are closest to His heart, know how to take advantage of His generosity for themselves and for others. It is a shame that so many graces intended for our benefit are left unclaimed and that, in effect, so many of God's gifts are refused and do not come to fruition.

Are we content with receiving just a few graces while missing so many? Or do we want to be like the soul who knows how to gather up in abundance the graces the Lord wants to give her, not only for herself, but for others as well? I know I can use all the graces I can get. I do not want to pass up any gift that the Lord wants to give me. I also want to receive the graces that God has in store for others through me. In short, I want to be one of the souls who know how to take advantage of the Lord's generous heart. Do you want to receive all the graces God wants to give you?

Response Required

Let us take a look at the definition of grace and focus on one element in particular that many people do not know about, one that makes a world of difference in whether or not God's gifts will bear fruit. Grace is a gift from God, but like any gift, it must be received, opened, and used. Otherwise, the benefits that go along with such a gift are not realized.

For instance, suppose I gave my brother a car rosary for his birthday. I put it in a box and left it on his living-room table because he was not home. But because he was so busy and distracted, he never noticed the box. In other words, my brother did not actually receive my gift. In another scenario, suppose that my brother did notice the box and opened it up and saw the car rosary, but then put it in his desk drawer and never used it. For all intents and purposes, he never used the gift and never enjoyed its benefits. In a third instance, suppose that my brother opened the box, took out the car rosary, and put it in his car. He enjoyed the rosary, and every time he drove somewhere, he would say a Hail Mary, asking Our Lady for protection. And whenever he had something on his mind, he would start praying the Rosary while driving. This habit of praying in the car would bring my brother closer to Mary and give him much consolation and peace. Furthermore, his friends might ask him about the rosary and then decide to purchase their own. Others, seeing the rosary hanging from the rearview mirror, might think about Mary and Jesus and prayer. In this last example, because my brother received and responded to the gift by using it, both he and others benefited from it, and these benefits multiplied.

So it is with grace. It is a gift from God that must be received, opened, and used for its benefits to be realized. Grace is a gift that calls for reception and response to be fruitful not only for its original recipient, but for others as well. The benefits of grace have the capacity to multiply and extend to others. Grace is not just something we *receive*, but we are invited to *use* that gift the way it was intended in order to attain and share its benefits. Because of this lack of understanding, many of us fail to have the proper disposition to receive and respond to God's grace and consequently miss out on fully enjoying the fruits of God's gifts.

The theological definition of grace is that it is a supernatural gift, which God in His benevolence bestows on human beings for their eternal salvation. The *Catechism* tells us: "Grace is *favor*, the free and undeserved help that God gives us to respond to his call to become children of God, adoptive sons, partakers of the divine nature and of eternal life."[3] Grace always calls for a response to

[3] CCC 1996.

make it fruitful. Grace is not forced upon us but is a gift that must be received and used. Otherwise, it does not fulfill its intended purpose.

Another analogy for grace is sailing a sailboat.[4] Imagine grace as the wind. The wind will come when God wants to lead us in a certain direction or guide us to a specific destination, which ultimately is heaven. But can we just sit there and do nothing and expect to get to our intended destination? Of course not. I do not know much about sailing, but I do know that we must at least pull up our anchor and then raise our sails. And not only do we have to raise and unfurl our sails, but we must adjust them accordingly in order to catch the wind and move where God wants to lead us. The more knowledgeable we are about how to respond and adjust our sails to take full advantage of the wind, or grace, the more quickly we will move and realize God's will for us. Cooperation with grace is always necessary in order to attain the fruits intended by God. St. Augustine tells us, "So while [God] made you without you, he doesn't justify you without you."[5] Response to grace is necessary for our salvation, for our sanctity, and for receiving more graces for our benefit and the benefit of others.

4 I think the sailboat analogy is most appropriate because grace is the work of the Holy Spirit, who is the wind or the breath of God. The Holy Spirit indeed appeared at Pentecost in the form of a noise like a strong driving wind that filled the house where the disciples were waiting. The Holy Spirit is also known as the gift and love of God, which is a description of grace itself. And the Holy Spirit is also known as the Sanctifier, which corresponds to sanctifying grace, which we will get to when we look at the different types of grace.

5 Augustine, "Sermon 169," in *The Works of Saint Augustine: A Translation for the 21st Century, Part III—Sermons*, ed. John E. Rotelle, O.S.A., trans. and notes Edmund Hill, O.P., vol. 5, *Sermons 151–183* (Hyde Park, NY: New City Press, 2018), 13.

Do Not Waste the Grace

In the Bible, St. Paul warns the Corinthians about the failure to respond to God's grace when he writes, "Working together with him, then, we entreat you not to accept the grace of God in vain" (2 Cor. 6:1). God worked through St. Paul and his preaching for the conversion of the Corinthians, but they needed to respond to this grace and be reconciled to God before they would truly benefit from His gift and have access to more graces. If they did not respond, St. Paul's words to them would have fallen on deaf ears, and they would not have received the benefits of God's grace.

St. Paul also speaks about his own response to God's grace, which enabled God to continue to work through him to bear much fruit: "But by the grace of God I am what I am, and His grace toward me was not in vain. On the contrary, I worked harder than any of them, though it was not I, but the grace of God which is with me" (1 Cor. 15:10). By generously responding to God's grace, Saul, the overzealous Pharisee who persecuted the early Christians, became *St. Paul*, the apostle to the Gentiles. Not only did St. Paul undergo a radical conversion, but the entire Church benefited from his ongoing and generous cooperation with God's grace. When we respond to God's grace, that initial grace becomes effective, and we merit additional graces not only for ourselves but also for others. In contrast, when there is a lack of response, the initial grace becomes ineffective and further graces are lost. If St. Paul had not responded to God's grace, the history and foundation of the Church and the Bible would be quite different.

Too often, many Christians fail to respond to grace as St. Paul did. It is true that many of us do not receive the same grace or vocation as St. Paul. Nevertheless, God has unique graces intended for each person: "But grace was given to each of us according to the measure of Christ's gift" (Eph. 4:7). Unfortunately, many of us do not cooperate with God's initial graces so that we may obtain benefits and merit more graces for ourselves and for others.

Effects of Grace

Now that we know that grace is a gift from God that requires a reception and a response in order for us to go where God leads us, let us examine the different effects of grace. Where does God want to lead us? What are the different functions of grace? What does God want to accomplish in and through us?

Grace Liberates

First, grace *liberates* us from the dominion of sin and concupiscence. It helps us to attain the true freedom of the children of God. The first effect of grace is conversion. God's grace helps us to see the harm caused by sin, as well as the goodness and mercy of God and His call to share in His life, love, and holiness. Grace gives us the desire and help to turn away from sin and to turn toward God for forgiveness and reconciliation. Because of our fallen human nature, we suffer the effects of concupiscence, which is the inclination to sin, to be puffed up with pride, and to rebel against God. The effects of concupiscence include inordinate self-love and disordered affections. We tend to love ourselves too much and to love created things more than we love God. Grace helps us recognize and fight against this tendency so that we may love Him rightly—that is, with all our mind, heart, soul, and strength—and love our neighbor as ourselves. In this way, our love and affections will become properly ordered.

The word for sin in Greek is *hamartia*, which literally means "missing the mark." Sin is when we fall short of our target. For example, instead of worshipping God at Mass on Sundays, we stay home to watch football or go shopping or go out with friends. By putting creatures before the Creator, we fall short of the true target and miss the mark of what is right and just and conducive to our greatest good. Our priorities get out of order, and we end up hurting ourselves and others and offending God. Grace helps us break free from the grip of sin and habitual vice and be reconciled with God, so that we are able to exercise control over our thoughts, words, and actions and live in a way that is most pleasing to God.

Grace Heals

A second effect of grace is medicinal; it *heals* the wounds caused by sin. Sin separates us from God, harms our dignity as His children, and wounds the Body of Christ. Grace restores our relationship with God and heals the wounds caused by our personal sins—wounds to ourselves, to our relationship with God, and to others. The wounds in our soul caused by sin tend to make it easier for us to continue to sin and to commit more-serious sins. Also, sin has a tendency to proliferate. For example, when we consider the matter of lying or using profanity, we see that if we do not lie or use profanity, we are less inclined to begin doing so. But if we start telling small white lies, we will find that lying becomes easier, and our lies get bigger and more serious. Before we know it, we are lying compulsively and simply out of habit. The same goes for using profanity. If we start using profanity, it becomes easier and more habitual, especially if we hear it commonly used in our surroundings. Again, before we realize it, we are using expletives routinely.

Grace heals the wounds caused by personal sin and helps us break the habit of sinning. Grace restores our dignity as children of God and helps us act and live in accordance with God's laws and commandments. Grace liberates us from the power and attraction of sin and strengthens our will to resist temptations and avoid becoming enslaved to the bondage of sin. Sin is addictive and has the power to pull us into a downward spiral, making us feel helpless and out of control and unable to free ourselves from the trap. Grace is needed to lift us out of the vicious cycle of vice and to liberate us from the dominion of sin. Grace also binds and heals our wounds so that we may become whole and spiritually healthy again.

To appreciate fully the power of grace to liberate and heal, ask anyone who engaged in a life of sin and then, through a powerful conversion, was liberated and set free. This includes anyone who suffered from addiction but, through the grace of God, was able to break his or her chains and embark on the path of recovery and true freedom. Grace is necessary to free us from the trifold spiritual enemy of the flesh, the world, and the devil. It is also necessary to heal us and make us whole so that we can properly order our loves, actions, and choices, and freely choose the good and reject the bad—or even a lesser good. Without grace, we would be enslaved to our passions and the works of the enemy, and our wounds would fester and spread. God, in His goodness and mercy, gives us grace so that we can put away the old self and put on Christ (see Eph. 4:22–24).

Grace Elevates

Third, grace *elevates* our human nature, enabling us to participate in the divine nature. Grace gives us a share in the divine life and gives us a new life in God. Indeed, at Baptism, we become a new creation; we are created anew to partake in the divine life. At Baptism, we are grafted onto Christ and truly become a son or daughter of God the Father. Then, God the Father sees not only us but also our oneness with Jesus. At Baptism, we begin to be transformed into the likeness of Christ. We become more like Jesus as we are sanctified and deified by grace and come to share in the life and love and grace of the Blessed Trinity. We can even participate in the divine life now, while we are still here on earth, which prepares us to experience its fullness in heaven.

During the Mass, the priest quietly says to himself several prayers that are inaudible to the congregation. One such prayer is said as he prepares the gifts and pours a little water into the wine and says quietly, "By the mystery of this water and wine, may we come to share in the divinity of Christ, who humbled Himself to share in our humanity." The water represents our humanity, and the wine represents Christ's divinity. By the action of mixing a little water with the wine and by his prayer, the priest is asking that the grace of the Eucharist elevate our human nature so that we may participate ever more fully in the divine nature of Christ.

This should not come as a surprise. In Scripture, St. Peter tells us, "[God] has granted to us his precious and very great promises, that through these you may escape from the corruption that is in the world because of passion, and become partakers of the divine nature" (2 Pet. 1:4). This is what it means to be holy, to be sanctified. Only God is holy, and so to become holy is to become like God. With the help of God's grace, we are able to become holy as the Father is holy by sharing in His divine nature. This is the reason Jesus became one with us and underwent His Passion, death, and Resurrection. St. Athanasius writes, "The Son of God became man so that we might become God."[6] This is possible through the Sacrament of Baptism, when we die to our old self and are re-created in Christ. We share in the divine nature by becoming one with Christ at Baptism and cooperating with grace throughout our life in order to grow in our conformity to Jesus.

Grace Empowers

Fourth, grace *empowers* us to do what is beyond our natural capacity. God knows, as do we, that our fallen human nature is weak and vulnerable, and so He helps us by guiding us and strengthening us

6 St. Athanasius, *De Incarnatione* 54, 3: PG 25, 192B, quoted in CCC 460.

to move in the right direction. Grace works with our human nature because God respects our free will. God may sometimes intervene and inspire us to desire something good that is beyond our natural human capacity. If we respond by pursuing the good yet difficult act, God will give us the necessary grace to accomplish the task that would normally be beyond our natural abilities. By cooperating with God's grace of inspiration, we merit additional graces, and our actions are meritorious for ourselves and others as well.

An example of this spiritual truth occurs when the angel of Satan gives St. Paul a thorn in the flesh. Three times, St. Paul asks the Lord to take it away, but the Lord says, "My grace is sufficient for you, for my power is made perfect in weakness" (2 Cor. 12:9). Thereafter, St. Paul willingly boasts of his weakness in order that the power of Christ may dwell in him. Grace allowed St. Paul to see the benefit of suffering and to be content to suffer so that the power of Christ might be manifested in him. This is like the martyrs' courage, faith, and even levity while enduring persecution, torture, and death. The martyrs' cooperation with grace not only benefitted the martyrs themselves but also helped to build up the Church. Tertullian wrote, "The blood of martyrs is the seed of Christians."[7] St. Paul speaks about how his suffering benefits the Church: "Now I rejoice in my sufferings for your sake, and in my flesh I complete what is lacking in Christ's afflictions for the sake of his body, that is, the Church" (Col. 1:24). Grace empowers us to accomplish things beyond our natural human capacity so that we may grow in holiness and contribute to the good of others.

[7] Tertullian, *Apology* 50, 13: PL 1, 603, quoted in Vicente Carcel Orti, "Pope John Paul II's teaching on the martyrs of our century," *Tertium Millennium*, March 1997, http://www.vatican.va/jubilee_2000/magazine/documents/ju_mag_01031997_p-56_en.html.

Types of Grace

So how do we know how to respond to God's grace, benefit from His gift, and receive even more gifts? This requires a look at the different types of grace and their intended effects.

The first is *sanctifying grace*, first given to us at Baptism. The purpose of this grace is to make us holy and pleasing to God. It is a gift that habitually transforms us into the likeness of Christ. It works in us slowly and gradually to make us perfect. With sanctifying grace, we develop good habits and grow in virtue. Sanctifying grace prepares us for the beatific vision as we begin to share in the life, love, and glory of God, and experience a taste of heaven on earth. *Sacramental graces* fall under this category, as each sacrament has its own particular gift: the graces of Baptism incorporate us into the family of God; the Eucharist nourishes us spiritually; Confession reconciles us with God; Confirmation strengthens us to bear witness to Christ; and the Anointing of the Sick heals us.

Within sanctifying grace, there is *habitual grace*, which is the permanent disposition to live and act in keeping with God's call to be His children and to share in His love, life, and eternal glory. This includes the infused theological virtues of faith, hope, and love; the moral virtues of prudence, justice, fortitude, and temperance; the gifts of the Holy Spirit, which are wisdom, understanding, counsel, fortitude, knowledge, piety, and fear of the Lord; and the fruits of the Holy Spirit, which are charity, joy, peace, patience, kindness, goodness, generosity, gentleness, faithfulness, modesty, self-control, and chastity. These infused virtues and gifts make the soul capable of loving God, following His commandments, and turning away from sin.

Besides *habitual grace*, there are *actual graces*, which are temporary interventions by God to inspire us to perform salutary acts and enable us to carry out the good deeds that will contribute to our salvation and the salvation of others. This is done at the beginning of conversion and in the course of sanctification.

Within *actual graces*, there is a distinction between *operating grace* and *cooperating grace*. *Operating grace* is when God begins to act within us to move our will and to inspire us to do something that is conducive to our sanctification. *Cooperating grace* is given to assist us in cooperating with God to respond to His inspiration and to carry out good deeds. When God gives operating grace, He also gives cooperating grace. But He respects our free will to cooperate with His inspiration or not. If we choose to cooperate, then the grace is there to assist us in performing the inspired act. But we can also reject God's inspiration, or not respond fully in carrying out the inspired deed, and hence not fully utilize or benefit from God's graces.

There is an order to God's work in sanctifying the soul, and this order is facilitated by graces called *prevenient grace* and *subsequent grace*. The order of the effects of these graces is as follows: first, God gives the grace to inspire us to conversion and to heal our soul. Next, He gives the grace to aspire to holiness. This is followed by His gift of grace to accomplish good deeds and grow in virtue. Finally, God gives us the grace to persevere in goodness and thereby attain eternal glory. At each stage, we are free to respond and cooperate with God's grace and advance in perfection or to reject and not cooperate with God's grace and not move forward on our spiritual journey.

Another other type of grace is a *charism*. St. Paul writes:

> To each is given the manifestation of the Spirit for the common good. To one is given through the Spirit the utterance of wisdom, and to another the utterance of knowledge according to the same Spirit, to another faith by the same Spirit, to another gifts of healing by the one Spirit, to another the working of miracles, to another prophecy, to another the ability to distinguish between spirits, to another various kinds of tongues, to another the interpretation of tongues. (1 Cor. 12:7–10)

These *charisms* are given to us for the benefit of others and to help build up the kingdom of God. Some of these charisms are more ordinary, such as teaching or administration, while others are more extraordinary and miraculous, such as healing and prophecy. Three indicators point to a possible charism: something we do exceptionally well and much better than the average person; something we enjoy doing because it comes naturally to us and we do not consider it burdensome work; and something others benefit from in a supernatural way and that contributes to the building up of the Body of Christ.

Lastly, there is the grace of the *state in life*, which helps us to fulfill our vocation in life, whether it be the priesthood, religious life, married life, or the single life. For married people, the grace of the Sacrament of Matrimony often remains untapped because of the failure of the parties to respond to and live out fully their vocation to the married life. Pope Pius XI writes:

> Since it is a law of divine Providence in the supernatural order that humans do not reap the full fruits of the Sacraments which they receive after acquiring the use of reason unless they cooperate with grace, the grace of matrimony will remain for the most part an unused talent hidden in the field unless the parties exercise these supernatural powers and cultivate and develop the seeds of grace they have received. If, however, doing all that lies within their power, they cooperate diligently, they will be able with ease to bear the burdens of their state and to fulfill their duties. By such a sacrament they will be strengthened, sanctified and in a manner consecrated.[8]

[8] Pope Pius XI, Encyclical Letter on Christian Marriage *Casti Connubii* (December 31, 1930), no. 41.

All graces, including those of Matrimony and Holy Orders, require our cooperation in order to bear fruit and achieve that which God intended.

All these different types of graces have much in common. They are God's gifts to help us grow in holiness and fulfill our vocation as God's children and as His instruments in the world. The more we use our free will and respond to and cooperate with each grace, the more fully we will share in the life and love of God and merit additional graces toward our own sanctification, as well as contribute to the sanctification of others.

In summary, grace is important and necessary for the following reasons: the goal in life is to be sanctified, and the means to sanctification is grace. Grace is the means by which we become holy, share in the life of God, and attain eternal life. Grace leads us to God, conforms us to God, and unites us to God, who is our end, our goal, our happiness, and the one for whom we were made. Grace empowers us with special charisms to build up the Church and live out our vocation and state in life.

Free Will and Merit

What sets us apart from the rest of visible creation is our free will and our intellect. Made in the image and likeness of God, we are rational, intelligent beings with a free will so that we may choose the good, reject the bad, love God and neighbor, and participate in God's eternal life, love, and happiness. God gives us free will because of His immense love for us. He knows that many will misuse it, choose sin and evil, and reject His love, but He wants us to resemble Him in a radical way. He wants us to be able to love and share in His friendship and to be creative and participate in His work of sanctification and salvation. Without free will and intellect, we would be less than human; we would be robots incapable of love and relationship.

Our free will can be misused and abused and become a cause of sin and evil and destruction. Yet at the same time, it can be strengthened and rightly ordered and conformed to God's will and become a source of life, love, and goodness. Our free will has the capacity to please God and to help others as we cooperate with Him in building His kingdom on earth. Our free will has the power to contribute to our own sanctification and help us become God's instrument for good in the world. In other words, our free will allows us to cooperate with God's grace and merit additional graces for our good and for His glory.

By giving us free will, God gives us the ability to merit the blessings that He wants to bestow upon us and the world. Our ability to merit is part of God's will, which is to include us in His work of salvation and sanctification. It pleases God when, using our free will, we choose to participate with His grace to grow in virtue and perform good deeds and acts of love. He then rewards our efforts and good intentions with more graces and gifts. St. Augustine said that in crowning our merits, God crowns His own gifts. We are incapable of meriting anything on our own. It is God who gives us the grace to desire, choose, and achieve the good. The *Catechism* explains our capacity to merit in this way: "Since the initiative belongs to God in the order of grace, *no one can merit the initial grace* of forgiveness and justification, at the beginning of conversion. Moved by the Holy Spirit and by charity, *we can then merit* for ourselves and for others the graces needed for our sanctification, for the increase of grace and charity, and for the attainment of eternal life."[9] Grace is the gift of God and the action of the Holy Spirit in our soul. It inspires us, sanctifies us, and empowers us to accomplish great things. If we cooperate with grace, we merit more graces. We must remember that our ability to merit is limited to our time on earth.

9 CCC 2010, emphasis original.

In the next life, we will be incapable of meriting additional graces for ourselves or for others.

After Vatican II, the word *merit* became unpopular and fell into disuse because it brought back memories of strict discipline, rigidity, and the false notion that we have to earn salvation; in its place, God's love, mercy, and grace were emphasized to the exclusion of our own role and participation in God's plan of salvation. There was a loss of the sense of personal sin, the acknowledgment of our fallen human nature, and the need to cooperate with God's grace. Slowly, the pendulum has started to swing back toward the center. People realized that it is not "either/or" but "both/and." Faith needs good works, Scripture needs Tradition, and grace needs cooperation. The revised translation of the Roman Missal in 2011 made the English closer and more faithful to the original Latin, and we started seeing the word *merit* more frequently. Know that God values our free will and desires our cooperation, and if we use our free will correctly and generously, we can merit tremendous graces for ourselves and for others.

Mary, Full of Grace

The angel Gabriel said to Mary, "Hail, full of grace, the Lord is with you" (Luke 1:28). How is it that Mary is full of grace? One reason is that she was chosen from all eternity to be the Mother of Jesus, not an insignificant role in the history of salvation. But did Mary have free will? Yes. Like every human person, Mary had free will. In fact, one can say that Mary's free will was *truly* free because she did not suffer from concupiscence. By her Immaculate Conception, Mary was free from the stain of Original Sin from the moment of her conception. By the grace of God and her free response, Mary remained free of any personal sin for her entire life. She exercised her free will in the most perfect way and merited for herself, and for the whole world, an abundance of grace. Our Blessed Mother conformed her will to God's will at each moment and cooperated perfectly with every grace given to her by God. She fulfilled her vocation faultlessly, and in doing so, Mary merited and obtained the fullness of grace fitting for her role as the Mother of God and Mother of the Church.[10]

Mary is full of grace not only because she is the Mother of God but also because she is the most perfect of all the disciples of Christ. In fact, Jesus pointed to Mary's discipleship, rather than her motherhood, as being worthy of praise. In the Gospel of Luke, we read: "A woman in the crowd raised her voice and said to him, 'Blessed is the womb that bore you, and the breasts that you sucked!' But he said, 'Blessed rather are those who hear the word of God and keep it!'" (Luke 11:27–28). Jesus was not saying that Mary is not blessed. He was saying that Mary *is* blessed not because she is His Mother but because she hears and observes the word of God in a flawless manner.

As Jesus was about to die, He gave a last commandment to St. John, His disciple standing at the foot of the Cross. This last commandment was meant not only for St. John but for all of Jesus' disciples, because St. John represents all of us. Scripture tells us: "When Jesus saw his mother, and the disciple whom he loved standing near, he said to his mother, 'Woman, behold, your son!' Then he said to the disciple, 'Behold, your mother!' And from that hour the disciple took her to his own home" (John 19:26–27). Before leaving this world, Jesus gave His Mother, Mary, to all of us to be our Mother, protector, and model.

10 In 2018, Pope Francis instituted a new memorial: Mary, Mother of the Church, to be celebrated on the Monday after Pentecost in the Roman Catholic Church. This may be a new memorial, but it is a traditional title for Mary and recognizes her role as the Mother and the model for all the disciples of Christ.

And because Mary is our Mother, we are to look up to her, learn from her, and take after her. Mary is not only our Mother but also our model. She is the most perfect model of discipleship, a chosen vessel and exemplar of all perfection. Mary is God's masterpiece, the finest of His creation, and the most perfect of human beings. St. John Vianney writes, "The Eternal Father delights in regarding the Heart of the Blessed Virgin Mary as the masterpiece of His hands."[11] If we want to grow in grace, we look to Our Lady, who received the fullness of grace and brought it to perfect fruition. Mary received the fullness of grace by responding to God's grace with her free will in the most sublime way. A loving and caring Mother, Mary is eager to help her children become everything God created them to be: holy and blameless in His sight. As Mary fulfilled her vocation as the Mother of God, she also wants to fulfill her vocation as our Mother and the Mother of the Church. But Mary can help us only to the extent that we accept her help, go to her, know her, love her, and desire to imitate her.

When we learn from Mary and imitate her qualities, we learn how best to respond to God's gifts and so attain the fullness of grace that He has in store for each one of us. God has different graces for each person. St. Thomas Aquinas confirms that the graces intended for each person are different and explains why: "Hence the first cause of this diversity is to be sought on the part of the God, Who dispenses His gifts of grace variously, in order that the beauty and perfection of the Church may result from these various degrees; even as He instituted the various conditions of things, that the universe

[11] *Mary Day by Day: Marian Meditations for Every Day Taken from the Holy Bible and the Writings of the Saints*, with an introduction by Rev. Charles G. Fehrenbach, C.Ss.R. (Totowa, NJ: Catholic Book Publishing, 1987), 8.

might be perfect."[12] The diversity we see in each other reflects God's own beauty, imagination, and creativity. Made in His image and likeness, each of us reflects certain attributes of God: kindness, humility, beauty, honesty, creativity, intelligence, and more.

Similarly, St. Thérèse of Lisieux writes:

> He [Jesus] set before me the book of nature; I understood how all the flowers He had created are beautiful, how the splendor of the rose and the whiteness of the Lily do not take away the perfume of the little violet of its scent or the delightful simplicity of the daisy. I understood that if all flowers wanted to be roses, nature would lose her springtime beauty, and the fields would no longer be decked out with little wild flowers. And so it is in the world of souls, Jesus' garden. He willed to create great souls comparable to Lilies or roses, but He has created smaller ones, and these must be content to be daisies or violets, destined to give joy to God's glances when He looks down at his feet. Perfection consist in doing His will, in being what He wills us to be.[13]

We are called to respond fully to the graces that God has in store for us individually. Each of us is unique and unrepeatable. In the history of the world, there will never be another you or another me. God has destined each one of us to exist at this particular time, in this place, and to grow in His grace and bear much fruit. Jesus tells us, "You did not choose me, but I chose you and appointed you that you should go and bear fruit and that your fruit should

[12] Thomas Aquinas, *Summa Theologica* I-II, q. 112, art. 4 (hereafter cited as *ST*).

[13] *The Story of a Soul: The Autobiography of St. Thérèse of Lisieux*, trans. John Clarke, O.C.D. (Washington, DC: ICS Publications, 1996), 14.

abide" (John 15:16). Like Mary, each of us has a role to play in God's plan of salvation. If we imitate our Blessed Mother, we, too, can fully live out our vocation and fulfill our role in God's ongoing work of redemption.

When we imitate our Blessed Mother, we do not lose our own identity. On the contrary, we discover our authentic identity as the person God created us to be, free from sin and capable of cooperating with His grace for our own sanctity and that of others. When we imitate our Mother and model, we acquire the temperaments, dispositions, and qualities that are most pleasing to God. The attributes of the Virgin Mary are most conducive to meriting more graces. Mary's soul is like the rich soil in which God is free to plant seeds of grace knowing that they will grow and flourish and blossom into beautiful trees that provide necessary shade and bear much fruit for the world. When our life takes on the qualities of our Blessed Mother, we become like porous sponges that can absorb all the graces that God wants to give us. These qualities make us most receptive to God's gifts. We will be like that one soul in St. Faustina's vision who was closest to the heart of Jesus, the one who gathered all the gifts for herself and for others.

The dispositions and actions of Mary are ideal for meriting an increase in graces. Remember, the graces we receive individually also affect the entire Body of Christ. We are all connected. When one member thrives, the whole Body benefits. And vice versa, when members do not live up to their potential, the Body suffers the consequences. Personal holiness contributes to the building of God's kingdom on earth both positively and negatively. God wants us not only to grow in holiness but also to become a channel of grace for others. As with Mary, God wants us to become His presence, His instruments, and His representatives, so that through us, He can dispense grace to others. When we go to heaven, we are not meant to go as a lone star but as one star leading a cluster of other stars. If we live out our vocation, we will be forming a new constellation of stars in the sky of heaven. We are called to lead our families, friends, and communities to God. Mary, as our Mother, guide, and example, shows us how to achieve the fullness of grace by meditating upon and imitating her qualities.

These attributes of Mary are not limited to her alone; they are also the attributes of Jesus and the saints. These qualities are pleasing to God, based on Scripture, and confirmed by the saints. It is my hope that some of you will learn something new or be reminded of an attribute that you would like to cultivate. You may already be familiar with these qualities and may be practicing them, but perhaps others will learn something new, or receive a heightened perspective, or be reminded of an area in their lives that needs more attention. And there may be some of you who will look at grace in a totally different way and learn the various practices by which you may even merit an increase in God's gifts.

By meditating on these attributes of the Blessed Virgin Mary and asking the Holy Spirit to enlighten us about the ones in which we are most lacking, we can then focus on and practice those qualities that are most difficult for us. Different qualities will come up at various times to remind us where we still need to grow. As we practice these qualities, they will become more ingrained and take on the form of habits, and we will develop a permanent disposition that is most conducive to an increase in grace. Once they become part of our personality and way of life, we will grow rapidly in grace and become God's instrument in the world. We will fulfill our vocation to holiness, bear witness to Christ, and build God's kingdom on earth.

1

Humility

The humbler we are, the more God will lift us up.

For he has regarded the low estate of his handmaiden. (Luke 1:48)

Humility Is Truth

Is humility a virtue? That depends on whom you ask. Jesus, St. Augustine, and St. Thomas Aquinas would definitely say that humility is a virtue, while most people in the world would probably say that it is not. Our culture does not view humility in a favorable light. Generally, humility has a negative connotation. It is often seen as weakness and timidity, as being a doormat, as being easily pushed around, stepped on, and taken advantage of by others. A humble person is regarded as one who does not have a backbone or the courage to stand up to others for what he or she believes. Humility is not usually viewed as a quality to be desired, but a personality flaw to be guarded against and overcome.

Many people, including Catholics, do not understand the *true* meaning of humility. To be humble is not to be weak or timid or to let others walk all over us. Instead, it is about recognizing the truth of who we are and who God is. St. Teresa of Avila describes humility as truth. Humility is knowing the truth that we are creatures, God is the Creator, and we are completely dependent on Him for everything. The truth is, not only did God create us out of nothing, but He continually sustains us. If God stopped thinking about us for one moment, we would cease to exist.

Our Lord said to St. Catherine of Siena: "Do you know, daughter, who you are, and who I am? If you know these two things you will be blessed. You are she who is not; whereas I am He who is. Have this knowledge in your soul and the Enemy will never deceive you and you will escape all his wiles; you will never disobey my commandments and will acquire all grace, truth, and light."[14] The truth is that we are nothing without God. We receive our being, our life, and all that is good from God as gifts.

Humility comes from the Latin word *humus*, which means "of the earth." The second chapter of the book of Genesis describes the creation of humankind: "The LORD God formed man of dust from the ground, and breathed into his nostrils the breath of life; and man became a living soul" (Gen. 2:7). Humble people are down-to-earth and grounded in the truth of their origin. When we receive ashes on Ash Wednesday, we are told, "Remember that you are dust and to dust you shall return." Humble people remember their roots, accept their mortal nature, and rely utterly on God.

Humility helps us recognize our nothingness. We are nothing without God. It also helps us realize the truth and effects of our fallen human nature: we are ignorant, weak, limited, and suffer from an inclination to evil. St. Paul speaks about this universal inner battle between right reason and the inclination to sin: "For I

[14] Raymond of Capua, *The Life of St. Catherine of Siena: The Classic on Her Life and Accomplishments as Recorded by Her Spiritual Director*, trans. George Lamb (Charlotte, NC: TAN Books, 2003), 62.

do not do the good I want, but the evil I do not want is what I do" (Rom. 7:19). When we recognize our capacity for evil, compared with God's mercy, goodness, and generosity, we cannot help but be humble.

Sometimes, it is easier to describe humility by describing what it is *not*. Humility is not about putting ourselves down or refusing to acknowledge the good that is in us. Sure, we all have different talents, gifts, and skills, which should rightfully be acknowledged. But we should also give credit where credit is due. Humility is realizing and acknowledging that everything we are and everything we have and all the good that we are capable of doing are gifts from the Lord. St. Paul asks: "What have you that you did not receive? If then you received it, why do you boast as if it were not a gift?" (1 Cor. 4:7). We do not let our talents and accomplishments go to our head, but know that God is the Giver of all that is good.

Humility is also not about putting ourselves down. Rather, it frees us from preoccupation with ourselves. One way to put it is that humility is not thinking less of ourselves; it is thinking of ourselves less. As a society, we tend to be self-absorbed. We are way too concerned about our own interests, image, and agenda. Humility takes our time, energy, and focus away from ourselves and orients them toward God and others. Humility frees us from our habit of self-preoccupation.

Humility is also not mediocrity. We do the best we can with our gifts and talents for the glory of God while acknowledging our limitations and need for grace. When we do something well, we know it is because of God's help. When we do something wrong, we rightfully attribute it to our shortcomings. Humility is the necessary disposition that puts everything in right order. A humble person recognizes that the Lord is in charge and deserves all the credit. The Lord is the artist, we are the brush; He is the musician, we are the violin; He is the sculptor, we are the chisel.

The Lord deserves all the praise and glory. Humility helps us to see ourselves as we really are—God's creation and instrument, called to cooperate with Him in His work in the world. But we are nothing without the Lord, and any good that we can do is because of God's grace.

Humility indeed is countercultural. The world tells us that we need to have *self*-confidence and *self*-esteem and believe in *our own* abilities to accomplish whatever we set our minds to. This may be nice to hear, but it is not true, and it creates a false sense of self. It is fine to dream, but we also must face reality. When I was a boy, I secretly wanted to be Michael Jordan, able to take off from the free-throw line and fly through the air and dunk the basketball. But then reality hit when I realized that I could not jump high enough to touch the rim of the basket. I also secretly wanted to be a rock star, and I would play air guitar to my favorite songs alone in my room and in front of a full-length mirror. But when I took guitar lessons, I discovered, to my dismay, that I was not musically gifted. Although I love music, I was not going to be the next rock star. The truth is that each of us is unique and has different gifts and talents, which also means that we have different weaknesses and limitations. An inflated sense of self creates an illusion of invincibility and blinds us to our need for God.

Contrary to our culture, Jesus tells us, "Take my yoke upon you, and learn from me; for I am gentle and lowly in heart, and you will find rest for your souls" (Matt. 11:29). When we are meek and humble, we do not have to prove anything to anyone. We peacefully accept our own limitations and weaknesses and trust in the Father. There is a peace that comes from surrendering to the Lord and relying on His grace rather than on our own abilities.

Unfortunately, as with humility, our culture associates *meekness* with weakness and timidity. But meekness is more like gentleness: the ability to be patient and to respond with composure, and even kindness, to a person or situation that is unjust or hostile. For instance, when Jesus was being interrogated by the high priest, He was struck by one of the temple guards, but He quietly responded, "If I have spoken wrongly, bear witness to the wrong; but if I have spoken rightly, why do you strike me?" (John 18:23). Rather than weakness, meekness requires tremendous strength to be calm and patient in the face of difficulties. It is easy to lash out, to react to anger and hostility with more anger and hostility. But we need to break the cycle of escalating rage and insults. Those who are meek speak the truth with love and work for peace and justice. But at the same time, they realize that God is ultimately in charge and will make all things right.

We do not have to wait for a hostile encounter or a major incident of injustice to practice meekness. We can learn to be meek and humble in everyday life by putting up with small inconveniences and annoyances patiently and by not demanding that our preferences, comfort, or desires be accommodated, but letting others have their way. Also, we can practice not being the center of attention. Let go of the need to impress or make a favorable impression. Try to become less self-conscious and more "God-conscious," seeing the spark of the divine in others. Regardless of the circumstances, try to see the image of God in each and every person, even in someone with a rough exterior or abrasive personality.

It should not come as a surprise that the teaching of Jesus is rejected by our culture. Jesus warned: "If the world hates you, know that it has hated me before it hated you. If you were of the world, the world would love its own; but because you are not of the world, but I chose you out of the world, therefore the world hates you" (John 15:18–19). In His farewell address at the Last Supper, Jesus prayed that His disciples, who remained *in* the world, would *not be of* the world: "I have given them your word; and the world has hated them because they are not of the world, even as I am not of the world. I do not pray that you should take them out of the world, but that you should keep them from the evil one. They are not of the world, even as I am not of the world. Sanctify them in the truth; your word is truth" (John 17:14–17). Because we live in the world, it is difficult for us not to be influenced by the world. Slowly, we tend to take on the prevailing views of society if we are not vigilant. Jesus knew this would happen, and so He prayed that the Father would consecrate us in the truth of His Word.

Clear the Ground

Humility is an essential disposition if we wish to lay the groundwork for a spiritual life. Before building a structure, we must first clear the ground, taking out all the weeds, rocks, and overgrown plants. If this is not done, the foundation cannot be laid. Humility, similarly, entails uprooting and clearing away unwanted pride and overgrown ego to prepare us to receive properly the other virtues as well as the gift of faith, which is the foundation of the spiritual life.

Where there is no humility, there is its opposite—pride—which is a huge obstacle to faith and the other virtues. One reason why the world does not have faith is because it does not have humility. As long as humility is shunned, pride will rear its ugly head, and the foundation of faith cannot be laid. Pride is excessive self-esteem and an inflated sense of one's own excellence. Vainglory, or vanity, which is a sister to pride, is being obsessed with parading our excellence and making a good impression. We want to exalt ourselves, and we want others to pay attention to us. But this can lead to self-indulgence and narcissism. Pride, in its fullest sense, is the refusal to acknowledge our subjection to God and is considered the worst of all vices. St. Gregory the Great and St. Thomas Aquinas call pride the "queen" or "mother" of all vices because it gives birth to other sins.

On the contrary, St. Bernard states, "Humility is the mother of salvation." Since humility is truth, it sets us free. Humility frees us to be ourselves. It frees us from the need to put up a facade, to pretend to be someone we are not, or to make a favorable impression. Are we too concerned about our image and what others think of us? Recall all the perfect images and selfies we post of ourselves on social media. A humble person does not need to be noticed, to impress others, or to receive compliments or accolades. Humility gives us true freedom to discover ourselves and to be comfortable in our own skin. As pride is the root of all sins, humility is the foundation of all virtues. Humility clears away pride to allow us to lay the foundation for the other virtues. St. Augustine observed: "It was pride that caused the Fall. If you ask me the ways to God, I would tell you the first is humility, the second is humility, the third is humility."[15] Humility is a prerequisite to the spiritual life and the other virtues, because without it, we do not get very far.

The Servant Handmaid

Is the Blessed Virgin Mary humble? How can we tell? From her own words, we come to know more about Mary—her thoughts, feelings, and dispositions. At the Annunciation, Mary refers to herself as "the handmaid of the Lord" (Luke 1:38). In her Magnificat, a spontaneous canticle that comes forth from her soul, we hear the same sentiment: "He has regarded the low estate of

[15] Augustine, "Letter 118," in *The Works of Saint Augustine: A Translation for the 21st Century, Part II—Letters*, ed. Boniface Ramsey, trans. and notes Roland Teske, S.J., vol. 2, *Letters 100–155* (Hyde Park, NY: New City Press, 2003), quoted in Timothy Cardinal Dolan, *Priests for the Third Millennium* (Huntington, IN: Our Sunday Visitor, 2000), 54.

his handmaiden" (Luke 1:48). A handmaid is a servant, a slave, someone who exists to serve others. Mary thinks of herself as the lowly servant of the Lord. The emphasis here is on her "low estate," which can be translated as her "poverty." Mary does not think of herself as important or worthy of praise or admiration, but as one who is poor and insignificant. Mary does not regard herself as a person of high status, but as one of low status, one who is there to serve, not to be served. Mary belonged to those who were called *anawim*: the poor and the outcast whom society looked down on. Yet they remained faithful to God despite difficulties and oppression. They relied on the Lord for their strength and longed for the coming of the Messiah. They were the people to whom Jesus came to announce the good news.

Mary's life imitated that of her Son, and their dispositions were the same. After James and John asked Jesus if they could sit at His right and His left in His kingdom, the other ten disciples became indignant. Jesus used the opportunity to emphasize the importance of being a servant in imitation of Him: "And Jesus called them to him and said to them, 'You know that those who are supposed to rule over the Gentiles lord it over them, and their great men exercise authority over them. But it shall not be so among you; but whoever would be great among you must be your servant, and whoever would be first among you must be slave of all. For the Son of man also came not to be served but to serve, and to give his life as a ransom for many'" (Mark 10:42–45). Like her Son, Mary gives her life in the service of God and others. So to be humble is to imitate Jesus and Mary in taking on the mindset and life of a servant. True greatness is measured in service.

To be a true servant, we must empty ourselves of all pride and ego and look to the interests of God and others. St. Paul reminds us to imitate Jesus' self-emptying, which is also called His *kenosis* or *condescension*:

> Do nothing from selfishness or conceit, but in humility count others better than yourselves. Let each of you look not only to his own interests, but also to the interests of others. Have this in mind among yourselves, which was in Christ Jesus, who, though he was in the form of God, did not count equality with God a thing to be grasped, but emptied himself, taking the form of a servant, being born in the likeness of men. And being found in human form he humbled himself and became obedient unto death, even death on a cross. Therefore God has highly exalted him and bestowed on him the name which is above every name, that at the name of Jesus every knee should bow, in heaven and on earth and under the earth, and every tongue confess that Jesus Christ is Lord, to the glory of God the Father. (Phil. 2:3–11)

Mary takes on this self-emptying quality of Christ in forgetting herself and focusing on how she can best serve and glorify God and help others. Mary considers herself as nothing compared to her Creator. Since the Lord has given her everything, our Mother wants to give back all she can to the Lord. Like Jesus, Mary empties herself of ego and self-preoccupation and makes herself available and ready to serve God and others. This self-emptying quality of Mary allows God to fill her with His grace so that she is overflowing with God's gifts and love. The Lord is able to live and work fully in our Blessed Mother precisely because she presents no obstacles or resistance to His grace. Her emptiness and poverty create the perfect abode where God is welcomed and invited to make His home. Mother Teresa once said to her sisters:

> I say it again and again, as I have said it so often, that even Almighty God cannot fill what is already full. We must be empty if we want God to fill us with His fullness. Our Lady had to be empty before she could be full of grace. She had to

> declare she was the handmaid of the Lord, before God could fill her. So also we must be empty of all pride, all jealousy, selfishness, and so on, before God can fill us with His love.[16]

Mary and the saints know how to create space within their being that is attractive and inviting to the Lord, so that He will come, visit, and make it His own.

This disposition of emptiness is often foreign to us because we are filled with ego and self-concern. As such, we leave no room or space for God. We tend to be so self-absorbed that we are not available to God or others. Our focus is on "me, my needs, my desires, and my agenda." We have no time to serve God, or anyone, because we need to concentrate on "number one." As a result, the Lord has little or no room to live and work in us. He will not force His way or His grace upon us. Only when we are ready and make room for God will He come and fill us with His gifts and with Himself. We should strive to be like St. John the Baptist, who said, "He must increase, but I must decrease" (John 3:30). God wants to live in us and transform us into Himself so that we may truly become His presence and instrument in the world. We must cooperate and desire the same.

When I was discerning the priesthood, I became friends with an elderly nun, Sr. Josephine. Sometimes, we would get together for breakfast at Denny's to catch up, and then we would go to Eucharistic Adoration together. One morning after Adoration, she asked me what I prayed for, and I told her. Then, I asked her what she prayed for, and she said, "I prayed that I may see Jesus in others, and that others may see Jesus in me." Indeed, the goal of apostolic work is to be Jesus for others, and that can happen only

16 Mother Teresa, *Where There Is Love, There Is God*, ed. Brian Kolodiejchuk, M.C. (New York: Doubleday Religion, 2010), 128.

if we empty ourselves and make room for the Lord to live in us and work through us.

For our Blessed Mother, humility was not just a lofty theory or a type of spirituality, but was lived out in actual service to God and others. Tradition has it that when Mary was about four years old, her parents, St. Joachim and St. Anne, presented her to the priests in the temple. There she lived, studied Scripture and the laws of God, and learned to serve the priests and others until her betrothal to St. Joseph at the age of fourteen. After her marriage to St. Joseph, Mary served her spouse and tended to his needs. Shortly after conceiving Jesus in her womb, Mary did not think of herself but instead went in haste to the house of Zechariah. There she stayed for three months to help her cousin Elizabeth, who was six months pregnant. After she gave birth to Jesus, Mary cared for her Son and her spouse during all those hidden years. During Jesus' public ministry, Mary served Him and His disciples by manual work and prayer. Even at the wedding at Cana, Mary was considerate of the newlywed couple and was the impetus for Jesus' first public miracle. These instances show that Mary's entire life was dedicated to the humble service of God and His plan of salvation.

Teaching His disciples about humility, Jesus washes their feet and gives them a concrete way to imitate Him: "If I then, your Lord and Teacher, have washed your feet, you also ought to wash one another's feet. For I have given you an example, that you also should do as I have done to you" (John 13:14–15). It is one thing to realize our complete dependence on God and refrain from conceit, but it is quite another to lower ourselves to perform manual labor and serve others in a way that may feel demeaning to us. But no type of manual work or service is considered too degrading for Jesus and Mary. Peter is appalled that Jesus would wash his feet because it is considered the job of a slave. But Jesus helps Peter understand that to be a servant and a slave to all is not just a hyperbole or a figure of speech: it is necessary if one is to be truly meek and humble like Jesus.

St. Teresa of Calcutta understood what it meant to live a life dedicated to serving others. No type of serving and caring for others was beneath her. Mother Teresa devoted herself to serving the poorest of the poor. She rejected no one who was suffering, dying, or in need. Mother Teresa explained to others that she saw Jesus Himself in the poorest of the poor and that her vocation was to serve Him by serving those who were most in need. Mother Teresa lived to serve, not to be served. She took on the same disposition as Jesus and Mary. The saints know the truth of who they are and who God is. They know that everything they have is a gift from God, and so they take credit for nothing and demand nothing. They know that their role is to imitate Jesus and Mary in serving the Father by serving others.

In another example of actual humility, Jesus tells His disciples to act and live like someone who is poor and insignificant:

> When you are invited by any one to a marriage feast, do not sit down in a place of honor, lest a more eminent man than you be invited by him; and he who invited you both will come and say to you, "Give place to this man," and then you will begin with shame to take the lowest place. But when you are invited, go and sit in the lowest place, so that when your host comes he may say to you, "Friend, go up higher"; then you will be honored in the presence of all who sit at table with you. For every one who exalts himself will be humbled, and he who humbles himself will be exalted. (Luke 14:8–11)

Humble people do not need to be noticed or made to feel important. They are comfortable within the group or even on its periphery. Mary has this quality about her because she wants to exalt God and not herself. She is comfortable with her lowliness and prefers not to be the center of attention. Whatever attention she receives, she refers to God for His glory.

In most images, the Blessed Virgin Mary is shown looking down, which is a sign of her humility.[17] She is grounded and down-to-earth and secure in her lowliness. Mary has no need to attract attention to herself and prefers not to be in the limelight, except when it is God's will and for His glory. Otherwise, Mary is completely comfortable staying behind the scenes, working quietly, and blending into the background while God takes center stage.

My grandmother also had this humble quality about her. She was always available to serve others. She had nine children and many grandchildren, and her focus was taking care of everyone except herself. She tended to the temporal and spiritual needs of the extended family. All her grandchildren were close to her because she was always close to them. There was also a gentle disposition about her. She never lost her temper or said a harsh word, but was always kind, patient, considerate, and attentive to the needs of others. She never wanted to draw attention to herself because she was always concerned with loving and serving God and others.

The Great Reversal

Humility is a disposition pleasing to God that moves Him to exalt us, while pride often leads Him to teach us a lesson that will humble us. The Lord wants us to be humble so that He can lift us up. In her Magnificat, Mary explains how God treats the humble and

[17] Some images show Mary looking up to God, which is also a sign of humility.

the proud: "He has shown strength with his arm, he has scattered the proud in the imagination of their hearts, he has put down the mighty from their thrones, and exalted those of low degree; he has filled the hungry with good things, and the rich he has sent empty away" (Luke 1:51–53). God favors the lowly, lifts them up, and exalts them, but the proud He casts down and humbles. The Lord supplies those in need, but He leaves the wealthy and powerful empty-handed.

It is incredible that the Lord humbles us only to exalt us. God is so rich in grace that He cannot wait to lavish us with His gifts. But we must have the proper disposition in order to receive His riches. St. James repeats an Old Testament truth: "God opposes the proud, but gives grace to the humble" (James 4:6). The Lord wants everyone to be happy, but He knows that selfishness and pride prevent that from happening. Humility is the only way to true happiness. Jesus Himself said, "Whoever exalts himself will be humbled, and whoever humbles himself will be exalted" (Matt. 23:12). God wants to shower His children with gifts, but He does not want to turn them into spoiled brats. Parents can relate to this predicament. Like God, many parents love their children and want to heap gifts upon them, but at the same time do not want to spoil them and so sometimes hold themselves back. Likewise, God wants our greatest good and happiness, and so He withholds His gifts if they will make us vain and prideful.

The meek and humble have a special place in the heart of God. Jesus explains to St. Faustina that the poor and humble most closely resemble Him and are most worthy of His blessings: "Today bring to Me the meek and humble souls and the souls of little children, and immerse them in My mercy. These souls most closely resemble My Heart. They strengthened Me during My bitter agony. I saw them as earthly Angels, who would keep vigil at My altars. I pour out upon them whole torrents of grace. Only the humble soul is able to receive My grace. I favor humble souls with My confidence."[18] Jesus reminds us that humility is a necessary disposition to obtain grace and that He wants to lavish the humble abundantly with His gifts.

In contrast, the proud are not capable of receiving grace. Jesus tells St. Faustina: "I have wanted to exalt this Congregation many times, but I am unable to do so because of its pride. Know, My daughter, that I do not grant My graces to proud souls, and I even take away from them the graces I have granted."[19] Not only do the proud *not* gain graces, but they even lose the graces they have received. Jesus wants to bless us and lift us up, but He will not do so if we are proud. That would only add to our pride, and He will not contribute to our sins.

In His Sermon on the Mount, Jesus tells us, "Blessed are the poor in spirit, for theirs is the kingdom of heaven" (Matt. 5:3). The poor in spirit are those who recognize their limitations, weaknesses, and poverty. They realize that they have nothing on their own, and their hands are empty. They look to God and completely depend on Him for all their needs. Jesus tells us that these humble souls will be abundantly blessed by God and will inherit the kingdom of heaven.

Moreover, it is in the humble souls that God's power and goodness can truly be manifested— there is no confusion that God is at work in one who is weak: "[God's] power is made perfect in weakness" (2 Cor. 12:9). The humbler we are, the more God's grace will work in us. The humble will not confuse God's gifts with their own abilities, and because of their utter need for God, the power of grace can be fully unleashed in them. St. Paul has the right attitude as he explains the correlation between humility and grace: "I will all the more gladly boast of my weaknesses, that the power of Christ

[18] *Diary*, no. 1220.

[19] *Diary*, no. 1170.

may rest upon me" (2 Cor. 12:9). The more we acknowledge our nothingness and complete dependence on God, the more He will live and work in us and manifest His power.

On the other hand, the proud think they are self-sufficient and have no need for God; they rely on their own abilities, and by doing so, they close the door to God's gifts. Those who rely on their own strength will be left to their own devices. The prideful will inevitably learn a hard but necessary lesson about their deficiency and complete dependence on God. Sometimes, God will allow us to fail miserably and hit "rock bottom," so that we may have a "wake-up call." The Lord would rather not humble us, but it is out of His goodness and mercy that He allows us to experience trials and suffering, so that we may turn to Him. Some people pray only when they are in a crisis or need something from God; otherwise, they rarely think of the Lord.

Imagine a seesaw with you on one side and God on the other. When you lift yourself up, you lower God. So when we lift ourselves up with pride and ego, in effect, we are saying to God: "I do not need you in my life. I can do it on my own." And the Lord will respect our wish and leave us to our own powers. But if you lower yourself, then you lift God up. In effect, you are saying to God: "I do not have what it takes. I am insufficient and weak. I need you to be present and active in my life. Because without you, I can do nothing." Then, the Lord will honor our wish and truly be present and active in our lives. The choice is up to us: Do we think we can do it all? Or do we know that we need God to live and act in our lives?

Children know their limitations and weaknesses and do not pretend to be self-sufficient. They know they must rely on their parents for help and are not afraid to ask for it. This is the type of disposition that Jesus wants us all to have. Jesus said to His disciples: "Truly, I say to you, unless you turn and become like children, you will never enter the kingdom of heaven. Whoever humbles himself like this child, he is the greatest in the kingdom of heaven" (Matt. 18:3–4). Mary and the saints know this secret and take it to heart. St. Thérèse of Lisieux in particular lived and promoted this way of spiritual childhood. Known as the Little Flower, St. Thérèse taught us her "little way." She sees herself the way that God sees her: as a little girl who cannot do much on her own, but falls often, and so needs the Father to help her, pick her up, and carry her in His arms. This saint said that she is not troubled by her weaknesses, but she rejoices in them because they cause God to reach down and come to her aid; He is happy to help His helpless little girl. St. Thérèse's confidence, therefore, is not in herself but completely in God. The more she depends on Him and not on herself, the more God is there to watch over her, protect her, and assist her.

Learning from the words of Jesus, the life of Mary, and the teaching of St. Thérèse, we should try to become humble like children again. One way for me to practice this aspect of spiritual childhood is to keep on my desk a picture of myself at nine months old. In this picture, I can barely stand on my own, but must hold onto the chair for support. This photo is to remind me that, in a way, I am still a little boy who can barely stand or walk, and I am not capable of doing much on my own. Therefore, I am completely dependent on God for everything and especially for accomplishing any good. This picture helps me to be humble and to see myself the way God sees me. Even though I am a grown man, I am still very weak and limited. I fall often and need God to help me, pick me up, and carry me. To tell you the truth, never a day goes by that I do not do something humiliating. I either say or do something ridiculous, which brings me back down to earth and makes me humble. Like St. Thérèse, we should not be surprised or upset by our inabilities, but we should just acknowledge them and remember our need for God. The more we acknowledge our nothingness, our weakness, and our complete dependence on God, the more He will come to our aid and pour out His graces upon us, as He did for Mary and the saints.

God rewards the childlike. There are a few times in the Gospel when we actually get to hear Jesus praying to the Father. This private conversation, which we are listening in on, reveals a lot about who God is and what is important to Him. The following words of Jesus to the Father confirm that God favors the lowly and the childlike over those whom the world admires: "At that time Jesus declared, 'I thank you, Father, Lord of heaven and earth, that you have hidden these things from the wise and understanding and revealed them to infants; yes, Father, for such was your gracious will'" (Matt. 11:25–26). Here is the great reversal of God: the last will be first, the weak will be powerful, and the childlike will be brilliant. Conversely, the arrogant will be humiliated, the rich will be empty, and the learned will be confounded. Such is the gracious will of God.

Lord, Have Mercy

When we see ourselves the way God sees us, we recognize not only our limitations as children but also our sins as adults. In a good examination of conscience, enlightened by the Holy Spirit, we will see another aspect of ourselves that we would rather not acknowledge. Some introspection should reveal that our weaknesses have led us to sinfulness. We have spurned God's generous love, made bad choices, hurt others and ourselves, and offended the Lord.

One of my favorite psalms is Psalm 51, which, as a priest, I pray every Friday morning in the Liturgy of the Hours. This is the psalm that David wrote after the prophet Nathan revealed to him how terribly he had sinned by killing Uriah and taking Bathsheba, Uriah's wife, as his own (see 2 Sam. 11–12). It is a psalm of true contrition, one that compelled the Lord to forgive David for his sin.

> Have mercy on me, O God, according to your merciful love; according to your abundant mercy blot out my transgressions. Wash me thoroughly from my iniquity, and cleanse me from my sin! For I know my transgressions, and my sin is ever before me. Against you, you only, have I sinned, and done that which is evil in your sight, so that you are justified in your sentence and blameless in your judgment. Behold, I was brought forth in iniquity, and in sin did my mother conceive me. Behold, you desire truth in the inward being; therefore teach me wisdom in my secret heart. Purge me with hyssop, and I shall be clean; wash me, and I shall be whiter than snow. Make me hear joy and gladness; let the bones which you have broken rejoice. (vv. 1–8)

True contrition is a gift from God to help us see ourselves for who we are and, at the same time, see the goodness and mercy of the Lord. Contrition is right and just and keeps us humble.

Although Mary did not sin, she was always afraid of offending God. Our Mother revealed to St. Bridget of Sweden: "As soon as I understood that there was a God, I was always solicitous and fearful for my salvation. And when I heard more fully that God was also my Creator and Judge of all my actions, I loved Him intensely, and every hour I feared and pondered lest I should offend Him in word or deed."[20] Mary received the plenitude of the gifts of the Holy Spirit, including fear of the Lord. This grace helps us to have a healthy fear of offending God because He is all-loving and deserving of all our love. We, too, should cultivate this fear

[20] *The Life of Mary as Seen by the Mystics*, comp. Raphael Brown (Charlotte, NC: TAN Books, 2012), 55.

of offending God because of the weaknesses of our fallen human nature. A humble and contrite heart is pleasing to the Lord.

Every morning, Blessed Columba Marmion made what he called the three stations of humility: the first station was to reflect on his past (how much he had sinned and offended the Lord); the second, to examine the present (how he was sinning against the Lord in the present moment); and the third, to look to the future (when he would continue to sin against the good God). Based on these honest examinations of his past, present, and future, he willingly accepted whatever form of death the Lord allowed him to experience that day to make reparation for his sins and to be purified. This is one way to keep our sins before our eyes, to be contrite for the multitude of ways and times in which we have offended God, and to accept peacefully whatever suffering or trials come our way. This sense of contrition helps us to see our capacity for sinfulness, be humble, and guard against our natural inclination toward pride and selfrighteousness.

In his book *A Guide to Living in the Truth: St. Benedict's Teaching on Humility*, Fr. Michael Casey, a Benedictine monk, shows us that we can use the words of Scripture as a way to meditate on our sinfulness and be truly contrite and humble. In one instance, he uses the following words from Psalm 22: "But I am a worm, and no man" (v. 6). These words may seem harsh and severe. But when we reflect on our vocation as rational human beings made in the image and likeness of God and destined for eternal life, we realize that our sins debase us and make us behave more like animals than human beings with God-given dignity. The saints know the gravity of sin, what it does to our soul, and how it hurts our dignity and our relationship with God. Accordingly, to remind me of my own sinfulness and keep me humble, I have posted this line from Psalm 22 on the wall next to my desk.

The saints are very aware of their limitations, weaknesses, and capacity to offend the Lord, and this disposition keeps them humble. In contrast, many people go through life oblivious of their sins. Some come to Confession for the first time in a long time and yet have little or even nothing to confess. They go to the Sacrament of Reconciliation because they are getting married or because they are pushed to go by someone else, and they do not make an examination of conscience or have contrition. Professor Peter Kreeft writes, "Sinners think they are saints, but saints know they are sinners."[21] How true it is. We are all sinners, yet some are completely clueless as to their own sins, while others, enlightened by the Lord, know their failings and are truly sorry.

In the parable of the Pharisee and the tax collector, Jesus warns us against self-righteousness:

> He also told this parable to some who trusted in themselves that they were righteous and despised others: "Two men went up into the temple to pray, one a Pharisee and the other a tax collector. The Pharisee stood and prayed thus with himself, 'God, I thank you that I am not like other men, extortioners, unjust, adulterers, or even like this tax collector. I fast twice a week, I give tithes of all that I get.' But the tax collector, standing far off, would not even lift up his eyes to heaven, but beat his breast, saying, 'God, be merciful to me a sinner!' I tell you, this man went down to his house justified rather than the other; for every one who exalts himself will be humbled, but he who humbles himself will be exalted." (Luke 18:9–14)

We should not feel smug just because we are Catholic, attend Mass, and pray. Vain complacency and self-righteousness harden the heart and the mind and block many graces from coming into our lives.

[21] Peter Kreeft, *Fundamentals of the Faith: Essays in Christian Apologetics* (San Francisco: Ignatius Press, 1988), 57.

And be careful not to look down on or judge other people, because they may be more pleasing to God than we are. Rather, take on the disposition of the tax collector, who knows that he is a sinner, unworthy to approach the sanctuary. Too ashamed even to look up to heaven, he beats his chest and asks God for mercy. This humble, contrite disposition is pleasing to the Lord and tugs at His heart-strings, causing Him to pour out an abundance of grace and gifts.

I try to say the Jesus Prayer every day. It goes like this: "Lord Jesus Christ, Son of the living God, have mercy on me, a sinner." It is a Christocentric variation of the prayer of the tax collector whom Jesus holds up as a model for His disciples. The more we make a habit of saying this prayer, the more we take on the disposition of the tax collector, which is most pleasing to God. This prayer keeps us grounded in the truth of our fallen human nature. No matter how virtuous we are or how much good we can accomplish, we should not let these things go to our head. Rather, say, "There but for the grace of God go I." Keep in mind that even with God's grace, we can fall at any moment. Never be complacent or smug, but always be meek and humble of heart, constantly relying on God's love and mercy.

Empty Hands

In his book, Fr. Casey also reflected on these words from Jesus to His disciples: "So you also, when you have done all that is commanded you, say, 'We are unworthy servants; we have only done what was our duty'" (Luke 17:10). Often, we give ourselves a pat on the back for doing something good. Sometimes, we take credit for accomplishing something worthwhile, but this can go to our head and inflate our ego. Remember that we have a tendency to congratulate ourselves, to be ruled by the need to feed our pride and the desire to feel good about our own abilities and accomplishments. Jesus reminds us that the perfection of charity—that is, loving God with all our heart, mind, soul, and strength, and our neighbor as ourselves — is an ongoing and lifelong process, during which we are doing only what God asks of us. To remind myself of this truth, I have this Scripture on my wall. It reminds me not to get conceited because of the good that I am able to do, but to remember that I am simply trying to live out my vocation as a priest and child of the Father.

St. Thérèse of Lisieux wrote that at the end of her earthly life, she would come before the Lord with empty hands. She would have no good works to show or call her own: only by the grace of God would she have accomplished anything worthy of praise. St. Thérèse merely tried to cooperate with God and do what she was supposed to do. She did not rest on her own merit but relied completely on God's mercy. She recognized her weaknesses, imperfections, and nothingness; therefore, she did not feel entitled to any reward, instead trusting in God's infinite love, goodness, and mercy.

Likewise, the Blessed Virgin Mary never takes credit for anything good. She knows that all the good she can do comes from God's grace and His goodness. It was the Lord who looked with favor on His lowly servant and lifted her up. It was God who filled her with grace and entrusted to her a special role in His plan of salvation. Some people think that by honoring Mary, we take away the honor that is owed to God. But there is never any competition: whatever honor we give to Mary, we give to God. Mary takes nothing for herself but gives credit where credit is due — to God alone.

Mary and the saints know their place, their nothingness, and their complete dependence on the Lord for all that is good. The prophet Isaiah acknowledges that God is behind all our good works: "O LORD, you will ordain peace for us, you have wrought for us all our works" (Isa. 26:12). Those who recognize the power of God working through imperfect human instruments stay grounded. Then, in turn, God lifts them up and works through them even more, because He knows that His gifts will not make them proud. We, too, should learn this truth, imitate Mary and the saints, and stay grounded. It is the Lord who has accomplished all the good that we have done.

Humility is not just the first virtue that we need in order to grow in the other virtues; it is also the virtue that is dearest to Mary and most pleasing to God. On the feast of the Immaculate Conception, St. Faustina saw the Blessed Mother, who said to her: "I desire, My dearly beloved daughter, that you practice the three virtues that are dearest to Me—and most pleasing to God. The first is humility, humility, and once again humility; the second virtue, purity; the third virtue, love of God. As My daughter, you must especially radiate with these virtues."[22] Mary, our Mother, has revealed to us that humility is the most pleasing virtue to God and most precious to her heart. The saints know how important humility is for growth in grace and holiness. Let us then ask for the grace to be humble like Jesus, Mary, and the saints, so that we might grow in virtue and be most pleasing to God.

Practical Suggestions

1. Every night, before going to bed, make an examination of conscience by reviewing your day and asking forgiveness for any ways you may have disappointed God.
2. Go to Confession monthly to cultivate awareness of your failings.
3. Display a childhood picture of yourself to remind you to be childlike and humble.
4. Say the Jesus Prayer often: "Lord Jesus Christ, Son of the living God, have mercy on me, a sinner."

[22] *Diary*, no. 1415.

2

Confidence in God

The more we trust in the Lord, the more He will act in our lives.

Blessed is she who believed that there would be a fulfillment of what was spoken to her from the Lord. (Luke 1.45)

In our culture, the word *confidence* usually refers to self-confidence, that is, confidence in one's own abilities. Sometimes, we have confidence in other people and their abilities, but rarely do we mention confidence in God. Political correctness eliminates the Lord from the equation. We cannot take the chance of offending an atheist, agnostic, or nonbeliever. But in the previous chapter on humility, we established the truth of our brokenness and complete dependence on the Lord for everything. Therefore, we acknowledge our limitations and do not rely on ourselves, but rightfully place our confidence in the Lord, the Giver of every good gift.

The more we rely on the Lord, the more He will act in our lives. There is a direct correlation between our confidence in God and the riches of grace we will receive. The more we believe, the more we will receive. Jesus tells St. Faustina: "The graces of My mercy are drawn by means of one vessel only, and that is—trust. The more a soul trusts, the more it will receive."[23] Trust is so important to the life of grace and our relationship with God that Jesus directed St. Faustina to place the following sentence at the bottom of the Divine Mercy image: "Jesus, I trust in you." This is to remind us to trust in the Lord, so that we may receive a superabundance of His grace and mercy.

The theme of trust appears throughout the Bible. In the Old Testament, we are told: "Trust in the LORD with all your heart, and do not rely on your own insight. In all your ways acknowledge him, and he will make straight your paths" (Prov. 3:5–6). Often, the Israelites, their leaders, and the prophets were tested by difficult circumstances and challenging commands, and they would entertain doubts or complain. But the Lord's response to them was always the same: "Trust in me, for I am always with you."

God Is Present and Active

To know God is to trust in Him. The Israelites came to know more about God when Moses encountered the Lord at the burning bush. During this encounter, Moses asked for God's name. His reply was mysterious yet profound and revealing: "I am who I am" (Exod. 3:14). In the Hebrew text, God's name consists solely of the consonants *YHWH* (transliterated *Yahweh*), which is called the *Tetragrammaton*, meaning "the four letters." In the ancient world, a person's name revealed his or her identity. Likewise, God's name reveals who He really is, that is, His nature and His attributes.

Yahweh is connected with the Hebrew verb *hayah*, which means "to be." The God of Israel is the one who *is*, namely, the absolute and unchangeable God. Everything but God has a beginning and an end. It is God alone who has always existed, presently exists,

[23] *Diary*, no. 1578.

and will exist forever. The first part of His name, *I* AM, means that God is truly present, not in some abstract or passive manner, but in a real way. The second part, WHO *I* AM, connotes that God does whatever He wills and acts according to His sovereign freedom. Therefore, we are to accept the Lord for who He is and not try to fit Him into our expectations or the image we have of Him.

The fact that *Yahweh* is a verb reveals the dynamism of the divine nature. The *a* vowel in the first syllable indicates a causative meaning. God not only *is*, but He causes *to be*. God is the origin of all that is. He creates and sustains all other beings. The verb *Yahweh* is in the form of an ongoing, continuous action. God, thus, continues to be. He is an active and living God. He is in the present, but He is also in the future. This verb form demonstrates the freedom and the mystery of God.

Because the definition of *Yahweh* includes "God *will be* present," another layer of meaning is added to His name. The Lord will be there for us when we are in need. By God's very name, He is saying, "I will be with you always," assuring us that we are never alone. He is always with us to help, guide, and protect us. The Lord is faithful forever.

In the call of Moses and the other prophets, we find the following pattern: God calls a person, the person responds with reluctance and fear, and then God reassures the person that He will be with him or her to offer His help. The Lord likewise assures us that He is always present to protect and to assist us. Indeed, Jesus tells His disciples, "Behold, I am with you always, to the close of the age" (Matt. 28:20).

Your Faith Has Saved You

St. Matthew shows that the prophet Isaiah foretold that God Himself would be with us in a radical way through the birth of Jesus:

"Behold, a virgin shall conceive and bear a son, and his name shall be called Emmanuel (which means, God with us)" (Matt. 1:23; cf. Isa. 7:14). Many times, Jesus referred to Himself as "I am," revealing His divinity. For example: "I told you that you would die in your sins, for you will die in your sins unless you believe that I am he" (John 8:24); "Jesus said to them, 'Truly, I say to you, before Abraham was, I am'" (John 8:58); and "I tell you this now, before it takes place, that when it does take place you may believe that I am he" (John 13:19).[24] In Jesus, the Word made flesh, God is truly with us, and He wants us to believe in Him: "Let not your hearts be troubled; believe in God, believe also in me" (John 14:1). And the more we believe in Jesus, the more His grace will work in our lives. In the New Testament, Jesus often points out that people are healed because of their strong belief. Faith is necessary to receive and experience the power of God's grace.

In one instance in the Bible, the father of a boy who was possessed by a mute spirit brought his son to the disciples of Jesus, but they could not drive it out. When Jesus learned this, He said: "O faithless generation, how long am I to be with you? How long am I to bear with you? Bring him to me" (Mark 9:19). Jesus was exasperated because His disciples and the boy's father lacked faith and thus could not heal the boy. Then, the father said to Jesus: "'If you can do anything, have pity on us and help us.' And Jesus said to him, 'If you can! All things are possible to him who believes.' Immediately the father of the child cried out and said, 'I believe, help my unbelief!'" (Mark 9:22–24). It was after this act of faith that Jesus healed the boy. Later, the disciples approached Jesus in

[24] See also "I am the bread of life" (John 6:35); "I am the light of the world" (John 8:12); "I am the door" (John 10:9); "I am the good shepherd" (John 10:11, 14); "I am the resurrection and the life" (John 11:25); "I am the way, and the truth, and the life" (John 14:6); and "I am the vine" (John 15:1, 5).

private and asked why they could not drive out the demon. Jesus said to them: "Because of your little faith. For truly, I say to you, if you have faith as a grain of mustard seed, you will say to this mountain, 'Move from here to there,' and it will move; and nothing will be impossible to you." (Matt. 17:20). Jesus explains that the disciples could not heal the boy because they lacked faith, whereas with a solid faith, they could do anything.

Similarly, when Peter had faith, he was able to walk on water toward Jesus. But when he saw how strong the wind was, Peter became frightened, started to doubt, and began to sink. At that time, Jesus said to Peter, "O you of little faith, why did you doubt?" (Matt. 14:31). When we have faith, the grace of God flows freely within us, and we can accomplish amazing things. But when we doubt, we prevent the supernatural gift of God from working in our lives.

In another instance, the Nazarenes' lack of faith prevented Jesus from performing many miracles there. The people in His hometown knew Jesus as the son of a carpenter and Mary, and they took offense at His public ministry. Consequently, we are told that "he did not do many mighty works there, because of their unbelief" (Matt. 13:58). Our doubts, worries, and lack of faith can limit the actions of grace in our lives. Jesus is often very demonstrative in His praise for those of great faith and, at the same time, expresses His utter disappointment in those who lack faith. There is a direct correlation between our faith and the grace that God bestows on our lives.

We all struggle with our faith at one point or another. The story of the boy possessed by a mute spirit gives us an example of how to handle a crisis of faith. We may want to seek the help of a priest, a religious brother or sister, or a knowledgeable person who has a strong faith. But we also must bring our problems and concerns to God in prayer with acts of faith by repeating the words "Jesus, I do believe; help my unbelief." When we say this seemingly contradictory statement, we are doing two things: first, we are making an act of faith. When we say "I do believe," we show God and ourselves that we do believe in God and that with Him anything is possible. But at the same time, we acknowledge that our faith is still weak and needs strengthening. The declaration "Help my unbelief" is a humble, honest act of faith that is pleasing to the Lord and brings down many graces both to strengthen our faith and to give us what we ask, if it is in accord with God's will.

So far, you may have noticed that different words are used to express the same idea: *faith*, *belief*, *trust*, *confidence*, and *hope*. These words may vary in meaning, but for purposes of this chapter, they are used interchangeably. By examining the definitions of the theological virtues of *faith* and *hope*, we get a better idea of the meaning behind the words.

Faith is defined as "the theological virtue by which we believe in God and believe all that he has said and revealed to us, and that Holy Church proposes for our belief, because he is truth itself."[25] With faith, we believe in God and everything He has revealed through His Church. God is credible: when He speaks, He does not lie. Everything the Lord reveals is worthy of belief because He is truth and the source of all that is true. We trust in the Church, founded by Jesus on the apostles, to communicate truth and grace. Jesus said to Peter, "I tell you, you are Peter, and on this rock I will build my Church, and the gates of Hades shall not prevail against it" (Matt. 16:18). Jesus also promised to send the Holy Spirit to lead the Church to all truth. He tells the disciples, "When the Spirit of truth comes, he will guide you into all the truth" (John 16:13).

Hope is a little different from faith: "Hope is the theological virtue by which we desire the kingdom of heaven and eternal life as our happiness, placing our trust in Christ's promises and relying

[25] CCC 1814.

not on our own strength, but on the help of the grace of the Holy Spirit."[26] The *Catechism* continues, "The virtue of hope responds to the aspiration to happiness which God has placed in the heart of every man; it takes up the hopes that inspire men's activities and purifies them so as to order them to the kingdom of heaven; it keeps man from discouragement; it sustains him during times of abandonment; it opens up his heart in expectation of eternal beatitude."[27] The theological virtues of faith and hope come from God as gifts; they are infused in us by sanctifying grace and lead us to God. The more we grow in these virtues, the more we will grow in sanctifying grace.

Blessed Is She Who Believed

Mary is a model of faith and hope because of her unwavering belief in God and complete trust in His goodness. Our first real introduction to Mary in the New Testament is in the first chapter of the Gospel of Luke, which recounts the Annunciation, when the angel Gabriel announced to the Virgin that she would conceive and bear a son. Mary's response to the angel is quite different than that of Zechariah, to whom Gabriel had announced the coming birth of John the Baptist. Mary said to the angel, "How will this be, since I do not know man?" (Luke 1:34). Mary's question is not one of doubt but of faith. In essence, Mary is saying, "I believe that what you tell me is true, but I am dumbfounded as to how this can happen." In contrast, Zechariah's response is: "How shall I know this? For I am an old man, and my wife is advanced in years" (Luke 1:18). In essence, Zechariah does not believe the angel and asks, "How do I know that what you are telling me is true?"

[26] Ibid., no. 1817.
[27] Ibid., no. 1818.

Because of his doubt, Zechariah was unable to speak until John was born: "And the angel answered him, 'I am Gabriel, who stand in the presence of God; and I was sent to speak to you, and to bring you this good news. And behold, you will be silent and unable to speak until the day that these things come to pass, because you did not believe my words, which will be fulfilled in their time'" (Luke 1:19–20). In contrast, Mary spoke freely, giving her unreserved assent: "Behold, I am the handmaid of the Lord; let it be to me according to your word" (Luke 1:38). Mary never doubts the words of the angel Gabriel for a moment because she knows that God, who is truth itself and the source of all truth, has sent Him. Although Mary considers herself unworthy of this honor, she also realizes that nothing is impossible with the Almighty God. Mary's consent is filled with faith, awe, and love at God's incredible graciousness.

After Mary's encounter with the angel, she goes to visit her cousin Elizabeth, who is six months pregnant with John. Elizabeth, enlightened by the Holy Spirit, knows that Mary is carrying Jesus in her womb and cries out: "Blessed are you among women, and blessed is the fruit of your womb! And why is this granted to me, that the mother of my Lord should come to me?" (Luke 1:42–43). Furthermore, Elizabeth knows that Mary never doubted but believed that what the angel told her would come to fulfillment. So Elizabeth said to Mary, "Blessed is she who believed that there would be a fulfilment of what was spoken to her from the Lord" (Luke 1:45). Mary, indeed, has the perfect disposition to receive this tremendous grace: she is humble and filled with faith. St. Augustine says that Mary conceived Jesus in her heart by faith before she conceived Him in her womb.[28] Mary's faith in

[28] St. Augustine, *Discourses* 215, 4, quoted in Pope Francis, Angelus, December 8, 2014, http://www.vatican.va/content/francesco/en/angelus/2014/documents/papa-francesco_angelus_20141208.html.

God never wavered but remained steadfast. Throughout her life on earth, Mary freely chose to believe and to trust in the Lord. The more she believed, the more she received.

Obstacles to Faith

The theological virtues are gifts from God infused into our souls to make us capable of acting as His children and meriting eternal life.[29] So why is it that some people have faith and others do not? And why do some people have great, strong faith, like Mary and the saints, while others have weak or little faith? Like all grace, the full gift of faith requires that we receive it and respond to it. We receive the virtues of faith, hope, and love at Baptism, but these graces may lie dormant, unable to grow or be effective until they are activated. For example, when we pour chocolate syrup into a glass of milk, the syrup sinks to the bottom and the milk remains white until we stir up the syrup. Then, the milk is changed into chocolate milk. Similarly, we receive graces and gifts in the sacraments, but that does not mean that they have been stirred up and are apparent and active. In order for graces and gifts to be active, we must stir them up. As St. Paul puts it, we must "rekindle the gift of God that is within [us]" (2 Tim. 1:6). In order to receive the fullness of this gift, we must be properly disposed; that is, we must be receptive and open to God and eliminate obstacles preventing us from receiving His gifts.

Pride

There are common obstacles that keep the gift of faith from blossoming. These obstacles overlap and reinforce one another. The first such obstacle is pride. One of the "deadly sins" or "capital

[29] CCC 1813.

vices," pride is considered the worst, and the root, of all the sins and vices. Pride, by definition, is excessive self-esteem and an inflated sense of one's own excellence. Pride blinds the mind and causes one to think that one is self-sufficient. Secular intellectual pride, for example, causes one to think that one is sufficiently intelligent and knowledgeable to explain everything from the viewpoint of the natural world and empirical data. A person with this closed mindset is not open to anything beyond the material world, such as God, grace, and the supernatural. Prideful people are not open or receptive to the full gift of faith; they have closed themselves off by thinking they already know it all. God will not force His gifts on anyone because He values our free will. This may explain why so many highly educated and intelligent people are atheists or agnostics. Their intellectual pride has become an obstacle to the full gift of faith. One must be humble in order to be properly disposed and receptive to the gift of faith being kindled into flame.

Attachments

The second obstacle is attachment. There are three types of attachments: to sin, to the world, and to oneself. People who are attached to sin have their minds and hearts darkened. They are not open to the light of faith, but would rather live in darkness. It is also difficult for worldly people to receive the full gift of faith because they are too attached to the things of the world, which are contrary to the things of God. Power, prestige, pleasures, and possessions dominate their minds and hearts and leave little or no room for God and His gifts. Then, there are those who are attached to themselves and their thoughts, ideas, and preferences. This is another form of pride by which people can become so self-absorbed and stuck in their ways that they are not open to the light of faith.

The parable of the sower illustrates these three attachments as different types of soil in which God wishes to sow the seed of faith. In the Gospel of Matthew, we read:

> And he told them many things in parables, saying: "A sower went out to sow. And as he sowed, some seeds fell along the path, and the birds came and devoured them. Other seeds fell on rocky ground, where they had not much soil, and immediately they sprang up, since they had no depth of soil, but when the sun rose they were scorched; and since they had no root they withered away. Other seeds fell upon thorns, and the thorns grew up and choked them. Other seeds fell on good soil and brought forth grain, some a hundredfold, some sixty, some thirty." (Matt. 13:3–8)

The seeds that fell on the path symbolize those who are attached to sin. They are not open to receiving the full gift of faith. Their hearts are hardened, and they are cut off from grace. Therefore, the seed of faith has no soil in which to grow and is eaten up by the birds. Jesus explains, "When any one hears the word of the kingdom and does not understand it, the Evil One comes and snatches away what is sown in his heart; this is what was sown along the path" (Matt. 13:19). The devil wants to enslave us to a life of sin. This keeps us from understanding the Word of God and receiving the gift of faith and other graces. We must be free from sin and in a state of sanctifying grace in order to be receptive to the seed of faith.

The seeds that fell among thorns symbolize those who are too attached to the things of the world. Jesus explains further: "As for what was sown among thorns, this is he who hears the word, but the cares of the world and the delight in riches choke the word, and it proves unfruitful" (Matt. 13:22). It is easy to be caught up in the things of the world. The secular world is an enemy of faith and has many temptations that lure us away from a life of faith in Jesus. It is easy to be influenced by the world because we live in it and are constantly exposed to its messages, which are contrary to the messages of the gospel. The world esteems wealth, fame, power, and sensual pleasures, all of which are fleeting and should not be desired for their own sake. Everything that God created is good, but these things are intended to lead us to the Creator. The world seeks these things in themselves rather than as reflections of their Creator. Jesus said: "No one can serve two masters; for either he will hate the one and love the other, or he will be devoted to the one and despise the other. You cannot serve God and mammon" (Matt. 6:24). The world loves and serves and is devoted to mammon (money); hence, it cannot serve or love or be devoted to God.

The seeds that fell on rocky ground symbolize those who are attached to themselves and their own will and comfort. Jesus continues to explain: "As for what was sown on rocky ground, this is he who hears the word and immediately receives it with joy; yet he has no root in himself, but endures for a while, and when tribulation or persecution arises on account of the word, immediately he falls away" (Matt. 13:20–21). Being too attached to themselves and their comfort and ideas, these people do not persevere through hardships because their faith is not deep. They enjoy the initial consolation of the gift of faith, but when that consolation goes away and they experience trials, they immediately fall away because their faith has not taken root. We must be detached from ourselves if we wish to become the rich soil in which the seed of the faith may take root.

St. John of the Cross explains the problem of attachment by giving us an image of a bird that is tied to the ground by a string on its leg. The bird cannot fly because it is attached to the ground by the string. As a result, the bird cannot do what it is made to do, which is to fly; therefore, the bird cannot really live the life of a bird. So it is with us: if we are attached to sin, to the world, or to ourselves, then we cannot do what we are made to do, which is to fly to the Lord in heaven. Attachments prevent us from becoming who we are made to be. God made us and calls us to be His children and live with Him forever. But we cannot become fully human and actualize our highest potential if attachments impede our ascent to the Lord. We need to cut the string that ties us down so that we can soar to the lofty heights to which we are called. Detachment from sin, the world, and the self allows the mind and heart to be free to receive the gift of faith and grow in virtue.

Apathy

The third common obstacle to the gift of faith is apathy, or indifference. Some people are just not very interested in having faith. They are happy-go-lucky and content with the way they are. They have no urgent need or immediate desire for faith, which they think is fine for others but not necessarily for themselves. They would rather pursue things that they consider more attractive and important. This lack of desire is a huge obstacle to faith. If people do not want faith, then God will not force it upon them. The Lord respects our free will. Only when we desire and ask for the gift of faith will the Lord grant it.

Apathy is repulsive to God. In the book of Revelation, the Lord chastises those who are indifferent: "I know your works: you are neither cold nor hot. Would that you were cold or hot! So, because you are lukewarm, and neither cold nor hot, I will spew you out of my mouth" (Rev. 3:15–16). Jesus revealed to St. Faustina that those who are lukewarm cause Him the most revulsion. He said: "These souls wound My Heart most painfully. My soul suffered the most dreadful loathing in the Garden of Olives because of lukewarm souls. They were the reason I cried out: 'Father, take this cup away from Me, if it be Your will.' "[30] Apathy, indifference, and tepidity cause the Lord the most pain, and these responses harden hearts and prevent people from receiving and growing in the gift of faith.

So receptivity, openness, and having the proper disposition are key to receiving the theological virtue of faith. In order to have a ripe condition for reception and growth, one needs humility, detachment, and desire. When the Lord finds us receptive, He will bless us with the infused virtue of faith.

The Testing of Faith

Our faith is meant to grow and blossom, and this requires testing. St. James tells us: "Count it all joy, my brethren, when you meet various trials, for you know that the testing of your faith produces steadfastness. And let steadfastness have its full effect, that you may be perfect and complete, lacking in nothing" (James 1:2–4). God will put us in situations that will require us to have faith and courage. Fear, in contrast, will keep us from growing in faith. Anxieties make us question and doubt the God who, by His nature, is always present to us. It is easy to have faith when everything is going well. But it is tougher when we are put in new, unknown, and challenging situations. However, this is necessary for our faith to mature. St. Peter confirms, "For a little while you may have to suffer through various trials, so that the genuineness of your faith, more precious than gold which though perishable is tested by fire, may redound to praise and glory and honor at the revelation of Jesus Christ" (1 Pet. 1:6–7). As gold is purified by fire, so faith becomes purer and more valuable when tested.

At the Annunciation, Mary was filled with the blessings of having been chosen to become the Mother of God. This joy

[30] *Diary*, no. 1228.

continued at the Visitation with Elizabeth. But before Mary gave birth to Jesus, her faith was tested. Shortly before she was due to give birth, a decree went out from Caesar Augustus that everyone must be enrolled in his or her native city. So Joseph and Mary had to leave Nazareth and travel to Bethlehem to be enrolled. This was not an ideal time, since it was the middle of winter and Mary was about to give birth, but she accepted this difficulty with trust in the Lord. With only a donkey and their own two feet to carry them, they had to travel about one hundred miles (the distance between Nazareth and Bethlehem), which would have taken several days. Mary and Joseph had to endure the rough and dangerous terrain and cold nights outdoors. Scripture tells us that there was no room for them at the inn, and so Mary had to give birth to Jesus in a manger (Luke 2:7). Yet amid all these difficulties, Mary remained steadfast in her faith. She did not give in to fear or worry or discouragement, but trusted wholeheartedly in the Lord. Mary's faith was tried and tested, and she responded with trust and acceptance.

We, too, need to be tested in order to grow in faith and trust. Those whose faith is weak fall away at the slightest hardship. But those whose faith is strong remain firm in times of challenges and difficulties, and this allows their faith to grow and blossom even more. It is tempting to give in to fear, doubt, and discouragement, but the Lord wants us to trust in His presence, power, and love. In times of need or uncertainty, we should turn to the Lord with faith, asking and trusting that He will supply our necessities.

Jesus tells us to have confidence in God's infinite love for us and to ask for what we need:

> Ask, and it will be given you; seek, and you will find; knock, and it will be opened to you. For every one who asks receives, and he who seeks finds, and to him who knocks it

> will be opened. Or what man of you, if his son asks him for bread, will give him a stone? Or if he asks for a fish, will give him a serpent? If you then, who are evil, know how to give good gifts to your children, how much more will your Father who is in heaven give good things to those who ask him! (Matt. 7:7–11)

We know that God is generous, but He is also all-knowing. Jesus tells us that God already knows our needs: "And in praying do not heap up empty phrases as the Gentiles do; for they think that they will be heard for their many words. Do not be like them, for your Father knows what you need before you ask him" (Matt. 6:7–8). Scripture even tells us to pray always (see 1 Thess. 5:17).

So, since God is generous, omniscient, and eternal, meaning we cannot change His mind, why is it necessary for us to pray at all? As St. Thomas Aquinas explains, God has ordained that certain effects shall result from secondary causes.[31] Specifically, God has ordained that by praying, we may obtain certain gifts that we would otherwise not obtain.[32] St. Thomas says: "We pray not that we may change the Divine disposition, but that we may obtain that which God has disposed to be fulfilled by our prayers. In other words, 'that by asking, men may deserve to receive what Almighty God from eternity has disposed to give.'"[33] It is true that we need to pray to God, not to make known to Him our needs or desires, but to remind ourselves of the necessity of having recourse to God's help. Out of His generosity, God bestows many things on us even without our asking, but He wishes to bestow certain things upon our asking. This is for the sake of our good, namely, that we may acquire confidence in having recourse to God and that we may

[31] Aquinas, *ST* II-II, q. 83, art. 2.

[32] Ibid.

[33] Ibid.

recognize Him as the author of our goods.[34] The act of praying helps us to be humble, to realize our need for the Lord, and to grow in our relationship with Him.

Jesus tells us that if we ask, we will receive. But we know from experience that there are times when we do not receive what we ask for in prayer. St. Thomas explains the reasons this sometimes happens. One reason is that we ask inconsistently or lightly.[35] An example of this is when St. Augustine prayed, "Lord, give me chastity, but not yet." Another reason is that we have not asked for what is truly good for us. A third reason is that we have stopped asking.

On the contrary, St. Thomas says that when the following four conditions are present, we always obtain what we ask for, if not something better: first, we ask for ourselves. This is because those for whom we pray may have some obstacle preventing them from receiving what we request. Nonetheless, we obtain graces when we pray for others out of charity. Second, we pray for the things necessary and conducive to our salvation. Third, we pray piously, that is, with humility, faith, and sincerity. And fourth, we pray perseveringly. Often, our prayer is not denied but deferred, so that it may be granted at a more suitable time. But this may not come to fruition if we lack perseverance and give up asking.

Sometimes, God will try our faith and the strength of our desire. If our faith and desire are protracted and increase over time, we will enjoy the blessings even more when we receive them. There are some prayers that may be meritorious and yet not granted. For example, one may pray to become a priest or a nun with the intention of dedicating one's life to God. This is laudable but may not be granted if it is not part of God's will for that person. The bottom line is that we should pray for ourselves and for others with the

[34] Ibid.

[35] *ST* II-II, q. 83, art. 15.

above criteria in mind and with the confidence that much good will come from our prayers.

We Are Royalty

If we truly know who God is and recognize His immense love for us, we will not let worries occupy our minds and hearts. A common theme in private revelations is trust in God's love for us.[36] God the Father told St. Catherine of Siena, "With the eye of your understanding you must see my affectionate charity, how unspeakably much I love you."[37] The Lord is calling us to have faith in His infinite love for us. Worries and fears place obstacles in our relationship with God. Scripture and the writings of the saints remind us to trust in the Lord's presence and care for our welfare. For example, St. John Paul II's motto was "Be not afraid." This is also a common theme in Scripture and should be our motto too.

Jesus tells us not to let the cares of daily life consume us but to focus on God and His glory, knowing that He will not abandon us:

> But if God so clothes the grass which is alive in the field today and tomorrow is thrown into the oven, how much more will he clothe you, O men of little faith! And do not seek what you are to eat and what you are to drink, nor be of anxious mind. For all the nations of the world seek these things; and your Father knows that you need them. Instead, seek his kingdom, and these things shall be yours as well. Fear not, little flock, for it is your Father's good pleasure to give you the kingdom. (Luke 12:28–32)

[36] For example, the Sacred Heart revelations to St. Margaret Mary Alacoque.

[37] Catherine of Siena, *The Dialogue*, trans. Suzanne Noffke, O.P., Classics of Western Spirituality (Mahwah, NJ: Paulist Press, 1980), 191.

St. Paul tells us, "He who did not spare his own Son but gave him up for us all, will he not also give us all things with him?" (Rom. 8:32). If God has given us His precious Son so that we may have eternal life, why would He not give us everything else that is conducive to our greatest happiness? And if it is not conducive to our greatest happiness, which is our salvation, then we do not need it anyway and should not desire it.

We must remind ourselves of how precious we are to the Lord. We are His children, His pride and joy, the apple of His eye. I found an image on Facebook of a girl wearing a royal gown and a crown on her head. Below were the words "On the darkest days when I feel inadequate, unloved, and unworthy, I remember whose daughter I am, and I adjust my crown." For us also, when we are tempted to give in to doubts, fears, and anxieties, let us remember whose sons and daughter we are and adjust our crowns. Our Father is the King of the universe, and we are princes and princesses. The King will not let anything harm His family but will do everything to protect and take care of His children.

The Father knows our weaknesses and vulnerabilities, and He has made provisions for our well-being. If we recognize our dependence on Him and trust in Him, we will not be disappointed. Here is an example: my office used to be in the same building as that of Fr. Robert Spitzer, S.J., who is blind. He must depend on his assistant, Joan Jacoby, to lead him. Fr. Spitzer trusts that Joan will not abandon him or lead him in the wrong direction or into a wall. Joan knows that Fr. Spitzer is blind, and so she becomes his eyes, tells him what he needs to know, and leads and guides him when necessary. There is mutual knowledge and trust between the two. So it is with us and God. He knows we need His help, and so He provides for our needs. We just have to acknowledge our dependence on Him, take Him by the arm, and trust that He will look out for us and lead us where we need to go.

Freedom of the Children of God

The Lord is ever calling us to greater faith and trust in Him. We all go through difficult times when we feel anxious and worried. When I find myself feeling afraid or uncertain, I am reminded of a song called "Trust" by Sixpence None the Richer. The words of the song are taken from Proverbs 3:5–6 and Matthew 6:34, and the refrain goes like this: "Don't worry about tomorrow; He's got it under control. Just trust in the Lord with all your heart and He will carry you through." After listening to the song or singing it to myself, I usually feel better. In time of need, is there a song or Scripture passage that can give you a boost of confidence in the Lord?

During my year as a transitional deacon, before I was to be ordained a priest, I went on a pilgrimage to the Holy Land with other seminarians and priests. Some of us had heard that the door to the Church of the Holy Sepulchre opened at 4:00 a.m. To avoid the crowd, a newly ordained priest and I got up early and arrived at the church in the wee hours of the morning. The whole church was practically empty. I went to the hill of Calvary and sat down and prayed. I poured my heart out to the Lord about the doubts and worries I was struggling with. Then, I heard the Lord say to me in my heart, "Take courage." And I heard it again: "Take courage." This reminded me of when Jesus told the disciples, "In the world you have tribulation; but be of good cheer, I have overcome the world" (John 16:33). This special gift gave me great comfort. It was a powerful moment of grace that gave me strength and hope that all would be well. So, when you experience hardships, disappointments, and doubts, as we all do, remember these words of Jesus.

The Lord is continually calling us to greater trust, courage, and freedom. The saints bear witness to Christ, especially in times of difficulty. St. Paul speaks of the "glorious liberty of the children of God" (Rom. 8:21). This is the freedom and courage that have been demonstrated by Mary and the saints, especially the martyrs. When we have faith in God, He will empower us with even more faith and grace to perform works that are beyond our natural abilities. Jesus said: "Truly, truly, I say to you, he who believes in me will also do the works that I do; and greater works than these will he do, because I go to the Father. Whatever you ask in my name, I will do it, that the Father may be glorified in the Son; if you ask anything in my name, I will do it" (John 14:12–14). To ask something in the name of Jesus means to ask on His authority, in union with Him, and with the confidence that He will not let us down.

As a priest, I administer the Sacrament of Anointing of the Sick on a regular basis. I do it on the authority of Jesus and in union with Him, with the confidence that Christ will heal the person according to His will. I have witnessed many powerful healings. There was one time when I was called to anoint a patient who was in a coma. During the anointing, the patient opened her eyes and came out of the coma. The family was ecstatic. Another time, I anointed a parishioner prior to surgery to remove a tumor. When I saw her again, she told me that she did not have to go through the surgery because the tumor miraculously disappeared.[38] If we

[38] Note that the primary grace that comes with the Sacrament of Anointing is the healing of the soul and the union of one's sufferings with Christ for the good of the person and the Church. While God can, and occasionally does, work healing miracles through the Sacrament of Anointing, such miracles are by no means the norm. While we can certainly hope that God will heal the physical ailments of those who receive Anointing of the Sick, we should not expect Him to do so, as the principal purpose of the sacrament is not ordered primarily to physical healing but to spiritual healing.

have faith in the Lord and pray in His name, He will accomplish incredible things through us. St. Paul had this freedom and confidence when he said "I can do all things in him who strengthens me" (Phil. 4:13). This is not self-confidence but confidence in the Lord, who leads us to true freedom and peace.

Those who have faith in the Lord exemplify great freedom and even levity. Pope St. John XXIII would say the following prayer every night before bed: "Lord, I did the best I could today. It's your Church; you take care of it. I'm going to bed." We should be as confident and carefree as our pope because we know the Lord has everything under control. We do our best and trust that God will take care of the rest. The more confidence we have in God, the more He will manifest His presence and His power in our lives.

Practical Suggestions

1. Display religious images, such as the image of Divine Mercy, which includes the words "Jesus, I Trust in You." You may also display inspiring Scriptural quotes, such as "I can do all things in Christ who strengthens me."
2. Find a song that you like and can listen to when you need that extra boost of faith.
3. Pray to God, Our Lady, and the saints.
4. Pray in the presence of the Blessed Sacrament, asking Jesus Himself to help you.
5. Remember that prayer increases grace, humility, and faith. Pray piously and perseveringly for that which is conducive to your salvation.
6. Eliminate pride, attachments, apathy, and fear, which are obstacles to faith.
7. Know that when you are experiencing trials, you are being asked to grow in faith.

8. Pray the Act of Faith:

   O my God, I firmly believe
   that you are one God in three Divine Persons,
   Father, Son, and Holy Spirit.
   I believe that your divine Son became man
   and died for our sins and that he will come
   to judge the living and the dead.
   I believe these and all the truths
   which the Holy Catholic Church teaches
   because you have revealed them
   who are eternal truth and wisdom,
   who can neither deceive nor be deceived.
   In this faith I intend to live and die.
   Amen.

9. Pray the Act of Hope:

   O Lord God,
   I hope by your grace for the pardon
   of all my sins
   and after life here to gain eternal happiness
   because you have promised it
   who are infinitely powerful, faithful, kind,
   and merciful.
   In this hope I intend to live and die.
   Amen.

3

Love of God

The more we love God, the more we will grow in holiness.

And Mary said, "My soul magnifies the Lord." (Luke 1:46)

Greatest Virtue and Commandment

As we grow in the theological virtues, we grow in sanctifying grace. Having covered the virtues of faith and hope in the last chapter, we now turn to the greatest of the three theological virtues, the virtue of charity. The *Catechism* states: "Charity is the theological virtue by which we love God above all things for his own sake, and our neighbor as ourselves for the love of God."[39] Charity is the last of the three theological virtues and the most important one. St. Paul writes, "So faith, hope, love abide, these three; but the greatest of these is love" (1 Cor. 13:13). And without love, says St. Paul, everything is meaningless:

> If I speak in the tongues of men and of angels, but have not love, I am a noisy gong or a clanging cymbal. And if I

[39] CCC 1822.

> have prophetic powers, and understand all mysteries and all knowledge, and if I have all faith, so as to remove mountains, but have not love, I am nothing. If I give away all I have, and if I deliver my body to be burned, but have not love, I gain nothing. (1 Cor. 13:1–3)

Charity is the preeminent virtue that gives life and meaning to the other virtues and orders them in perfect harmony.

Not only is charity the greatest virtue, but it is also the greatest commandment in both the Old and New Testaments. In Judaism, the commandment to love God is known as the *Shema*, which refers to the first two words: "Hear, O Israel." This most important commandment remains the centerpiece of Judaism and its liturgical and prayer life. God gives the great commandment through Moses to His people:

> Hear, O Israel: The LORD our God is one LORD; and you shall love the LORD your God with all your heart, and with all your soul, and with all your might. And these words which I command you this day shall be upon your heart; and you shall teach them diligently to your children, and shall talk of them when you sit in your house, and when you walk by the way, and when you lie down, and when you rise. (Deut. 6:4–7)

The *Shema* is recited at every Jewish morning and evening prayer service and is considered the most important part of the prayer service by observant Jews.

In the New Testament, Jesus confirms that to love is the most important of all the commandments:

> But when the Pharisees heard that he had silenced the Sadducees, they came together. And one of them, a lawyer, asked him a question, to test him. "Teacher, which is the great

> commandment in the law?" And he said to him, "You shall love the Lord your God with all your heart, and with all your soul, and with all your mind. This is the great and first commandment. And a second is like it, You shall love your neighbor as yourself. On these two commandments depend all the law and the prophets." (Matt. 22:34–40)

These two commandments form the two parts of the virtue of charity: love of God and love of neighbor. We will see more clearly that the two cannot be separated. To love God is to love our neighbor, and we love our neighbor because of our love for God. This chapter focuses on the love of God, while chapter 8 will focus on the love of neighbor.

In order to love God, we have to know and experience His infinite love for us. Many people do not love God because they do not know Him and have no knowledge or experience of His love for them. How can you love someone whom you do not know? The Jewish people first had to learn that there is but one God. God chose to reveal that He is the only true God to the Israelites and, ultimately, to the whole world. He made a covenant with the chosen people: He would be their God, and they would be His people. In this covenant, God revealed His love and care for His people, liberating them from slavery in Egypt and bringing them to the Promised Land. In return, the people were to be faithful to the Lord by loving Him with all their heart, soul, mind, and strength.

In a polytheistic world, it was earth-shattering to discover that there was but one God. This meant that the Lord created every person and everything in the universe, and that He sustains and keeps everything and every person in existence. Through His providence, the Lord protects and provides for every living creature. As such, each person owes his or her entire life to the Lord and is to love God with his or her entire being.

Let us examine what it means to love God with all our heart, soul, mind, and strength. First, the heart is the innermost part of the person. It is where we decide to respond to God's love or to reject it. If we love God with all our heart, then every decision or choice we make must be consistent with our love for God; that is, it must be pleasing to God and bring us closer to Him. Second, the soul is the life-force of a person. To love God with all our soul is to give our time and our life over to the Lord. This entails sacrificing our own interests in order to serve the Lord's interests. It means dying to self and living for God alone. Third, the mind includes our thoughts, imagination, knowledge, understanding, and memory. Do we use all our mental faculties for the praise and glory of God? How often do we think about God, contemplate His goodness, or seek to know and understand Him? Do we entertain selfish thoughts and sinfully indulge our imagination? How often do we dwell on negative experiences rather than God's blessings? All our mental abilities should be animated and directed toward the love and glory of God. And fourth, to love God with all our strength is to be our best in everything for the glory and honor of His name. This includes refraining from doing anything that is sinful or displeasing to God and going out of our way to show our love for God by acts of worship and charity.

Blessed Are the Pure of Heart

Because of our fallen human nature, it is difficult for us to love God with all our heart, mind, and soul. Rather, we suffer from inordinate self-love; that is, we love ourselves too much, and we do not love God enough. We also have disordered affections and tend to love created things more than God. Created things are meant to lead us to God, but too often, we love things for themselves and forget about the Creator, without whom those things would not exist. We have a divided heart. Instead of loving God with all our heart, we divide our hearts between ourselves, the things of the world, and even sin. Thus, the motivations behind our choices and actions are often based on self-interest or the interests of others, rather than our love for God.

Imagine that we could take a spiritual X-ray of our heart. We would see its divisions: one part loves ourselves, another loves sin, yet another loves the things of the world, and one last part is dedicated to loving God. To love God with all our heart means we have to purify our heart of attachment to sin, self, and the things of the world. To love God with our whole heart is to seek to do His will in all things. We put aside our own will and the temptations of sin and worldly allurements to do the will of God, because we want to please our Father.

Once, I preached about the image of a spiritual X-ray in my homily. A woman came up to me after Mass and told me that as I was speaking, God revealed to her an image of her own heart. She saw that about half of it was filled with clear running water, while almost the entire other half was filled with sand, rocks, and gravel. One small part was filled with what looked like black mud. We understood together that the flowing clear water represented her pure love for God, the sand and gravel represented her love for the things of the world and for herself, and the black mud represented her love for sin.

Although we do not have such a spiritual X-ray machine, we can ask the Lord in prayer to reveal what our heart looks like to Him, so that we may have a better idea of how much of our heart belongs to the Lord and how much belongs to other competing interests. In this way, we can purify our love and give our heart wholly to God by rightly ordering our affections. In the Beatitudes, Jesus tells us, "Blessed are the pure in heart, for they shall see God" (Matt. 5:8). To be pure in heart means that our love is pure, not contaminated by self-love or disordered affections. We love God purely and completely for His sake, and we love all others because of our love for Him.

Mary's love for God is pure because she loves God for His sake, above all things and in all things. Mary's love is rightly ordered; that is, she loves the Lord with all her heart, mind, and soul. There is no taint of sin or inordinate love of self or the things of the world in Mary's Immaculate Heart. Our Lady revealed to St. Bridget of Sweden that her love for God has always been spotless: "When I had attained an age to know something of my Creator, I turned to Him with unspeakable love and desired Him with my whole heart."[40] Mary's heart is not divided; rather, it is completely whole and entirely at the service of the Lord.

We, too, ought to love God for who He is: the Creator of all that is good. He is goodness, truth, and life itself. All that is good comes from God's overflowing love. The love of the Trinity is so powerful that it cannot be contained, but overflows into creation. God, by nature, is constantly giving of Himself. Therefore, we love God because He is all good and deserving of all our love. To love God for His sake is to love the Lord for who He is and all that He is. The Lord is pure goodness, love, and life, and is worthy of all our affection.

Mary sees people and things as they are — as created by God out of His love so that He can lead us to know Him, love Him, and enjoy eternal beatitude with Him forever. Mary has no excessive self-love or disordered affections for things. Her love of God is so pure that she developed an aversion to the things of the world. Our Blessed Mother told St. Bridget of Sweden, "Then when I heard that He had given a Law to His people and wrought so many wonders with them, I firmly resolved in my mind to love naught but Him, and worldly things became most

[40] *Life of Mary*, 47.

bitter for me."[41] Mary wanted to give her heart to God alone. She saw that worldly things should not be loved for themselves but only in relation to the Creator and the purposes for which He created them. Nothing should obstruct our love for the Lord; instead, everything should increase our love for Him.

Do Everything for the Glory of God

But because we tend to have a divided heart, we must make a conscious effort to purify our intentions. St. Paul tells us that the love of God must be the central motivation for all our actions: "So, whether you eat or drink, or whatever you do, do all to the glory of God" (1 Cor. 10:31). To love God is to do everything well with the intention of pleasing and glorifying Him. We need to be aware of why we do what we do. What is the intention or motivation behind our action or inaction? Is it to glorify God or ourselves? Often, we have mixed motives or even ulterior motives. The more an action is done purely for the love and glory of God, the more pleasing it is in His sight.

Mary's love for the Lord is the motivation behind all her choices and actions. She wants to glorify the Lord in her life and in her whole being. The first words of her Magnificat reveal this desire: "My soul magnifies the Lord" (Luke 1:46). Another translation is "My soul proclaims the greatness of the Lord" (NABRE). Mary desires only God's glory. All her thoughts, words, and actions are aimed at pleasing the Lord.

Mother Teresa reminds us that we do not have to do great things, but just little things with great love. It is the love behind the action that gives the action its value. For example, if I wash the dishes by hand, I can do so without putting any thought or

[41] Ibid., 55.

intention into the action, or I can do the dishes carefully and well with the intention of offering this small act of love to God. In the latter case, my action is *sanctified* in that it is pleasing to the Lord, contributes to my holiness, and merits more graces, while the former has little or no merit in the eyes of God because I lack love and right intention. When we do something well out of love for God, our actions take on supernatural value. Our pure intention of doing something well for God's glory is most pleasing to Him and merits an increase in grace so that we may grow in charity. God desires that we grow in love, and hence, in holiness. Therefore, the more we try to do everything out of love for God, the more He will bless us with His graces.

In my office, I have a plaque with the letters *AMDG* within the four quadrants of a Jerusalem cross. The letters stand for *Ad Maiorem Dei Gloriam*, a Latin phrase that means "For the Greater Glory of God," which is the motto of the Society of Jesus, also known as the Jesuits. This plaque helps remind me to do everything not for my glory, but for the glory of God. We tend to seek attention and praise to feel affirmed, encouraged, and good about ourselves, but selfish motives diminish the supernatural value of our actions and reduce our capacity to merit more graces. However, if we are motivated by love for God and His glory, our actions take on supernatural value and merit an increase in grace. There are many times when we must do things that we would rather not do. We should view these occasions as opportunities to show our love for God by doing them well for His glory, thereby growing closer to the Lord and becoming more pleasing to Him. As a priest, I often have to do things I would prefer not to do—for example, waking up at 2:00 a.m. to give someone the Sacrament of the Anointing of the Sick. To tell you the truth, I would rather go back to sleep. But I get up anyway, telling myself, "I was ordained to be inconvenienced," and telling God, "I'm doing this out of love for you."

There is a phrase credited to Meister Eckhart that helps me sanctify my time and actions: "Holiness is doing the next thing that has to be done with your whole heart and finding delight in it." Sanctification is found in living out our state in life and fulfilling our daily duties with love and joy. The disposition of the heart is more important than the action itself when it comes to the Lord. "For the LORD sees not as man sees; man looks on the outward appearance, but the LORD looks on the heart" (1 Sam. 16:7). The Lord looks at the intention, love, and disposition behind our every action. May our heart and motives always be pleasing to the Lord.

Holiness Is the Perfection of Charity

St. Thomas Aquinas describes holiness as the perfection of charity. This makes sense because Scripture tells us that God is love and that He is holy.[42] Therefore, to be holy is to be like God and to love perfectly. But how do we know of God's love? And what does perfect love look like? St. John tells us, "For God so loved the world that he gave his only-begotten Son, that whoever believes in him should not perish but have eternal life" (John 3:16). God's love is revealed in the Paschal Mystery, that is, the life, Passion, death, and Resurrection of Jesus. St. Paul adds, "God shows his love for us in that while we were yet sinners Christ died for us" (Rom. 5:8). In other words, when we look at a crucifix, we see what love looks like. There is no greater love than to lay down one's life for another. By His life, death, and Resurrection, Jesus reveals the Father to us in His Person: "[Jesus] is the image of the invisible God" (Col. 1:15). The Son has shown us the love of the Father by becoming human and suffering and dying for our redemption.

[42] 1 John 4:8, 16; Lev. 19:2; 1 Pet. 1:16.

When we look at God's love, we see three essential qualities, the first being *sacrifice*. God the Father sacrifices His only begotten Son and sends Him into the world to become human, to suffer and die, so that we may have eternal life. The Father cannot possibly sacrifice any more—He is giving us *everything* by sacrificing what is most precious to Him: His only begotten Son. We see the same sacrifice in the Son, who, out of love for the Father and for us, becomes incarnate to suffer and die so that we may live. The Son cannot possibly sacrifice any more for us.

In this sacrifice, we see the necessity of *self-forgetfulness*, which is the second quality of God's love. Part of the great mystery of the kenosis, or self-emptying, of the Son of God in the Incarnation is that He humiliates Himself completely by taking a created human nature. This kenosis is heightened even more by the Lord's Crucifixion in His human nature. While the incarnate Word always knows Himself to be one of the Trinity by virtue of the beatific vision He possesses at every moment—even on the cross—we might analogically or metaphorically say He "forgets Himself" insofar as He empties Himself in total humility to assume our nature and suffer on our behalf.

The third quality of God's love is *acceptance*. The Father has created us with free will, and He accepts the fact that many will reject the gift of His only Son for our eternal life. Similarly, the Son accepts that many will spurn His love and reject the complete gift of Himself. Even those who believe in and accept God's love experience weaknesses, ingratitude, and sinfulness, which He lovingly accepts.

Nevertheless, we are called to imitate and reciprocate that perfect love. St. John puts it this way: "We love, because he first loved us" (1 John 4:19). We try to love God with the same kind of love with which He loves us. This calls for sacrifice, selfforgetfulness, and acceptance. For love to be authentic, there must be an element of sacrifice. We must give up something that is valuable and dear to us. Love is not just a warm and fuzzy feeling; it must cost us. Many Catholics are not even willing to sacrifice one hour a week to go to Mass; still others are unwilling to sacrifice time to pray, to do works of charity, or to give up meat on Fridays during Lent. Similarly, love requires that we forget ourselves to consider the good of others. But we tend to be self-absorbed. To love God is to forget our self-interest and think of honoring and glorifying the name of the Lord. With trust in God's providence and goodness, we must accept all the pain, confusion, and desolation that may accompany self-forgetful love. It is easy to say, "Lord, I love you," but God tells us, "Show me your love." Indeed, actions speak louder than words. Our love for God must be manifested in our lives by concrete actions performed as gifts of self to the Lord. Everything we do can become a gift for the Lord when we do it with that specific loving intention.

We have only our time on earth to perfect our love. In heaven, we can neither grow in love nor merit an increase in virtue. Our time to merit graces and grow in charity and holiness is limited to this life. If we have not yet reached perfection when we die, we will have to be purified in purgatory before we can see God face-to-face in heaven. The *Catechism* tells us: "All who die in God's grace and friendship, but still imperfectly purified, are indeed assured of their eternal salvation; but after death they undergo purification, so as to achieve the holiness necessary to enter the joy of heaven."[43] We have a limited time on this earth to perfect our charity. We do so by loving, that is, by performing acts of charity, purifying our motives, and living for God and His glory. The more we perform each action with the intention of doing our best out of love for God, the more the action is sanctified and has value in God's eyes, *and* the more we merit graces to

[43] CCC 1030.

continue to grow in charity. It is the exercising of our free will for the greater honor and glory of God that helps us perfect our charity and grow in holiness.

Mary and the saints are models of the perfection of charity and holiness. They have conformed their love to that of Jesus in a radical way. All the martyrs throughout the history of the Church refused to deny Christ. They sacrificed their lives, forgetting themselves and accepting suffering and death. Likewise, Mary gave herself completely to the Lord, forgetting herself and living only for the honor and glory of God, while accepting whatever pain and suffering God allowed to come her way. Mary imitates and reciprocates God's perfect sacrificial love; hence, she is showered with graces from above. In turn, Mary does not waste an ounce of grace but responds even more generously in loving and living for the Lord.

We can never really have enough time to show God our love for Him. The prolific writer Fr. Henri Nouwen stressed this reality to his students at Yale Divinity School. On the first day of his theology class, he would take chalk and draw a long horizontal line from one end of the chalkboard to the other. Then, he would explain that this long line represented God's love for us: "God loved you before you were born, and God will love you after you die. In Scripture God says, 'I have loved you with an everlasting love.' This is a very fundamental truth of your identity. This is who you are whether you feel it or not."[44] Then, in the middle of the horizontal line, he would draw two small vertical lines to indicate our limited time on earth. Fr. Nouwen would tell his students, "Your time on earth is just a short opportunity for you to say to God, 'I love you, too.'"[45] Truly, we do not have enough time in this short life to show our

[44] Henri J.M. Nouwen, *Finding My Way Home: Pathways to Life and the Spirit* (Chestnut Ridge, NY: Crossroad Publishing, 2018), 129.

[45] Ibid., 130.

love for God. We can never return to God the love He has given us. Therefore, we must not waste a single minute by not loving the Lord.

Self-Gift

To love consistently, we need to have a certain mindset to offset our tendency toward selfishness. The opposite of love is not hate, but selfishness or inordinate self-love. It is love turned inward rather than outward toward God and others. We need to understand that our life is not our own. Scripture tells us that we have been purchased at a price: "Do you not know that your body is a temple of the Holy Spirit within you, which you have from God? You are not your own; you were bought with a price. So glorify God in your body" (1 Cor. 6:19–20). Mary and the saints understand that their lives are not their own: they belong to the Lord. St. Peter explains that we have been purchased with the infinitely precious blood of the Lamb: "You know that you were ransomed from the futile ways inherited from your fathers, not with perishable things such as silver or gold, but with the precious blood of Christ, like that of a lamb without blemish or spot" (1 Pet. 1:18–19). As we do not belong to ourselves, but to God, we no longer live for ourselves, but for God.

God wants us to live for Him willingly, not out of a sense of duty, but out of love. We give ourselves back to the Lord not only because He has purchased us by the blood of Christ but because He deserves all our love. Out of His love and goodness, He has given us everything we have. We have nothing to call our own. Everything we have, and everything we are, belongs to the Lord. But He wants us to make a *gift of ourselves* to Him. He values our free will and does not force us to do anything, but if we truly love Him, we want to give ourselves completely back to Him. Mary and the saints are the perfect examples of this because they have freely given themselves to Him out of love.

For example, after his radical conversion, St. Ignatius of Loyola wrote his famous *Suscipe* prayer, in which he gave his entire being back to the Lord:

> Take, Lord, and receive all my liberty,
> my memory, my understanding,
> and my entire will,
> all I have and call my own.
> You have given all to me.
> To you, Lord, I return it.
> Everything is yours; do with it what you will.
> Give me only your love and your grace,
> that is enough for me.

St. Ignatius simply wants to live for God alone. He no longer wants to do anything for himself, but desires only to dedicate his life and use everything in his power for the glory of God. This is true love — to give oneself entirely to another.

Mary did not have to undergo a conversion before giving her life to the Lord. At a very early age, when she came to know God, she decided to give herself to Him. Mary revealed to Venerable Mary of Jesus of Agreda, "At the first sight of the Highest Good, my heart was wounded with love and I gave myself entirely to Him."[46] Mary gives herself to God out of pure love and lives her entire life for Him alone. In giving herself to the Lord, she is prepared to serve Him in whatever capacity He deems best. Hence, she refers to herself as the "handmaid" or "servant" of the Lord. Mary lives not for herself, but to serve the Lord.

To love is to serve and to forget oneself. There is a story about St. John Paul II that illustrates this concept. During one of his visits to another country, at the end of a long day with many stops,

[46] *Life of Mary*, 41.

a reporter asked him, "Holy Father, how do you feel after such a long hard day with so many visits?" His spontaneous answer was "I don't know." St. John Paul II did not have time to think about how he felt. He was so focused on loving God through loving others that he forgot about himself. A similar story is told about St. Teresa of Calcutta, who was so focused on serving Jesus in the poorest of the poor that she forgot herself entirely. As a culture, we tend to be consumed with ourselves, our wants, and our needs. However, the saints, who have given themselves to the Lord out of love, tend to forget about themselves and instead are willing to sacrifice their interests in the service of the Lord.

Giving oneself to God may be compared to giving oneself to a spouse in marriage. People who marry are usually in love with each other and describe this feeling as being on cloud nine. Truly, the emotion of love is intoxicating. One cannot help but think about the other person and look forward to seeing and pleasing him or her. Fr. Pedro Arrupe, S.J., superior general of the Society of Jesus from 1965 to 1983, is known for his quote about falling in love with God:

> Nothing is more practical than finding God, than falling in Love in a quite absolute, final way. What you are in love with, what seizes your imagination, will affect everything. It will decide what will get you out of bed in the morning, what you do with your evenings, how you spend your weekends, what you read, whom you know, what breaks your heart, and what amazes you with joy and gratitude. Fall in Love, stay in love, and it will decide everything.

Many saints have described falling in love with God. Falling in love changes your life because you become consumed with the other person. You start to live for this person, you want to be with him or her always, and you want to make him or her happy. In other words, this person makes you feel alive.

To Know God Is to Love Him

When you love someone, you want to know everything about him or her. You want to know what this person likes and dislikes and what is important to him or her. The same goes for God. To love God is to seek to know Him more and more. One cannot love someone one does not know. The more one knows God, the more one will love Him. Brother Lawrence of the Resurrection suggests: "Let us occupy ourselves entirely in knowing God. The more we know Him, the more we will desire to know Him. As love increases with knowledge, the more we know God, the more we will truly love Him."[47] There are different ways for us to seek to know God. One way is to read and study what saints, theologians, and other spiritual writers have written about Him. Therefore, we should make time for some spiritual reading every day. We can never stop learning and growing in our knowledge and love of God. There are many good spiritual books out there. Even if I have not done any spiritual reading all day, I can read a little right before going to bed because I always have a spiritual book on my nightstand.

Another way to learn more about God is to read, study, and meditate on Scripture. St. Jerome said, "Ignorance of Scripture is ignorance of Christ." So, to know Jesus, one must be familiar with the Bible. Peter Kreeft says that the Bible contains God's love letters to us. In it, the Lord reveals Himself, His love, and His plan for us. Therefore, have your own personal Bible. Buy a nice one to keep near you out in the open. Treasure this sacred book; be familiar with it. You might choose a study Bible or find biblical commentaries to help you better understand the meaning of the Scriptures.

Our Blessed Mother was well versed in the Old Testament. This is evident in her Magnificat, which is taken from different

[47] Brother Lawrence, *The Practice of the Presence of God* (New Kensington, PA: Whitaker House, 1982), 55.

psalms and other Scriptures and woven together in her own heart and soul. Mary probably memorized much of the Old Testament, and it became a part of her soul, her prayers, and her life. Mary and Joseph probably studied the Scriptures with Jesus. We know that Jesus was very familiar with the Old Testament because He quoted it throughout the New Testament. He used Scripture when He resisted the temptations of the devil, debated with scholars, and taught the crowds. In particular, Jesus prayed the Psalms, especially during His Passion. On the Cross, Christ made the words of Psalm 31 His own when He said, "Into your hands I commit my spirit" (v. 5; cf. Luke 23:46). He did the same with Psalm 22, praying, "My God, my God, why have you abandoned me?" (v. 1; cf. Matt. 27:46). We, too, should know the Word of God, for that is one way He speaks to us.

There are different ways for us to meditate on Scripture. One way is *lectio divina*, which literally means "divine reading." There are different ways to practice *lectio divina*, but the basic method is the same. Mine is as follows: first, I slowly *read* the Scripture passage I have chosen, usually one of the readings for Mass. I ask the Holy Spirit to enlighten me as to a word, phrase, or idea to which I should direct my attention, and then I continue reading a few more times to see what "jumps out at me" or "speaks to me." Second, I *reflect* on what God may want me to take away from this word, passage, or idea. I ask God to reveal to me what He wants me to know or understand about this point. After a few moments, I may make some notes. Third, I *respond* to God by trying to live out whatever message He gives me. For example, perhaps God is calling me into a deeper union with Him. I respond by thanking Him and resolving to unite myself to Him more consistently through prayer. These are my steps, and they are easy to remember: (1) read, (2) reflect, and (3) respond—three Rs. When we meditate on Scripture daily, we come to know God more intimately and grow in our love for Him.

Hatred of Sin

As we come to know God, we begin to conform ourselves to Him. We start to take on His dispositions, His likes and dislikes. To love God is to learn to love what He loves and to hate what He hates. Mary and the saints hate sin because they know how much sin offends God and separates us from Him. Scripture tells us, "The Lord loves those who hate evil; he preserves the lives of his saints; he delivers them from the hand of the wicked" (Ps. 97:10). Love of God requires a hatred and removal of sin, because sin and love do not mix. Mary revealed to St. Elisabeth of Schoenau: "A soul cannot have any virtue if it does not love God with all its heart, for from this love the abundance of grace descends into the soul. But after descending it does not remain, but flows away like water, if the soul does not hate its enemies, that is, its sins and vices."[48] Because we love the Lord, we should make every effort to avoid the near occasion of sin. Just as we seek to avoid a contagious disease, so too we should flee from sin, which is a disease of the soul.

We do not think about sin often because we do not think about our soul often. We take care of our body because we are constantly reminded of it. We take showers and brush our teeth every day. We try to eat healthy foods and exercise to keep our body looking and feeling good. When we suffer pain or have an injury or become ill, we tend to the problem with rest or medical treatment, but unfortunately, we tend to neglect our soul. Our body will age and die and decay, but our soul lives on forever. Sin harms and disfigures the soul. St. Teresa of Avila had a vision in which the human soul, created by God in His image and likeness, appeared as a beautiful sparkling diamond. Then, she saw the same soul in a state of mortal sin, covered with the most disgusting dirt, grime, and filth. Similarly, St. Christina

[48] *Life of Mary*, 56.

the Astonishing could smell sin. Whenever she was near someone in mortal sin, she could not handle the awful stench and did everything she could to get away from the sinner. Such is the reality and the nastiness of sin. Yet many people are oblivious to the state of their soul. They rarely go to the Sacrament of Confession, choosing instead to immerse themselves in a life of sin. Sin is to the soul what cancer is to the body. If not removed, it spreads and destroys. In our love for God, we should detest sin because it defaces the beauty of God in us and destroys our relationship with Him. Sin is contrary to the holiness and goodness of God. When we love someone, we never want to do anything that will displease him or her. Therefore, an authentic love of God carries with it an aversion to sin and evil.

Mary and the saints fled from sin as they tried to love God with their whole being. They teach us how to love the Lord. One of my favorite images of the Blessed Virgin Mary is the "Tenderness" icon, in which she is holding the child Jesus with their cheeks pressed together and their arms wrapped tightly around each other. Jesus is looking at His Mother with great love and affection, and Mary is looking at us, as if saying, "Imitate me in loving Jesus with all your heart." Mary, indeed, shows us how to love and embrace her Son, and Jesus teaches us how to love and embrace His Mother.

Mary and the saints know the preeminence of love. On the eve of her death, St. Thérèse said, "It is love alone that counts."[49] Similarly, another Doctor of the Church, St. John of the Cross, reminds us, "In the evening of life, we shall be judged on our love."[50] Love needs to inform everything we do. Love sanctifies all our actions and our soul. The love of God must permeate every aspect of our lives. Our love of God calls down ever more graces to help us grow

[49] *St. Thérèse of Lisieux: Her Last Conversations*, trans. John Clarke, O.C.D. (Washington, DC: ICS Publications, 1977), 262.

[50] St. John of the Cross, *Dichos* 64, quoted in CCC 1022.

in charity. The greater our love for the Lord, the greater the graces we will receive. So let us be creative and bold in loving the Lord.

Practical Suggestions

1. Hang a crucifix in every room as a reminder of the suffering that Jesus endured to reveal the love of God.
2. Practice self-denial and detachment from all that is not of God.
3. Have your own Bible, and read it often.
4. Get to know the Lord intimately through meditating on Scripture and spiritual reading.
5. Make time to be with God in prayer, especially in the presence of the Blessed Sacrament.
6. Purify the intentions behind your every action by choosing that which is most pleasing to God.
7. Try to do everything to the best of your ability out of love for God and for His honor and glory.
8. Strive to give more time to God and divine things, and eliminate all that is unnecessary.
9. Pray, "May all of my thoughts, words, and actions aim at doing what is most pleasing in your sight, O Lord."

4

Union with God

The more united we are to the Lord,
the more we will become like Him.

But Mary kept all these things,
pondering them in her heart. (Luke 2:19)

When we love someone, we want to be united with him or her always. That goes for loving God as well. When we are in love with God, we cannot imagine being apart from Him. We are united to the Lord with all our mind, heart, and soul. A key part of love is to be one with the beloved, and the more united we are to the one we love, the more we will become like him or her. In the last chapter, we talked about loving God, wanting to know Him, and conforming ourselves to Him. We also discussed the concept of holiness, which is taking on the likeness of Christ as we perfect our love. This chapter continues the theme of becoming like God by uniting ourselves to Him. But what does union with God look like? There are several aspects that are related, but the main idea is to be one with the Lord at all times in mind, heart, and soul.

Recollection

Recollection is the state of being calm, quiet, and present to the Lord as we acknowledge His presence. It is about having an interior life and a prayerful disposition in which we are in tune with God. Recollection is especially challenging in our society because of the prevalence of digital devices and easy access to media. Mobile phones, computers, and the Internet are constant sources of distraction. It is difficult for people to go a long time without giving in to the temptation of checking their email, social media apps, or favorite websites. This constant exposure to media makes us restless and keeps us on edge. Added to that is our hectic and fast-paced life, which is filled with many responsibilities and deadlines. There is a dearth of leisure, solitude, and peace. But having a quiet interior disposition is essential if we are to grow in grace and in our relationship with the Lord.

Jesus warns us about getting caught up in busyness and losing our peace, and He emphasizes the importance of being recollected and present to Him. In the biblical story of Martha and Mary, Jesus drives home this point:

> Now as they went on their way, he entered a village; and a woman named Martha received him into her house. And she had a sister called Mary, who sat at the Lord's feet and listened to his teaching. But Martha was distracted with much serving; and she went to him and said, "Lord, do you not care that my sister has left me to serve alone? Tell her then to help me." But the Lord answered her, "Martha, Martha, you are anxious and troubled about many things; one thing is needful. Mary has chosen the good portion, which shall not be taken away from her." (Luke 10:38–42)

How many of us can relate to Martha? Indeed, many of us are busy, restless, and anxious about many things. But Jesus emphasizes that "one thing is needful." We are called to imitate Mary, to choose the better part, and to be recollected, present, and attentive to Jesus; otherwise, we miss out on His presence, His Word, and His love.

A tension exists between *doing* and *being*. Our society highly values productivity. We are praised for working hard, being efficient, and being productive. If we are not working or *doing* something, we are considered lazy, wasteful, or unproductive. There is a sense that we must be *doing* something, or else we are not using our time wisely. But there is something to be said for just *being*. There is a benefit to being still and present to ourselves, those around us, and God, who is always with us. Scripture reminds us of the importance and value of peace and solitude: "Be still, and know that I am God" (Ps. 46:10). It is in stillness that we come to know God, to perceive His presence, and to hear Him speak. Without this peace and tranquility, we cannot truly be present to the Lord, and we are incompletely united to Him.

Blaise Pascal observed, "All the unhappiness of men arises from one single fact, that they cannot stay quietly in their own chamber."[51] We are so used to living and moving at a fast pace that we forget what it is like to slow down, to breathe, and to be still. We are habitually restless and agitated and cannot be at ease. This inability to be tranquil makes it difficult to pray. Jesus teaches His disciples the importance of solitude in prayer: "But when you pray, go into your room and shut the door and pray to your Father who is in secret; and your Father who sees in secret will reward you" (Matt. 6:6). Prayer unites us with the Lord, but we are often so restless that we cannot find the proper disposition even to begin to pray.

In addition, the activities and demands of our lives leave us with little or no time for prayer. In essence, many of us are telling God, "I

[51] Blaise Pascal, *Pensées*, trans. W. F. Trotter, Dover Philosophical Classics (Mineola, NY: Dover Publications, 2003), no. 139, p. 39.

am too busy for you." We are always in a hurry and cannot find the time to slow down and be recollected with the Lord. Yet it is God who has given us life, a family, a career, and everything else. All these gifts are given to us to lead us to the Lord, but we get so consumed with work and family that we forget about the Giver of every good gift. Yet without God, we would not even have time at all. Time is given to us by the Lord to be used in a way that leads us closer to Him. With time, we come to know the Lord and His love for us and begin to love Him in return. But we frequently misuse our time. We focus on the gifts rather than the Giver, the creatures rather than the Creator, and the temporary rather than the eternal. In a way, we turn the means into ends in themselves. We fill our life with passing matters that distract us and constantly demand our attention. We become enslaved to technology and a lifestyle that is focused on the material and the superficial rather than the true, the good, and the enduring. We crave fleeting pleasures that keep us hooked but never really satisfy us, because we are made for so much more.

We are body and soul, and we need spiritual nourishment and life. We are made to know God and share in His life and love, yet our hearts are set on passing things and have no room for God. Yet God respects our free will. He wants to liberate us from enslavement to the things of the world, but we must want to be liberated. The Lord patiently waits for us to realize our need for Him; turn away from all the noise and distractions; and seek peace, rest, and solitude in Him.

The Holy Spirit is subtle, gentle, and unobtrusive. God does not force His way into our lives, and He does not demand our attention. Rather, He comes to us softly, gently nudging us, inviting us to notice Him. This is how the prophet Elijah came to know the Lord:

> And he said, "Go forth, and stand upon the mount before the LORD." And behold, the LORD passed by, and a great

> and strong wind tore the mountains, and broke in pieces the rocks before the LORD, but the LORD was not in the wind; and after the wind an earthquake, but the LORD was not in the earthquake; and after the earthquake a fire, but the LORD was not in the fire; and after the fire a still small voice. And when Elijah heard it, he wrapped his face in his mantle and went out and stood at the entrance of the cave. (1 Kings 19:11–13)

Only when we are quiet, still, and recollected can we recognize God's presence and hear His "still small voice" speaking to our hearts. Only then can we come to know God, recognize His love for us, and desire to be in communion with Him.

Mary Kept All These Things in Her Heart

Our Blessed Mother has a quiet, recollected disposition, and she is comfortable with solitude. This quiet disposition allows her to perceive God's subtle presence and respond by uniting herself to Him. Her mind, heart, and soul are always connected to the Lord. Her love for God compels her to be one with Him. Truly, when we love someone, we want to be united to him or her always. Mary never leaves God's presence but uses her faculties to be in communion with the Lord. Many images of the Annunciation show Our Lady kneeling in prayer. Also, our Blessed Mother was not shocked that the angel Gabriel came to her, but was surprised at his greeting: "Hail full of grace, the Lord is with you." It seems as if Mary was accustomed to communicating with angels. Many times in the Bible, people are terrified when angels visit them because they are not used to seeing or hearing from spiritual beings. But in the Gospel, Mary appears rather at home with the angel Gabriel, as if she was familiar with the presence of angels. Actually, the mystics tell us that Mary did speak regularly to the angels.[52] In addition, as a woman of prayer, Mary turned her heart and mind to God frequently. When she was not speaking, praising, or singing hymns to the Lord directly, Mary pondered the things of God in her heart.

St. Luke also tells us that Our Lady was a contemplative, frequently reflecting on the marvels of God in her mind and heart. At the birth of Jesus, the shepherds came to visit the newborn Jesus lying in the manger: "And when they saw it they made known the saying that had been told them concerning this child; and all who heard it wondered at what the shepherds told them. But Mary kept all these things, pondering them in her heart" (Luke 2:17–19). Mary often reflects on the words and the actions of Jesus. In another example, after looking for the child Jesus for three days, Mary and St. Joseph find Him in the temple listening and speaking to the teachers. St. Luke describes the scene:

> And when they saw him they were astonished; and his mother said to him, "Son, why have you treated us so? Behold, your father and I have been looking for you anxiously." And he said to them, "How is it that you sought me? Did you not know that I must be in my Father's house?" And they did not understand the saying which he spoke to them. And he went down with them and came to Nazareth, and was obedient to them; and his mother kept all these things in her heart. (Luke 2:48–51)

Mary is always in communion with the Lord, either in prayer or by contemplating His mysteries. As Mary's children, we are called to learn her ways and imitate her quiet, contemplative disposition so that we may be united to the Lord at all times.

[52] Some saints, such as St. Padre Pio, were used to communicating with their guardian angel.

Indwelling of the Holy Trinity

God is always present to us, even when we are not present to Him. The Lord is actually closer to us than we think. In fact, God is closer to us than we are to ourselves. Sometimes, we are so distracted or consumed with our thoughts that we are not really present to ourselves. But when we are in the state of grace, the Holy Trinity dwells within us. We are indeed a temple of the Holy Spirit. Jesus promises: "If you love me, you will keep my commandments. And I will ask the Father, and he will give you another Counselor, to be with you for ever, even the Spirit of truth, whom the world cannot receive, because it neither sees him nor knows him; you know him, for he dwells with you, and will be in you" (John 14:15–17). Wondrously, the Father and the Son as well as the Holy Spirit come to dwell in us: "Jesus answered him, 'If a man loves me, he will keep my word, and my Father will love him, and we will come to him and make our home with him'" (John 14:23). We often forget that the Holy Trinity dwells in our soul. How often do we acknowledge God's presence, speak to Him, and spend time with Him? When we have guests in our home, we are expected to be attentive to them, speak to them, and care for their needs. We do not just ignore them and go about our own business. So it must be with the three Persons of the Holy Trinity, who are guests in our soul. We should acknowledge our guests, speak to the triune God, and get to know each Person of the Holy Trinity. Let us not neglect our divine guests but treat the Father, Son, and Holy Spirit with attention, affection, and gratitude.

The *Catechism* confirms that our union with God starts now: "The ultimate end of the whole divine economy is the entry of God's creatures into the perfect unity of the Blessed Trinity. But even *now* we are called to be a dwelling for the Most Holy Trinity."[53]

[53] CCC 260, emphasis mine.

St. Elizabeth of the Trinity was known for her spirituality and reflections on the intimacy of the indwelling of the Lord. She wrote, "It is there in the depths, in the heaven of my soul that I love to find Him, since He never leaves me: God in me, me in Him, oh that is my life."[54] Mary and the saints teach us that in a way, we can experience heaven on earth. We are called to a perfect union with God in heaven, but that reality starts the day we are baptized. Sanctifying grace allows us to share in the life of the Blessed Trinity on earth and to experience its fullness in heaven. Our life on earth is a process of growing in knowledge, intimacy, and conformity with the ever-present triune God. It would be a shame for us to forget our lofty vocation. St. Elizabeth of the Trinity left us a prayer to help us develop an intimate, peace-filled union with the Lord, even in our noisy and chaotic world:

> O my God, Trinity whom I adore; help me forget myself entirely that I may be established in you as still and as peaceful as if my soul were already in eternity. May nothing trouble my peace or make me leave you, O my unchanging One, but may each minute carry me further into the depths of your mystery. Give peace to my soul, make it your heaven, your beloved dwelling and your resting place. May I never leave you there alone but be wholly present, my faith wholly vigilant, wholly adoring, and wholly surrendered to your creative action.[55]

Many saints speak about a sanctuary in their heart where God resides. They come to this sanctuary often to speak to the Lord, to spend time with Him, and to rest in His love. Truly, the Lord waits

[54] Elizabeth of the Trinity, *Always Believe in Love*, ed. Marian T. Murphy, O.C.D. (Hyde Park, NY: New City Press, 2009), 40.

[55] Ibid., 130.

for us in the deepest part of our being to share with us His peace, consolation, and joy—if only we would remember to visit Him. I know it is difficult to turn inward when the busyness of our lives makes turning outward so tempting. But knowledge, remembrance, and practice make it possible to be united to the Lord even amid the noise of everyday life. It takes a conscious effort and much practice to have an interior life. Imagine the waters of the ocean: if we live mostly on the surface, we will be tossed about by storms, winds, waves, and unpredictable weather. But if we go deep beneath the surface, we will find a place that is tranquil, calm, and serene. Likewise, when we turn to the Lord in the quiet sanctuary of our heart, we can experience calm, rest, and peace—a taste of heaven on earth.

We do not have to take off work to tend to our divine guests. Wherever we are, whatever we are doing, God is always with us. He sustains us in all that we do. We should turn to Our Lord often throughout the day and seek His help in our work, our family, and our social life. Brother Lawrence teaches us about the practice of the presence of God. He describes it in this way:

> God does not ask much of you. But remembering Him, praising Him, asking for His grace, offering Him your troubles, or thanking Him for what He has given you will console you all the time. During your meals or during any daily duty, lift your heart up to Him, because even the least remembrance will please Him. You don't have to pray out loud; He's nearer than you can imagine.[56]

It does not sound very difficult for us to practice the presence of God according to Brother Lawrence. Yet not many people turn to the Lord throughout the day. Instead, we usually separate our time

[56] Brother Lawrence, *Presence of God*, 37.

according to work, family, and prayer. But Mary and the saints tell us that it is possible to include prayer in all aspects of our lives. In fact, St. Paul tells us to "pray constantly" (1 Thess. 5:17). This is possible only if we pray while performing all the different duties and activities of life. Even while Mary was busy taking care of St. Joseph and Jesus, she was in prayer. The saints tell us, "She spent every moment in profound inner recollection, prayer, and spiritual communion with God in her heart."[57] It takes a conscious effort to cultivate and develop a recollected interior disposition. But God gives us the grace, and if we do our best, He gives us even more graces to grow in contemplation and union with Him.

Relationship

One of the graces that God gives us when we turn to Him is the grace to grow in our relationship with Him. The more we unite ourselves to the Lord, the more we will know Him, love Him, and become like Him. In order to know someone, we have to spend time with that person. By spending time with the Lord, we come to know Him not so much intellectually, but intuitively and personally. This is the friendship that Jesus speaks of to His disciples: "No longer do I call you servants, for the servant does not know what his master is doing; but I have called you friends, for all that I have heard from my Father I have made known to you" (John 15:15). Jesus desires an intimate friendship with each one of us. He offers us His friendship and invites us to come to Him, to be with Him, to know Him, and to love Him. This friendship is not so much for His benefit as it is for ours. We are made to know God, to love Him, and to share in His eternal life and happiness.

[57] *Life of Mary*, 70.

We are made to have a loving relationship with each of the three Persons of the Holy Trinity: Father, Son, and Holy Spirit. We are called to know the Father as *Abba*, which is a term of endearment that signifies intimacy and tenderness. It is the Holy Spirit that helps us to call God *Abba*: "For you did not receive the spirit of slavery to fall back into fear, but you have received the spirit of sonship. When we cry, 'Abba! Father!' it is the Spirit himself bearing witness with our spirit that we are children of God" (Rom. 8:15–16). The image of a father may have negative associations for some of us, but the Holy Spirit helps us to have a new understanding of our true Father in heaven, who is full of tenderness and compassion. The all-knowing Father is full of goodness and cannot wait to lavish His gifts on His children. This filial relationship changes our view of our own identity, worth, and dignity. We learn that we are the apple of God's eye and precious in His sight. We have God's DNA because we are His sons and daughters, made in His image and likeness. Knowing God as *Abba* changes our outlook on life: we become more confident, knowing that the Creator of the universe loves us personally, passionately, and infinitely. The more we remain united to the Father, the more we discover our true identity and lofty vocation as His sons and daughters.

We are also called to unite ourselves to the Holy Spirit, the Lord, the Giver of Life. The Holy Spirit is the *breath* of God, and He gives us a new *life* in the Lord. The Spirit re-creates and transforms us into His holy temple, a sanctuary for His dwelling, where He lives and breathes the divine life into us. The Spirit gives us a share in the eternal life and love of the Blessed Trinity. The Holy Spirit is God's *love* poured into our hearts (Rom. 5:5), enabling us to experience the immense love of the Holy Trinity and allowing it to overflow to others. The love of the Spirit sets us on fire for love of God and neighbor as we become zealous for the glory of God and the salvation of souls. Jesus says, "I came to cast fire upon the earth; and would that it were already enkindled" (Luke 12:49). The fire of the Holy Spirit also purifies us and makes us holy, for He is known as the *Sanctifier*. In addition, the Holy Spirit empowers us with His gifts and charisms and enables us to participate in building up the Body of Christ on earth. Also known as the *Advocate* and the *Consoler*, the Spirit of God enlightens us to the truth of God and comforts us in our need.

Union Transforms and Perfects

Union with the Lord allows us to know and experience the love of God, which transforms us into His likeness. We tend to become like those whom we love and with whom we spend our time. Spouses tend to take on each other's qualities. They tend to like the same types of food, vacation spots, or forms of entertainment. Close friends also tend to like the same things and may even begin to look and act alike. They may wear the same kinds of clothes, use the same vocabulary, and act in similar ways. So it is with God: when we spend time in union with the Lord, we tend to become like Him and take on His qualities. The Church teaches, "Christ . . . fully reveals man to man himself and makes his supreme calling clear."[58] In Jesus, we see who we are made to be. By taking on the likeness of Christ, we reclaim the image of God in us that has been defaced by sin and trauma, and we become who He created us to be.

The more we are united to the Lord, the more He actively and effectively transforms us into His likeness. In her *Dialogue*, St. Catherine of Siena asks the Father how she can grow in perfection. The Father tells her:

[58] Vatican Council II, Pastoral Constitution on the Church *Gaudium et Spes* (December 7, 1965), no. 22.

> See that you remain united with me in loving affection for I am supreme and eternal purity. I am the fire that purifies the soul. So the nearer the soul comes to me the more pure she will become, and the more she departs from me the more unclean she is. This is why worldly folk fall into such wickedness because they have left me. But the soul who unites herself directly with me shares in my own purity.[59]

The more we are united to the Lord in love, the more we will grow in purity and holiness. This is one of the secrets to sanctity and a more intimate union with God. When we are united to God in loving affection, we take on His likeness, which is all-good, holy, and perfect. This is why Mary and the saints are holy—because they are united to the Lord, they love Him, and they are conformed to His likeness.

The Holy Trinity reveals that God is not an isolated individual but a communion of Persons. God Himself is a reciprocal relationship of self-giving love. From all eternity, the Father gives Himself, all that He is, and all that He has to the Son. The Son receives everything from the Father and gives Himself completely to the Father in return. The bond of love between the Father and the Son is so complete, so real, and so powerful that it becomes life-giving in the Person of the Holy Spirit. St. Augustine says that the Father is the *Lover*, the Son is the *Beloved*, and the Holy Spirit is *Love*. So, made in the image and likeness of God, we too are made for relationship. We are made to love and to be loved. We are incomplete until we give ourselves in love. The Church teaches, "Man . . . cannot fully find himself except through a sincere gift of himself."[60] We are made to have self-giving relationships with God and with

[59] Catherine of Siena, *Dialogue*, 191.

[60] Vatican Council II, *Gaudium et Spes*, no. 24.

one another. Fr. Norris Clarke, S.J., puts it this way: "To be is to be together." In other words, to exist is to be in relationship, and to be fully human is to give and receive love.

We are made to participate in the reciprocal self-giving love of the Trinity, to know each of the Persons intimately, and to share this love with others. Husbands and wives, in particular, are called to this oneness. In the book of Genesis, we learn that from the beginning, God created Adam and Eve to come together as man and wife and thus become one: "Therefore a man leaves his father and his mother and clings to his wife, and they become one flesh" (Gen. 2:24). This reciprocal self-giving love between husbands and wives comes from the unity of the Trinity and is meant to reflect the love of God in the world. Married love shares in the fecundity of God's love and takes physical form in the couple's children. The family unit reflects the love and unity of the Holy Trinity. Each of us is called to cling to God and become one with Him, just as a husband clings to his wife and becomes one with her. In our oneness with God, we do not lose our identity but discover who we truly are as we share in His life-giving love.

Mary is always intimately united to the Lord and never loses her identity but, on the contrary, fulfills her unique vocation as the Mother of God and as our Mother and model. Analogically, Catholics frequently speak of Mary's cooperation with the Holy Spirit in marital or spousal terms. As such, some popular devotions may refer to Mary as the Spouse of the Holy Spirit. This is not meant literally; rather, it reveals how Mary's will is always conformed to God's will, which produces a certain unity between her and God. The more closely we are united to the Lord, the more we fulfill our vocation as His children and bring glory to His name.

The spiritual masters speak about the three stages of the spiritual life through which we are called to advance: the *purgative*, the *illuminative*, and the *unitive*. The *purgative* stage marks the initial conversion in which one turns away from sin and toward God in prayer and the practice of virtue. In the *illuminative* stage, one grows in the knowledge and love of God and advances to a quieter, more contemplative way of prayer. A person in this stage is practicing high levels of virtue and conformity to God's will. In the *unitive* stage, heroic virtue and contemplative prayer are the normal way of life, and one experiences what is called the *mystical*, *transforming*, or *spousal* union with the Lord. We are called to this highest level of union with God on earth as a preparation for our union with Him in heaven. Unfortunately, many do not reach this *unitive* stage because they insufficiently recognize and respond to God's grace. But the saints, who respond fully to God's grace, are invited to this perfect union with the Lord as a prelude to eternal life. To the extent that we are united to the Lord, we can experience heaven on earth.

As we grow in the spiritual life and come closer to the Lord, the expressions of our prayer evolve. We start with *vocal* prayers, conversing with the Lord and the saints through the words of common prayers such as the Our Father, the Hail Mary, and the Act of Contrition. These prayers help us express what we want to say when we do not know how to formulate our words. These prayers also form us to acquire the proper disposition for addressing the Lord and Mother Mary. The next level of prayer is *meditation*, which involves using our mind to reflect on the Word of God and the mysteries of our redemption.

In the highest level of prayer, *contemplation*, we are united with God. Speaking and thinking cease, and pure love abounds. In contemplation, the focus is not on our words, or even on God's Word, but on God Himself. It is a quiet prayer in which our gaze is on the Lord as we rest in His goodness and love Him without words. When two lovers are together, words sometimes get in the way, for love at this level is more effectively communicated directly from heart to heart. Once, St. John Vianney saw a farmer spending time in the presence of the Blessed Sacrament without ever moving his lips. When the saint asked him what he was doing, the man replied, "I look at Him, and He looks at me." Contemplation is being present to the Lord, marveling at His beauty, and embracing Him with all our heart.

The *Catechism* defines prayer this way: "Prayer is the raising of one's mind and heart to God or the requesting of good things from God."[61] Regrettably, most people raise their mind and heart to God *only* to request something. We often take our relationship with God for granted. We turn to the Lord when we are desperate or in need of something. Then, when everything is going well, we do not even think of the Lord. We tend to treat our relationship with God like one of utility. We turn to the Lord only when it is beneficial for us. How would you like it if a friend thought of you and contacted you only when he or she wanted something from you? You would not consider that person a true friend but one who takes advantage of you. So it is with God and us. Although God knows our weaknesses and forgives us, He desires a true friendship with us. To be friends with someone is to like and esteem the other person for who he or she is, not just what he or she can do for us. We enjoy being with the other person, whose good and happiness we desire. We enjoy union and goodwill with each other.

As everyone knows, relationships need to be fostered and tended to if they are to grow. Relationships require faithfulness. Imagine what would happen if you never talked to your spouse or your best friend. The relationship would suffer, and undoubtedly, you would grow apart. In the same way, we must spend time with the Lord for our relationship to develop. St. Luke tells us that Jesus often went before dawn to a secluded place by Himself to be alone with the Father in prayer. Like her Son, Mary also had a practice of rising

[61] CCC 2559.

in the middle of the night to be alone with God in prayer. Some religious communities continue this practice by praying the Divine Office in the middle of the night.

The saints love God for who He is, they enjoy being in His presence, and they take every opportunity to be united with Him. They teach us that when we make an effort and take time to be with and united to the Lord, He blesses us abundantly.

Apart from Me You Can Do Nothing

Our union with the triune God is essential if our work is to bear fruit that will last. The Martha in us is restless and wants to work, be active, and get things done. But Jesus reminds us that we need to be united to Him if our work is to bear fruit for the kingdom. Not being united with God, we can still accomplish much in the world, but these are secular accomplishments that hold little value in the eyes of the Lord. If we want to be effective in bearing witness to Christ and building His kingdom on earth, we must be in union with Him. Jesus tells us: "Abide in me, and I in you. As the branch cannot bear fruit by itself, unless it abides in the vine, neither can you, unless you abide in me. I am the vine, you are the branches. He who abides in me, and I in him, he it is that bears much fruit, for apart from me you can do nothing" (John 15:4–5). The word *abide* is also used by Jesus to describe His intimate union with the Father. Therefore, Jesus is calling us to the same intimacy with Him that He has with the Father. This is necessary if we are to bear lasting fruit for the kingdom.

When Jesus called the Twelve to be His apostles, He first wanted them to spend time with Him, get to know Him, and be united to Him: "And he appointed twelve, *to be with him*, and to be sent out to preach and have authority to cast out demons" (Mark 3:14–15, emphasis mine). Jesus knew that without an intimate knowledge of and union with Him, the apostles would fail in their apostolic work and would not be able to fulfill their mission. The apostles first had to enter into this close friendship with Christ and remain in this bond if they were to be effective witnesses to the gospel. So, when Jesus sent them out, He instructed them, "Take no gold, nor silver, nor copper in your belts, no bag for the journey, nor two tunics, nor sandals, nor a staff" (Matt. 10:9–10). Without material goods, the apostles were forced to remain united to Jesus and rely on His strength and grace. It was the Holy Trinity who dwelled in the apostles, worked through them, and brought success to their work. Remember, the apostles were fishermen and tax collectors by trade. They would not have stood a chance if they were not united to Jesus and did not allow His grace to work in and through them. Abiding in Jesus and relying on His grace, the Twelve were able to spread the gospel message to the whole world.

Likewise, though we are weak and limited, God can accomplish incredible things through us if we abide in Him and He in us. We must rely not on our own skills and strength, but on the power of God, who lives and works in us. When we are intimately united to Jesus, not only will His power be manifested in our work but His presence will be revealed in our being. When we see saintly persons, we detect the presence of God in them. God's presence was undeniably clear in St. Teresa of Calcutta, St. John Paul II, and St. Pio of Pietrelcina. When we are closely united to the Lord in love, others will tend to perceive the spark of the divine in us. Truly, we are called to be God's instruments in the world. Our lives must bear witness to Christ, bring glory to God, and overflow with His presence.

The Grace of the Present Moment

God gives us grace at each moment of our lives. But if we are distracted or preoccupied, we are not truly present to the Lord in the here and now, and we can miss out on His grace. Fr. Jean-Pierre de Caussade, S.J., called this grace "the sacrament of the present moment." Often, we are preoccupied with what has happened in the past, or we are distracted by thoughts of the future. As a result, we are not truly living in the present moment. St. Faustina tells us that although life may seem routine sometimes, every moment is precious if we understand the life of grace. The saint writes:

> O life so dull and monotonous, how many treasures you contain! When I look at everything with the eyes of faith, no two hours are alike, and the dullness and monotony disappear. The grace which is given to me in this hour will not be repeated in the next. It may be given me again, but it will not be the same grace. Time goes on, never to return again. Whatever is enclosed in it will never change; it seals with a seal for eternity.[62]

When we are not living in the present moment, united to the Lord, we can miss the valuable graces that He gives us at each moment. On the contrary, each moment of the day is sanctified when we are one with the Lord in love.

In Greek, there are two words for time: *chronos* and *kairos*. *Chronos* is chronological or sequential and is measured in minutes, hours, days, months, years, and so on. *Kairos*, on the other hand, is the *eternal now* where God lives and acts. *Chronos* has a quantitative nature, while *kairos* has a qualitative and permanent nature. The two interact because God acts in human history. But to realize this interaction requires an awareness of the *eternal now* in which God is present.

St. Augustine advises us to live fully in the present moment in order to experience God's love fully. He writes, "Surrender the

[62] *Diary*, no. 62.

past to God's mercy, the future to His providence, and the present to His love." If we live too much in the past or the future, we miss out on God's precious love in the present. Mary and the saints keep their eyes on God's abundant love and receive all that He wants to shower upon them at each and every moment. Jesus reminded the French mystic Gabrielle Bossis to "give all your loving attention to each little moment. Think of this all your life through. Nothing of the past. Nothing of the future. Only the present moment of love."[63]

We need to remember that God is constantly gazing at us with loving attention. How He wishes we would return that gaze. The Lord pursues us like an impassioned lover. St. Catherine of Siena writes:

> O eternal Father. O fiery abyss of charity.... O mad lover. And you have need of your creature? It seems to me, for you act as if you could not live without her.... Why then are you so mad? Because you have fallen in love with what you have made. You are pleased and delighted over her within yourself, as if you were drunk [with desire] for her salvation. She runs away from you and you go looking for her. She strays and you draw closer to her.[64]

Like a mad lover, the Lord does not give up on us, but pursues us because He created us for Himself, and He is consumed with our salvation, eternal happiness, and union with Him.

In our world of constant distraction, which includes a heightened focus on digital devices and media consumption, one can see how easy it is not to be truly present in the moment. Everywhere we go, people are constantly looking at their phones and are not

[63] Gabrielle Bossis, *He and I*, trans. Evelyn M. Brown (Sherbrooke, QC: Médiaspaul, 1985), 142.

[64] Catherine of Siena, *Dialogue*, 325.

really present to each other or their surroundings. One day, while at a restaurant, I saw a young mother and her daughter having lunch together. The whole time, the mother was on her cell phone. The daughter was very patient and tried talking to her mother. She would sometimes say something back but would not take her eyes off her phone. After a while, the daughter realized that her mother was preoccupied, gave up trying to talk to her, and just sat there pretty much by herself. It was sad to see the mother and daughter miss out on the grace of the present moment, their chance of spending some quality time together, and the opportunity to bond while sharing a meal. Imagine the conversation and the connection that could have taken place had the mother put her phone away. That is sometimes how it is with God and us. God is present and sitting across from us, waiting for our attention, wanting to talk to us. But we are preoccupied with our phone or our thoughts, and we tune Him out. But we are the ones that miss out on the precious love and grace of that moment forever.

In his Encyclical on Care for Our Common Home *Laudato Si'*, Pope Francis talks about the danger of digital distractions. He writes, "When media and the digital world become omnipresent, their influence can stop people from learning how to live wisely, to think deeply and to love generously."[65] We need quiet and solitude in order to think and contemplate. Silence, which is so elusive, is necessary for us to get in touch not only with God and others but also with ourselves. Perhaps we are uncomfortable with getting to know ourselves. We may harbor fears, insecurities, and shame that we would rather ignore, suppress, and hide. At the same time, it is important to reflect on our deepest desires, dreams, and hopes. Therefore, we need silence, solitude, and recollection to get in

[65] Pope Francis, Encyclical Letter on Care for Our Common Home *Laudato Si'* (May 24, 2015), no. 47.

touch with who we are and what we are about. Perhaps we do not want to be vulnerable, or we think it is silly to reflect on our struggles, dreams, and purpose in life. But by denying time and space for introspection, we miss out on the wonder of our being. Psalm 139 speaks about the amazement of discovering ourselves through the eyes of God: "For you formed my inward parts, you knitted me together in my mother's womb. I praise you, for I am wondrously made" (vv. 13–14). We come to know God better when we know ourselves better. Noise, distractions, and preoccupations rob us of the chance to step back, breathe, and ponder.

Our world's many distractions can really make us miss out on so much that life has to offer. It is indeed difficult to be united to the Lord at all times and to receive all that He wants to give us if we are constantly checking our phones. A recent study reveals that on average, Americans check their phones once every twelve minutes—which adds up to eighty times per day.[66] When we are connected to our phones, we are disconnected from the one who matters most. God will not compete with our mobile phones. We must make a conscious choice to know, receive, and respond to His love instead of checking the number of "likes" we received for our last post on social media.

Even our prayers emphasize the importance of the present moment. In the Hail Mary, we pray, "Holy Mary Mother of God, pray for us sinners, *now* and at the hour of our death." These words mean that we are asking Mary to pray for us at *this moment*, as we are reciting the prayer. In effect, we are asking for all the graces we can receive at this particular moment in time. *Now* is an essential

[66] This study was conducted by Asurion, a global tech protection company. "Americans check their phones 80 times a day: study," *New York Post*, November 8, 2017, https://nypost.com/2017/11/08/americans-check-their-phones-80-times-a-day-study.

time, as well as the hour of our death. These are the two times we need Mary's prayers the most. As another example, in the Glory Be, we pray: "Glory be to the Father, and to the Son, and to the Holy Spirit. As it was in the beginning, is *now*, and ever shall be, world without end. Amen." By these words, at this present moment, we are honoring the glory of the Holy Trinity as it existed from the beginning and will be forever. *Now* is a unique and precious moment in which we want God to be glorified.

Likewise, in the Our Father, Jesus teaches us to pray: "Our Father, who art in heaven.... Give us *this day* our daily bread." By these words, Jesus teaches us to focus on the present moment and live one day at a time, asking God for enough bodily and spiritual food for each day. Furthermore, we have the Morning Offering, which helps us concentrate on each particular day: "O my Jesus, through the Immaculate Heart of Mary, I offer you my prayers, works, joys, and sufferings of *this day* for all the intentions of your Sacred Heart." The prayers given to us by Scripture and the Church express the centrality of focusing on the here and now.

Scripture is filled with passages that emphasize the primacy of the present moment. Priests and religious recite Psalm 95 as the very first prayer every morning. It reads: "O that *today* you would listen to his voice! Harden not your hearts, as at Meribah, as on the day at Massah in the wilderness, when your fathers tested me" (vv. 7–9, emphasis mine). Here, God is reminding us to have an open, docile, and attentive heart every day. Also, in the New Testament, we hear, "*Today*, when you hear his voice, do not harden your hearts" (Heb. 4:7, emphasis mine). Jesus Himself tells us: "Therefore do not be anxious about tomorrow, for tomorrow will be anxious for itself. Let *the day*'s own trouble be sufficient for the day" (Matt. 6:34, emphasis mine).

Everything takes on new meaning when done or experienced in union with the Lord because His merits become our merits. In St.

Thérèse of Lisieux's Morning Offering prayer, she prays, "I desire to sanctify every beat of my heart, my every thought, my simplest works, by uniting them to [the Sacred Heart's] infinite merits." All our thoughts, words, and actions can be sanctified when united to Jesus for love of Him. Our goal is to be so united and conformed to Christ that when the Father looks at us, He sees His Son, Jesus, and His Son's merits in us.

Our Mother and model, Mary, lives moment to moment in God's presence, receives all His graces, and responds fully to His love. She is always in union with the Lord, through good times and difficult times. Mary is always one with the Lord in mind, heart, and soul. We, too, are called to have this intimate union with the Lord at all times. My spiritual director tells me that God is always lovingly attentive to us and our needs. In return, we should pay devoted attention to the Lord as He gazes lovingly at us and blesses us with His gifts. In this way, we will be able to grow closer to the Lord and increase our ability to recognize and respond to His gifts from moment to moment.

Practical Suggestions

1. Reduce your screen time.
2. Make prayer your first activity of the day. Set aside some quiet time in the morning to be alone with the Lord. If you can do so in the presence of the Blessed Sacrament, all the better.
3. Practice deep breathing with prayer. Start by sitting in a comfortable position (preferably in front of the Blessed Sacrament, a crucifix, or another Christian image); then, breathe in and out deeply and slowly through your nose. As you breathe in, you can say in your mind, "Lord Jesus Christ, Son of the living God," and as you breathe

out, "Have mercy on me, a sinner." This is known as the Jesus Prayer. Alternatively, as you breathe in, you can say, "Come, Holy Spirit, fill the hearts of us your faithful," and as you breathe out, "And enkindle in us the fire your love." As you are doing this, you can have an image in your mind of Jesus, the Holy Spirit, or the Holy Trinity filling you up as you breathe in, and as you breathe out, think of letting go and releasing all your sins and anxieties.

4. Take a yearly silent retreat.
5. Take time to rest, recuperate, and rejuvenate.

5

Gratitude and Praise to God

The more gratitude and praise we express to God, the more He will bless us.

For he who is mighty has done great things for me, and holy is his name. (Luke 1:49)

The Source of All That Is Good

The secular world speaks a lot about gratitude, but never about gratitude to God. Rather, our culture promotes a general attitude of being thankful for what we have. We are encouraged to practice gratitude not so much because it is right, but because it makes us happy. Many psychologists and self-help authors tell us that if we want to be happy and feel better about ourselves, we should practice gratitude. They tell us to identify and name the things for which we are grateful, and the process will give us a greater sense of overall well-being.

The definition of *gratitude* is "the quality of being thankful; readiness to show appreciation for, and to return kindness."[67] But

[67] Lexico.com, s.v. "gratitude," accessed May 6, 2020, https://www.lexico.com/en/definition/gratitude.

popular authors do not speak about identifying the source of our blessings. Therefore, their definition of gratitude is incomplete. How are we supposed to show appreciation and return kindness when no person or source is identified? To whom shall we go to give thanks and show appreciation and return kindness? For the secular world, it does not matter. Gratitude is more about making ourselves happy than acknowledging the goodness of another. The source of our blessings remains a mystery and is considered irrelevant. We are thankful for what we have because this attitude makes us feel good about ourselves, not because we want to acknowledge Someone's goodness and show our appreciation for His kindness.

The world does not want to talk about the source of our blessings because the topic of God may come up, which is a taboo in our politically correct society. Besides, the aim of gratitude is about what I can do for myself and how I can most benefit. My end is my happiness, and gratitude is a means to that end. It is ironic that gratitude is valued not because it is virtuous or morally correct, but because it is self-beneficial and self-gratifying. Instead of being a virtuous practice, gratitude actually becomes an occasion for selfishness. The psychological view of gratitude is that it is not a matter of justice (rightfully thanking the person who helped us), but a matter of making *us* happier, which is the bottom line. To heck with righteousness and justice — it is all about me.

In contrast, Scripture reminds us that it is important to know that God is the source of all that is good: "Do not be deceived, my beloved brethren. Every good endowment and every perfect gift is from above, coming down from the Father of lights with whom there is no variation or shadow due to change" (James 1:16–17). Ultimately, all gratitude should rightly be given to God, the Author of every good gift. Even if we identify persons in our lives to whom we should be grateful, ultimately, the source of all goodness can be traced back to the Lord. We can thank our spouse, friends, teachers, or parents for their goodness, but the source of all that is good is the Lord Himself. God is the Creator of all that is good, and all creation takes its goodness, beauty, and truth from Him. Each creature participates in God's goodness and reflects His qualities. Just as an artist leaves his mark, something of himself in his work, so the Lord leaves His imprint, His mark, something of Himself, in all His creation. Therefore, as we acknowledge and thank the people in our lives for their goodness, we should also give thanks to the Lord.

But how often do we give thanks to God? How often do we go back to the source of all that is good? We may be grateful for the gift of life, health, family, career, or friends. But we often forget to acknowledge and thank the Giver of these gifts. Every sentiment of gratitude ought rightfully to be traced back to the Author of life and all that is beautiful, true, and good. We ought to thank God for all that we have and all that we are, because everything comes from Him as a gift.

God's usual way of giving is by a proximate cause; that is, He tends to use an intermediary, another person, as an instrument to show forth His goodness: a stranger who gives you an unexpected smile, a spouse who forgives when you make a mistake, or a friend who is there to support you when you need it most. All these people are instruments of God's love. When we are grateful for a person's kind act, we should thank not only him or her but also the Lord, because He brought that person into our life and gave him or her the inspiration and opportunity to do good.

Even when God does not work through an intermediary, He blesses us with His gifts. When we see a beautiful sunset, when we receive a promotion at work, when we enjoy a good movie—these are gifts from the Lord. Often, we attribute our good fortune to happenstance, luck, or coincidence. But an accident avoided, an unexpected encounter with an old friend, or a song on the radio that moves your heart—these are all part of God's providence. Many times, we chalk these occasions up to our being at the right place at the right time. We rarely think that God is present and active, aware of every detail in our lives and always blessing us with His gifts. The Lord is subtle, gentle, and inconspicuous with His gifts, and yet a spiritually perceptive person can recognize the hand of God behind the scenes and give credit and thanks to the Lord for His graces. He is constantly watching over us, is attentive to our needs, and is always providing for our welfare, even if we never notice.

Ingratitude

We see that the Lord blesses us even without our asking; therefore, many gifts may go unnoticed and unappreciated. But there are times when we come to the Lord in prayer asking for His assistance. The Lord then answers our prayers and gives us the assistance we need. Yet oftentimes, we fail to see His help and do not acknowledge and thank Him for answering our prayers. An example of this reality is provided in the Gospel:

> As he continued his journey to Jerusalem, he traveled through Samaria and Galilee. As he was entering a village, ten lepers met [him]. They stood at a distance from him and raised their voice, saying, "Jesus, Master! Have pity on us!" And when he saw them, he said, "Go show yourselves to the priests." As they were going they were cleansed. And one of them, realizing he had been healed, returned, glorifying God in a loud voice; and he fell at the feet of Jesus and thanked him. He was a Samaritan. Jesus said in reply, "Ten were cleansed, were they not? Where are the other nine? Has none but this foreigner returned to give thanks to God?" Then he said to

him, "Stand up and go; your faith has saved you." (Luke 17:11–19, NABRE)

In the time of Jesus, those who had leprosy suffered tremendously because they were ostracized from the rest of society. They had to be separated from their family, friends, and community and live outside the village because of the widespread fear that leprosy was contagious. They could not even get physically close to another person. If anyone approached them, they had to yell out, "Unclean, unclean." Perhaps the most painful aspect of leprosy was that lepers were not allowed to worship God in the synagogues and temple. Hence, they felt alienated and rejected by God Himself. Therefore, when the lepers saw Jesus, they were desperate to be healed and begged Jesus to have pity on them. Jesus, moved with compassion, healed them and restored them to health so that they might resume their normal lives. Yet only one of the ten, a Samaritan, came back to thank Him. Jesus was disappointed by the ingratitude of the other nine whom He had healed. Our Lord had given all ten lepers their lives back, yet nine of the ten did not even bother to return and give Him thanks. As for the one who did return to express his gratitude, Jesus told him that because of his gratitude and faith, he was not only healed: he was saved (the word *saved* has a double meaning in Greek—"healed" and "saved"). Because of his gratitude, this leper received even more graces than the other nine who did not give thanks. When we thank God for His goodness, our blessings will be multiplied. But those who are not grateful will miss out on additional blessings that God had in store for them.

Remember the Goodness of the Lord

Often, we can be like the other nine lepers. We turn to the Lord when we are in need, and He answers our prayers and helps us. But then, we forget to acknowledge and thank God for what He has done for us. When I was in the seminary, I would pray especially hard to do well on an exam. But then, after I received a good grade, I usually spent little or no time giving thanks to the Lord for His help. I would give myself the credit for studying hard and knowing the answers. But I rarely thanked the Lord for giving me the opportunity and ability to study hard and know the correct answers. So it is with other important events in my life. If something significant is about to happen, I turn to the Lord in prayer for His assistance. Most of the time, things turn out the way I had hoped. But then, I forget to thank and praise the Lord for answering my prayers. I know that I am not alone in this way of responding. Most of us turn to the Lord when we are in need but then fail to return to the Lord in praise and thanksgiving after we receive what we wanted.

Worse still, I know some people who never even think of the Lord *until* they need something. It is only in desperate times that some people remember to turn to the Lord and ask for His help. But after things get better, they fail to give God His due. Often, when these people come to me asking for help in a crisis, I discover that they are fallen-away Catholics and have not been practicing their faith. I encourage them to go to Reconciliation and turn back to the Lord, and He will help them. Many take my advice and start to go to Mass and pray again. Ultimately, their situation gets better. But then, guess what? I never hear from them or see them again. These people not only forget to thank me, but also they stop going to Mass to thank the Lord now that their life is back in order.

How would we feel if people we know never acknowledged us until they wanted something from us? They approach us to ask for a favor, and we go out of our way to help them. But they never thank us, and we never hear from them again until they need something else from us. My friend Jenny Cochrane says, "I wouldn't have warm fuzzy feelings, and that's for sure." But that is how most people treat God. They turn to Him only when they need or want something, and after getting what they want, they never thank Him. Instead, they forget Him altogether until the next time they need something. Ingratitude is a sin because it violates justice. We owe it to God to give Him thanks and praise for His goodness, just as we owe appreciation and thanks to others who help us.

Memory Problem

Some people are grateful for our help and God's help and do say thank you, but often, their gratitude is short-lived. For example, I know a person named Jim[68] who suffered from insomnia and could not fall asleep until the early morning hours. As a result, he could not wake up in time to get to work. Eventually, he was dismissed from his job. I discovered what happened and introduced him to a friend of mine who is a therapist. I also encouraged him to go to Confession, receive the Sacrament of the Anointing of the Sick, and go back to Mass (he had stopped attending for some time). The therapist was able to help him sleep better at night, and for the first time in a long while, Jim went to Confession and attended Mass. The next day, he received a job offer. He was very grateful to God for helping him get his life back together. He promised God and me that he would go to Mass every weekend from then on. But the following weekend, he did not attend Mass, and he has completely stopped attending, as before. Many people may be grateful to God once they get what they want, but then, they quickly forget Him.

God has given us the capacity to remember so that we may not forget all His goodness. But how easy it is for us to forget God's goodness after He grants our request. This is a common theme in

[68] The names of all persons mentioned in this book have been changed to preserve their anonymity.

the Old Testament. God made a covenant with the Israelites: He would be their God, and they would be His people. God delivered them from slavery, fed them in the desert, and brought them to the Promised Land. Yet the Israelites kept grumbling and provoking the Lord and turning their backs on Him, the one who was always faithful to them. Over and over, Moses and the other prophets encouraged the Jewish people to remember God's goodness and remain faithful to Him. The Psalms urge all people to give thanks and praise to the Lord for His goodness and fidelity: "O give thanks to the LORD, for he is good; his mercy endures forever!" (118:1). But like the Israelites, we have a short-term memory. One moment, we are praising God for His goodness; the next, we are complaining that He is unfaithful. In reality, we are the ones who are unfaithful.

Truly, many of us act like spoiled children. We rarely think of, let alone thank, God our Father, yet we are always making demands of Him, and when we do not get what we want, we throw a tantrum. A family friend told me that all her children are mad at God and have stopped going to Mass. They said this is because God did not answer their prayers to heal their father. When their father died of cancer, they stopped believing in God altogether. Their father was a medical doctor with a thriving practice, and the family was well-to-do. The children grew up very comfortably and became highly educated, successful professionals. Yet when they perceived that the Lord did not answer their prayers for their father's healing, they quickly abandoned God and forgot all the blessings He had bestowed on them and their family.

When it comes to God's goodness, not only do we have short-term memory, but we also have selective memory. We tend to remember the times when our prayers were not answered exactly the way we asked, and we tend to forget all the times God provided for us, with or without our asking. I see this pattern over and over not only with others but with myself. Sometimes, we can be so focused on getting what we want that we dwell on the negative and fail to recognize the good of a particular situation.

It is difficult and yet essential for us to keep in mind the blessings we have received from the Lord. Had the children whose father passed away kept in mind all of God's past blessings, they probably would not have left the Church. Had the Israelites remembered God's fidelity, they probably would not have grumbled and worshipped idols. Had Jim remembered God's provision for his health and career, he probably would not have stopped going to Mass. Had the lepers remembered that Jesus healed them, they probably would have come back to give Him thanks and praise. God has given us our ability to remember His goodness, yet we are quick to forget all the gifts we have received from His loving hand. Instead, we use our memory to retain trivia, such as lyrics to pop songs, statistics of baseball players, famous lines from movies, sins of our past, and other things that take us away from the Lord.

Give Thanks in All Circumstances

There are times when we can see *some* good even though our prayers were not answered in the way we had hoped. One parishioner told me that she had been away from the Church for many years, but when her mother was diagnosed with cancer, she returned to the Lord to pray for her mother's recovery. Although her mother did not survive, the parishioner grew in faith through the adversity and continues to attend Mass regularly. She accepts her mother's passing, and because she returned to the Lord in prayer and the sacraments, her faith has flourished.

This parishioner was not stuck in her ways; therefore, she was able to see God's goodness. She told me that she can see how much God has blessed her life. She sees even her mother's passing as a gift from God, because she is no longer suffering but is probably in heaven praying for her family. It takes maturity to remember all the Lord's goodness to us and to be grateful for all His blessings. Even when we do not get what we ask for, God still blesses us in different ways because He knows better than we do what is best for us. Indeed, St. Paul reminds us to be grateful always, regardless of the situation: "Rejoice always, pray constantly, give thanks in all circumstances; for this is the will of God in Christ Jesus for you" (1 Thess. 5:16–18). It is pleasing to the Lord when we acknowledge and remember His gifts, because this helps us to grow closer to Him and trust in Him, knowing that He is always close to us, loves us, and provides for our needs.

Besides the gifts from God that are readily apparent to us, we should remember that everything is a gift from the Lord. St. Thérèse tells us:

> Everything is a grace, everything is the direct effect of our father's love—difficulties, contradictions, humiliations, all the soul's miseries, her burdens, her needs—everything, because through them, she learns humility, realizes her weakness. Everything is a grace because everything is God's gift. Whatever be the character of life or its unexpected events—to the heart that loves, all is well.[69]

Suffering, trials, and annoyances are given to us by God out of love. These are opportunities to practice patience, faith, and love. Challenges also offer us an opportunity to unite our suffering with that of Jesus on the Cross for His ongoing work of redemption and sanctification in the world. Even in the midst of difficulties and challenges, we can know that God is using them to bring about a greater good. Therefore, we should learn to give thanks always.

[69] *Her Last Conversations*, 57.

It Is Truly Right and Just

In all circumstances, God wants us to give Him thanks and praise not for His benefit but for ours. By offering praise and thanksgiving to God, we fulfill our duty and satisfy justice. In the Liturgy of the Eucharist, we pray, "It is truly right and just, our duty and our salvation, always and everywhere to give you thanks, Lord, Holy Father, almighty and eternal God." Thanksgiving and praise to God are right and just because they give God His due. We owe it to the Lord to thank Him for all He has done and continues to do for us and for the world. The Eucharist is the highest form of praise and thanksgiving. In fact, *Eucharist* is a Greek word that means "thanksgiving." The Eucharist is the re-presentation of the one sacrifice of Jesus to the Father on our behalf to satisfy divine justice and offer praise and thanksgiving. To offer praise and thanksgiving in union with Jesus is the highest form of expressing our gratitude and is right and perfect worship.

In the Old Testament, God tells His people that He does not desire the sacrifice of animals but instead the sacrifice of praise and thanksgiving.

> I will accept no bull from your house, nor he-goat from your folds. For every beast of the forest is mine, the cattle on a thousand hills. I know all the birds of the air, and all that moves in the field is mine. "If I were hungry, I would not tell you; for the world and all that is in it is mine. Do I eat the flesh of bulls, or drink the blood of goats? Offer to God a sacrifice of thanksgiving, and pay your vows to the Most High." (Ps. 50:9–14)

The sacrifice of praise and thanksgiving is what every person owes to God because of everything the Lord has given us and continues to give us. We are always indebted to God for all that we have and all that we are. We can never thank or praise Him enough. It is proper and right worship to offer ourselves with the self-offering of Jesus in the Holy Sacrifice of the Mass in praise and thanksgiving to the Father. We satisfy justice and our duty to God by continually giving thanks and praise to the Father through Jesus Christ.

Even in the Old Testament, the proper way to show gratitude to God for all His goodness is to offer a sacrifice of praise and thanksgiving. There is a whole series of psalms dedicated to offering praise and thanksgiving to the Lord:

> What shall I render to the Lord for all his bounty to me? I will lift up the cup of salvation and call on the name of the Lord, I will pay my vows to the Lord in the presence of all his people.... You have loosed my bonds. I will offer to you the sacrifice of thanksgiving and call on the name of the Lord. I will pay my vows to the Lord in the presence of all his people, in the courts of the house of the Lord, in your midst, O Jerusalem. Praise the Lord! (116:12–14, 16–19)

The New Testament confirms that we ought to give continual thanks and praise to God through Jesus: "Through him then let us continually offer up a sacrifice of praise to God, that is, the fruit of lips that acknowledge his name" (Heb. 13:15). God has given us the ability to speak and sing; therefore, we should use these gifts for the glory and honor of His name by proclaiming His praises.

When I first came back to the Faith, I had a tough time with the concept of praising God. I understood that we should thank the Lord for all His blessings, but it seemed as though God wanted us to heap compliments on Him to make Him feel good about Himself. I thought this was strange and egotistical. But then, I realized that praise and thanksgiving go hand in hand. We praise God for who He is, and we thank Him for all that He has done for us. When we are grateful to God, we thank and praise Him for His goodness. It is less about heaping compliments upon God and more about adoring all His incredible attributes and perfection. We often forget that prayer is not limited to petitions, that is, asking God for what we need. Prayer includes giving thanks and praise to God for all His goodness.

In heaven, the angels and saints praise God as they see Him face-to-face. They marvel at His beauty, goodness, and holiness and cannot help but pour forth hymns of endless praise. We, too, can experience to a certain degree the life of heaven *now* when we join the heavenly court in praising the Lord. This is a way for us to prepare for heaven—to do now what we will be doing for all eternity: contemplating God in His majesty and singing aloud His praises.

The words we pray at Mass confirm that God does not need our praise, but it is His gift to us for our benefit. "For although You have no need of our praise, yet our thanksgiving is itself Your gift, since our praises add nothing to Your greatness but profit us for our salvation through Christ Our Lord."[70] Not only do we satisfy justice by offering to God our thanks and praise, but in the process, we become holier and more devoted to the Lord, which ultimately leads us to our salvation. St. Thomas Aquinas explains: "Consequently we need to praise God with our lips, not indeed for His sake, but for our own sake; since by praising Him our devotion is aroused towards Him.... And forasmuch as man, by praising God, ascends in his affections to God, by so much is he withdrawn from things opposed to God."[71] By praising the Lord, we are changed for the better; we grow closer to Him and withdraw our affections from sin and the things that are opposed to God. As with all gifts, the gift of thanksgiving requires a reception and a response on our part in order to be realized.

[70] *Roman Missal: English Translation According to the Third Typical Edition* (Totowa, NJ: Catholic Book Publishing, 2011), 468.

[71] *ST* II-II, q. 91, art. 1.

Similarly, when St. Catherine of Siena asked God the Father how she could grow in perfection, God told her: "Unite yourself to me with loving affection, keeping in mind the blessings you have received from me." The way to perfection is to increase our union with God and love of Him. What helps to draw us closer to the Lord in love is to remember the blessings He has bestowed upon us. So many people are distant from God because they do not think about or reflect on all the blessings they have received from the Lord. So, many become lukewarm and distant from the Lord and instead immerse themselves in sin, the world, and all that is not of God. In contrast, Mary and the saints do remember God's goodness; hence, they are filled with love and gratitude for the Lord and are drawn closer to Him with much tenderness and affection. As they deepen their union with God, they become like Him—that is, holy and perfect.

Mary Is Filled with Praise and Thanksgiving

Our Blessed Mother is always filled with praise and gratitude to God because she remembers all His goodness toward her and the people of Israel. Mary is perfectly holy in part because she has a perfect memory of God's goodness and perfectly unites herself to the Lord in love and gratitude. The words that flow forth from Mary's soul reveal this abundant gratitude: "And Mary said, 'My soul magnifies the Lord, and my spirit rejoices in God my Savior, for he has regarded the low estate of his handmaiden. For behold, henceforth all generations will call me blessed; for he who is mighty has done great things for me, and holy is his name'" (Luke 1:46–49). Mary sings God's praises when Elizabeth acknowledges her as the Mother of the the long-awaited Messiah. Elizabeth praises our Blessed Mother for her faith. But Mary redirects the praise to the Lord because she knows that it is God in His goodness who has blessed her with the privilege of becoming the Mother of His Son. Therefore, Mary pours forth praise and thanksgiving to the Lord for exalting her, a lowly handmaid, as the Mother of God.

Mary remembers not only God's goodness to her but also His faithfulness to the people of Israel: "He has helped his servant Israel, in remembrance of his mercy, as he spoke to our fathers, to Abraham and to his posterity for ever" (Luke 1:54–55). Mary is able to see God's hand in the history of the Jewish people. God promised to send the Israelites the Anointed One to liberate them from their enemies. And then, He fulfilled His promise by making Mary the Mother of the Redeemer. Mary perceives, acknowledges, and give thanks to the Lord for His ongoing love and fidelity to her and the chosen people. She marvels at what God has done and, from the bottom of her heart, pours forth torrents of praise and thanksgiving to the Lord.

Gratitude to God is the proper disposition that animates our life and gives it purpose. Being perceptive of and grateful for God's constant love gives us direction and motivation. Filled with gratitude, we want to live for the Lord and use all His blessings to serve Him, build up the Body of Christ, and glorify His name. G. K. Chesterton proposes, "Praise should be the permanent pulsation of the soul."[72] This indeed is the disposition of our Blessed Mother, and so it should be ours, since we are her children. The more we grow in gratitude to God, the more we will grow in perfection and in our union with and love for God.

As Mary's children, we are called to imitate our Blessed Mother in always remembering God's goodness to us and His fidelity to all mankind. Then, we should give thanks and praise to the Lord, for it is right and just to acknowledge and express our gratitude for all

[72] G. K. Chesterton, *Orthodoxy* (London, 1908; Digireads.com Publishing, 2018), 119.

His generosity and love. When we live with continuous gratitude, we grow closer to the Lord and take on His likeness. We benefit and grow in grace when we properly thank the Lord for His providence in our lives, and He, in turn, pours out more graces upon us to bless and to perfect us even more.

God has indeed done great things for Mary and for His people. What great things has He done for you? How can you become more grateful to God for all His goodness? Remembering God's goodness may not be natural for us because of our fallen human nature. Therefore, we do have to make a conscious effort to bring to mind the blessings we have received from the Lord. Practicing giving thanks and praise to God on a regular basis helps us to form a habit and grow in this virtue of gratitude. Below are some suggestions about things for which we should be grateful and occasions when we should make acts of praise and thanksgiving.

Practical Suggestions

1. First thing in the morning, give thanks to the Lord for the gift of sleep and for a brand-new day, a fresh start, and an opportunity to live for and serve Him.
2. Say grace before every meal. You may say the following prayer: "Bless us, O Lord, and these thy gifts which we have received from thy bounty, through Christ Our Lord. Amen." Give thanks after each meal by saying the following prayer: "We give you thanks, Almighty God, for these and all thy gifts, which we have received from thy bounty, through Christ Our Lord. Amen."
3. At the end of each day, make an Examen, asking the Holy Spirit to reveal to you the blessings He has given you throughout the day. Then, write down these blessings in a journal and thank the Lord.

4. Make a list of people and blessings for which you are grateful. Keep adding to this list and look at it often. Thank the Lord for each person and each blessing on this list.
5. Thank the Lord for all the *material gifts* you have received, such as your life, health, family, friends, house, car, food, and all that you can recall. Remember the people in the world who do not have even a portion of all that you have received.
6. Thank God for your *mental gifts*, such as the ability to read, understand, or speak a second language. Not everyone has all the mental gifts that God has given to you.
7. Thank God for your *spiritual gifts*, such as the gift of faith, unique charisms, the Church, the sacraments, your prayer life, the angels, and the saints. Many people do not have the spiritual gifts that you possess.
8. Before you make a specific request in prayer, develop the habit of starting every spontaneous prayer by praising and thanking God for His goodness.
9. Keep in mind that God is always with you, looking out for you and providing for your needs. Make a habit of constantly thanking God throughout the day—a simple "thank you, Lord" is enough.

6

Joy in the Lord

The more joyful we are in the Lord, the more we please Him.

My spirit rejoices in God my Savior. (Luke 1:47)

The Source of True Joy

With gratitude comes joy. We are joyful because of God's goodness, our blessings, and our knowledge and experience of God and His closeness. Everyone wants to be happy, and we all look for ways to find happiness because God has put into our hearts a yearning for true joy. In fact, we are made for the fullness of joy. There are tons of books about achieving happiness, and people buy them in search of contentment. Tremendous amounts of money are poured into scientific research, psychological studies, and seminars in the quest for happiness. People spend their entire lives in pursuit of happiness but often come up disappointed. This is because true joy can be found in God alone. We are made for joy because we are made for God. True joy comes from knowing and loving God.

In 1975, Pope St. Paul VI published his Apostolic Exhortation on Christian Joy *Gaudete in Domino*. In it, he distinguishes between pleasure and joy. His words are even more relevant today:

> Technological society has succeeded in multiplying the opportunities for pleasure, but it has great difficulty in generating joy. For joy comes from another source. It is spiritual. Money, comfort, hygiene and material security are often not lacking; and yet boredom, depression and sadness unhappily remain the lot of many. These feelings sometimes go as far as anguish and despair, which apparent carefreeness, the frenzies of present good fortune and artificial paradises cannot assuage.[73]

Our society has advanced technologically by leaps and bounds since 1975. Instantaneous pleasures are readily available at our fingertips, yet we are more disconnected and alienated from true joy than ever before. Searching for joy in a world without God often leaves us disillusioned and depressed.

One day, a young man named Bob came to me for spiritual direction. He explained that he was brought up Catholic, but for many years, he had not practiced his faith because he was focused on his career. He worked very hard, advanced quickly in his company, and made a lot of money. But at the same time, he was very stressed and burned out. About a year before our meeting, he had taken a leave of absence from his job, and during that time, he attended a retreat. As he sat and prayed in the presence of the Blessed Sacrament, he started to feel a peace and joy that he had never experienced before. It was the peace and joy that he had been working so hard to find in worldly success but that had eluded him until his encounter with Jesus in the Blessed Sacrament. After that epiphany, he began thinking about leaving his fast-paced career behind. Now he wanted me to help him discern a possible

[73] Pope Paul VI, Apostolic Exhortation on Christian Joy *Gaudete in Domino* (May 9, 1975), pt. 1.

vocation to the priesthood or religious life. About a year after our first meeting, Bob applied to enter a religious order.

Bob's story is not unusual. Many people think they can find happiness through wealth, status, possessions, and power, but they all end up disheartened because we are made for so much more. True peace and joy can be found only in the Lord. This is the serenity that the world cannot give. Jesus tells His disciples, "Peace I leave with you; my peace I give to you; not as the world gives do I give to you" (John 14:27). Similarly, before his conversion, St. Augustine indulged in the things of the world in the hope of finding meaning and happiness. But it was only after his conversion that he attained the true joy for which he longed. In his *Confessions*, he pours out his soul to the Lord: "For Thou hast made us for Thyself and our hearts are restless till they rest in Thee."[74] Indeed, nothing in this world can satisfy our deepest hunger for the infinite, the perfect, and the eternal. Only in the Lord can we discover the fulfillment for which we are made.

Levels of Happiness

Fr. Robert Spitzer, S.J., speaks about the four levels of happiness.[75] The first level is the most basic and deals with sensual pleasures and material comfort, including food, sex, and material possessions. The gratification at this level can be intense and immediate, but the satisfaction is rather superficial and short-lived. When there is an overemphasis on finding happiness on this level, the individual will ultimately experience profound emptiness because these things do not begin to satisfy our capacity for happiness. Ultimately, all forms

74 Augustine, *Confessions*, bk. I, 3.

75 Robert Spitzer, *Finding True Happiness: Satisfying Our Restless Hearts* (San Francisco: Ignatius Press, 2015).

of joy come from the Lord and are meant to lead us to Him. The problem is that most people pursue pleasures for themselves — that is, as their own ends — instead of seeing them as a means to bring us to God. These fleeting pleasures are God's gifts to us to help us know Him and love Him and grow closer to Him. Yet tragically, we get so caught up in the gifts that we forget about the Giver.

The second level has to do with self-esteem. We achieve a certain level of satisfaction when we attain worldly success and the esteem of others. But focusing too much on success can lead to stress and a constant feeling of having to compete and win all the time. The contentment at this level is still rather shallow and does not truly satisfy our deepest desires. But unfortunately, most people in our world try to find happiness and fulfillment at these first two levels. Power and honor are not bad in themselves. Indeed, we can use power and influence for the good of others and the glory of God. In fact, they are God's gifts for us to use in a way that builds up His kingdom. But people tend to seek accolades for their own ego and selfish pursuits.

The third level Fr. Spitzer identifies is more meaningful and altruistic. We all have an innate desire to give back to society, to help others, and to contribute to the good of someone or something greater than ourselves. Being made in the image and likeness of God, we are made to give of ourselves, and it is only by this self-gift that we are fulfilled and become the person that God made us to be. The happiness at this level is deeper and lasts longer than that of the first two levels as the person fulfills his or her vocation to serve and give of himself or herself. Nevertheless, this gratification is still not enough because it lacks a transcendent dimension.

When God created us, He put in our hearts a desire for the infinite, the eternal, and the sacred. There is a longing in every heart for perfect beauty, truth, justice, and love, which can be found only in God Himself. We have a transcendent dimension to our being because we are made of body and soul, flesh and spirit. We have a need to know God and His love for us and to love Him in return. Unfortunately, most people never get to this level because they are stuck in the first two or three levels or because they deny God altogether. But those who seek their highest good and allow themselves to be drawn to their deepest desire experience a joy that is deep, pervasive, and enduring. This fourth level is most difficult to attain, but the reward is more than worth the time and the effort. St. Paul tells us, "What no eye has seen, nor ear heard, nor the heart of man conceived, what God has prepared for those who love him" (1 Cor. 2:9). Those who ardently and perseveringly seek the Lord with all their heart will not be let down.

Product of Love

The chapters of this book build upon one another. There is a natural progression from one theme to the next. We started with humility, which is necessary to build a foundation based on faith and hope; and then we moved through the love of God, union with God, and gratitude. All these qualities, individually and collectively, lead us to experience joy in the Lord. But the main cause of joy is our love of God and our union with Him.

St. Thomas Aquinas tells us that joy is a product of charity, which is given to us by the Holy Spirit through the outpouring of God's love into our hearts (Rom. 5:5).[76] The proper names for the Holy Spirit are *Love* and *Gift*. He is the love of God—the bond of love between the Father and the Son—given to us. When the Holy Spirit descended upon the disciples at Pentecost, He appeared as tongues of fire (Acts 2:3), which represent the burning love of God. The hearts of the disciples were set aflame. When one is filled

[76] Aquinas, *ST* II-II, q. 28, art. 1.

with the Holy Spirit and on fire with the love of God, he experiences true joy. It is the Holy Spirit who gives us consolation: "For the kingdom of God does not mean food and drink but righteousness, peace, and joy in the Holy Spirit" (Rom. 14:17). The Holy Spirit is also known as the *Consoler* or *Comforter*. Furthermore, the fruits of the Holy Spirit include peace and joy: "The fruit of the Spirit is love, joy, peace, patience, kindness, goodness, faithfulness, gentleness, self-control" (Gal. 5:22). The Holy Spirit—the love of God—is the key ingredient to heavenly bliss.

It is important to distinguish between the supernatural joy of the Holy Spirit, which is the love of God poured into our hearts, and merely a naturally cheerful disposition. Many people are naturally cheerful, easygoing, and happy-go-lucky. But this is not the same as the felicity that comes from God. An atheist can be jovial, and a saint can be dour (at times). That is not what I am talking about. The supernatural bliss that comes from God is not a sensible feeling or a passing emotion but a deep, abiding joy that comes from the knowledge and love of God. The joy of the Holy Spirit is noticeably different from a cheerful personality.

It is true that sometimes the spiritual consolations of God can be felt in a very powerful and real way and the mind, heart, body, and emotions are affected. But even when the feelings go away, the deep joy remains. Many times, I have felt an overwhelming feeling of God's love that causes me to smile or cry or fall to my knees in love and gratitude. The Lord gives these gifts periodically to strengthen and encourage us to progress in our spiritual life. And yes, we should savor these precious moments and thank the Lord for His love. Sometimes, this special grace will remain with us for a long time. As I am typing this, I am staying with the Carmelite Sisters of Los Angeles at their Sacred Heart Retreat House. Just a few days ago, one of the sisters made her first vows, and she is still radiating the joy that came from that special occasion. At some point, I am sure, she will come down from the clouds of spiritual consolation, but if she stays close to the Lord, the joy will remain in her and will grow.

Those who are authentically joyful are filled with the Holy Spirit and on fire with the love of God. Although these Carmelite sisters all have different personalities and temperaments, they consistently radiate a blessedness that is not often found in the secular world. It is a supernatural joy that comes from the indwelling of the Holy Spirit that causes their hearts to be on fire with the love of God. They exude the happiness that comes from knowing God, possessing Him, and loving Him. Because God and His love are truly present to these sisters, they radiate the love and joy of God Himself.

Where there is the Holy Spirit, there are the Father and the Son because there is one God in three Divine Persons. When we are in the state of grace, each Person of the Holy Trinity dwells in us, and this union with the Lord by which we share in His love is the cause of our joy. When someone we love is present to us, we are delighted. For example, I love my mom, and once a week on my day off, I go home to visit her. We spend the day together, and I am content. I feel blessed by her company, her love, and her presence in my life. Likewise, if we love God, we will experience gladness when He is present. If we love the Lord, we will enjoy being close to Him, spending time with Him, and interacting with Him. It is in God's presence and in sharing His love that we partake of His supernatural joy. Even before the first coming of Jesus, the Jewish people knew this truth. We read in the Psalms that true delight is found in being in God's presence: "You show me the path to life; in your presence there is fulness of joy, in your right hand are pleasures for evermore" (16:11). True joy is found in being in the presence of the Beloved.

Nevertheless, the Lord respects our freedom and will not force Himself or His love upon us. He will come to stay and share His love to the extent that we welcome Him. We are made to be temples of the Holy Spirit, but this is not automatic. We have to make a conscious effort to prepare a place in ourselves that is suitable and welcoming to the Lord, and not to do anything that will drive Him away. St. Paul reminds us, "Do not quench the Spirit" (1 Thess. 5:19). Sin quenches the Holy Spirit. Committing a mortal sin severs our relationship with God and cuts us off from His life, love, and grace. Also, worldly anxieties can quench the Holy Spirit. Attachments to things or to self can quench the Holy Spirit. We need to become a welcoming abode for the Lord, a place He can come, stay, and make His home. In our world of distractions and preoccupations, we need to empty ourselves of all that does not belong to God and allow Him to fill us up with His Holy Spirit. Then, we can share in His love and abide in His tranquility.

Besides acknowledging and loving God, who is always with us, we can also meditate on His qualities. When you love someone, you admire and love the goodness he or she possesses. For example, even when I am away from my mom, I find joy in thinking about her and her goodness. My mom is kind, gentle, and loving. Thinking about her and her qualities brings me joy because I love her, and I am happy that God has endowed her with many wonderful attributes. This is all the truer with God because He is infinitely good and perfect. I take great delight in contemplating God and His attributes, such as His mercy, wisdom, and generosity. So, by loving the Lord, abiding in His presence, and marveling at His perfection, we can find joy in Him.

Because God is infinite and perfect love, He is infinitely and perfectly joyful. And the incredible thing is that He wants to share His love and joy with us so that we may experience the fullness of joy. Jesus says: "As the Father has loved me, so have I loved you; abide in my love. If you keep my commandments, you will abide in my love, just as I have kept my Father's commandments and abide in his love. These things I have spoken to you, that my joy may be in you, and that your joy may be full" (John 15:9–11). Jesus loves us with the same love He shares with the eternal Father and the Holy Spirit. And if we remain in His love, our joy will overflow. The fullness of joy is reserved for us in heaven, where we see God face-to-face and know Him as He is. But in a real way, we can start to experience His presence, His love, and His joy *now*. God wants us to experience all these things now and know that we will experience their fullness in the next life. Just imagine: Jesus wants to share with us the same eternal and perfect joy that exists between the Father and the Son and the Holy Spirit. This is the supernatural beatitude for which we are made.

God is joyful, and He wants us to be joyful. He created us precisely to share in His blessedness. Speaking through the prophet Isaiah, God tells us: "Be glad and rejoice for ever in that which I create; for behold, I create Jerusalem a rejoicing, and her people a joy. I will rejoice in Jerusalem, and be glad in my people" (Isa. 65:18–19). When we are joyful, God is joyful. God takes delight in us and in our happiness. St. Irenaeus tells us, "The glory of God is man fully alive." We most resemble God when we are filled with His attributes, including His joy. In our preparation for eternal bliss in heaven, we must become fully alive and joyful in the Lord while still on earth. When we are intimately united to God in love, we share in His eternal joy and become more and more like Him. Just as parents want their children to be happy, so too the Lord desires our happiness; and just as parents find joy in their children's happiness, so does the Lord delight in our bliss.

The Lord calls His people to rejoice in Him, for He delights in them: "Let Israel be glad in his Maker, let the sons of Zion rejoice in their King! Let them praise his name with dancing, making melody to him with timbrel and lyre! For the LORD takes pleasure in his people; he adorns the humble with victory. Let the faithful exult in glory; let them sing for joy on their couches" (Ps. 149:2–5). All the more are we called to rejoice in the Lord now that the time of fulfillment has dawned. The long-awaited Messiah has come. The joyful hope of God's chosen people grows even stronger in the New Testament because Jesus has come and will come again. Therefore, St. Paul commands us to "rejoice in the Lord always; again I will say, Rejoice" (Phil. 4:4). Each Advent, on Gaudete Sunday, we are reminded to rejoice in the Lord for all He has done for us, for all He is doing for us now, and for all He will bring to fulfillment in the future. Rejoice and be glad, for yours is the kingdom of heaven.

Joy in Suffering

Because God's joy arises from His love, which is abiding and eternal, it is not incompatible with suffering. In his Encyclical on Christian Joy *Gaudete in Domino*, Pope St. Paul VI speaks of God's joy as a deep, supernatural inner peace that endures even in the midst of natural suffering. As Christians, we are not immune to trouble, sadness, or distress, but we do not let these situations rob us of our inner peace. When I am called to give the Sacrament of the Anointing of the Sick, the recipient is usually suffering from pain, preparing for a major surgery, or about to die. Yet oftentimes, the person who has a strong faith and relationship with God is not agitated or worried but is at peace and even serene. It amazes me to see the power of grace at work in these people. No amount of pain and anguish can eliminate the serenity and intimacy they have in the Lord.

Unlike the fleeting pleasures of the world, the elation that comes from the Lord is everlasting. Pope Francis observes, "Joy adapts and changes, but it always endures, even as a flicker of light born of our personal certainty that, when everything is said and done, we are infinitely loved."[77] True joy comes from the knowledge and conviction that no matter what happens, we are infinitely and passionately loved by the Creator of the universe. Nothing can rob us of this gift. It is an internal and abiding elation that comes from a life spent in union with the Lord.

Jesus, Mary, and the saints endured much suffering, but at the same time, they experienced happiness because they endured their suffering for the sake of love. "[Love] rejoices in the right. Love bears all things, believes all things, hopes all things, endures all things" (1 Cor. 13:6–7). When we accept everything for the love of God, we can find sweetness even in sorrow. We are able to suffer with joy because of love. To love is to sacrifice and to suffer for the good of the other. When we are hurt, we can offer our pain to God out of love and unite it to the suffering of Jesus for His ongoing work of redemption. Suffering has value in that it allows us to participate with Christ in His work of redemption and sanctification. It also helps us to be conformed to Christ as we grow in holiness and virtue. We can suffer with joy because we have the knowledge that God has allowed this opportunity for us to expiate sins, participate in His work of redemption, and be conformed to His Son.

The secret to finding joy in suffering is to go deep—where God is. There, His love will sustain us. It all depends on whether we lead a mostly exterior life, in which our environment dominates our well-being, or a deep interior life to which we can turn to find calmness in God's presence at any time. Imagine a bicycle wheel: if we exist on the surface of a tire, we will experience the conditions of the terrain. If the terrain is rough, we will experience many bumps, rocks, and potholes, and we will feel a great volatility of highs and lows. But if we live at the center of the wheel, the

[77] Pope Francis, *Evangelii Gaudium*, no. 6.

hub—where God is—we will remain relatively stable regardless of what is happening on the surface. So, if we abide in God and He abides in us, we can let all of life's fluctuations come and go and remain centered in the Lord, who is our peace.

Those who are close to the Lord do not lose their equanimity regardless of the circumstances of life. Our strength, our hope, and our delight are in the Lord. In the Old Testament, we hear much about rejoicing in God, even when times are tough:

> Though the fig tree does not blossom, nor fruit be on the vines, the produce of the olive fail and the fields yield no food, the flock be cut off from the fold and there be no herd in the stalls, yet I will rejoice in the Lord, I will joy in the God of my salvation. God, the Lord, is my strength; he makes my feet like deer's feet, he makes me tread upon my high places. (Hab. 3:17–19)

There is no contradiction between experiencing the difficulties and challenges of life and finding strength and encouragement in the Lord.

Even when we experience trials, we should rejoice in the Lord because of the abiding presence of the Holy Trinity in us. Jesus gives us His abiding peace and tells us not to give into anxiety or fear: "Peace I leave with you; my peace I give to you; not as the world gives do I give to you. Let not your hearts be troubled, neither let them be afraid" (John 14:27). Jesus gives us His joy and peace, the same perpetual bliss of the eternal Godhead. This supernatural consolation is ours to sustain us through all that the world can throw at us. Jesus did not promise us that we would be free from travail but that His power would sustain us: "In the world you have tribulation; but be of good cheer, I have overcome the world." (John 16:33). Rest in the Lord, and He will supply you with the grace you need to ride out any storm in life.

Mary Rejoices in God Her Savior

Mary radiates the joy of God from the depths of her soul. The Magnificat is a hymn of joy and praise that flows naturally from Our Lady's heart. When Mary heard that Elizabeth received from the Holy Spirit the insight that Mary was carrying the Messiah in her womb, she cried out spontaneous words of joy, praise, and thanksgiving to God. The Blessed Virgin cannot contain her joy, for it flows from her entire being: "My soul magnifies the Lord, and my spirit rejoices in God my Savior" (Luke 1:46–47). Truly, the joy of God is within her. God's joy pervades her body and soul, causing her to share this jubilation with her cousin Elizabeth, St. John the Baptist, and, ultimately, with the rest of the world.

Mary is delighted because she is overflowing with God's love. The Holy Spirit overshadowed her and made her His dwelling, and she is on fire with the love of God. The love of God completely fills Mary and is perfected in her. The presence of the Father, the Son, and the Holy Spirit fills Mary and unites her to the Godhead in complete intimacy. God and His love are truly present and active in Our Lady in the most profound way, and the abundance of joy naturally flows from God into Mary as the two become inseparable.

Mary's happiness also comes from her continuous contemplation of God and His goodness. In the Magnificat, Mary recounts God's goodness to her and to the people of Israel. She especially expresses how God is present and faithful to His covenant and how His love and generosity exceed all expectation:

> For he who is mighty has done great things for me, and holy is his name. And his mercy is on those who fear him from generation to generation. He has shown strength with his arm, he has scattered the proud in the imagination of their hearts, he has put down the mighty from their thrones, and

> exalted those of low degree; he has filled the hungry with good things, and the rich he has sent empty away. He has helped his servant Israel, in remembrance of his mercy, as he spoke to our fathers, to Abraham and to his posterity for ever. (Luke 1:49–55)

Throughout the Gospels, we read that Mary ponders in her heart all the things of God. The contemplation of God's goodness, wisdom, and mercy is a constant source of delight for Mary. She marvels at God's perfection and treasures all His attributes. The secret to Mary's jubilation is her boundless love for the Lord. Mary is immersed in God's love and taken in by His fulfillments.

Mary's joyfulness does not cease as she braves hardships, because her love for God and awareness of His presence are always before her. Through it all, Mary maintains a certain equilibrium because of her adherence to God and His will. These qualities mirror those of Jesus as He endured His Passion for our salvation. There was joy in Jesus' agony because of His oneness with and love for the Father and the Spirit, as well as His love for us. This is also true of the saints, especially the martyrs, who experienced jubilation even in the midst of torture because of their abiding love for God and His Church. We, too, can learn from Mary, Jesus, and the saints to abide in God's overwhelming love, to contemplate His goodness, and to endure hardships cheerfully for love of Him.

God Loves a Cheerful Giver

Although this supernatural bliss, which comes from the love of God, is deep, abiding, and internal, it is not meant to be kept hidden. The divine felicity is meant to pervade all our actions and form every aspect of our lives. Joy, by nature, cannot be contained but overflows and multiplies. It is meant to be expressed and shared with others. In fact, if we imitate Mary, Jesus, and the saints, then our joy needs to be outwardly visible in our daily lives and impact the lives of others. Just as Mary shared her elation with St. Elizabeth and St. John the Baptist, we are called to bring our joy to every place we go and share it with others.

When we live for the Lord, love Him, and serve Him, we ought to do everything with cheerfulness. The happiness given to us by the Lord is not meant for us alone but has been entrusted to us so that we may cultivate and increase it by revealing it to others for their benefit and for the glory of God. Our radiance must be apparent to all with whom we come into contact: "You are the light of the world. A city set on a hill cannot be hidden. Nor do men light a lamp and put it under a bushel, but on a stand, and it gives light to all in the house. Let your light so shine before men, that they may see your good works and give glory to your Father who is in heaven" (Matt. 5:14–16). Like Mary, who brought Jesus to the entire world, we are called to bring the warmth of Christ to as many people as possible. Our flame is a sign of the divine spark and marks us as His servants, His instruments of light, peace, and love.

St. Paul reminds us, "Each one must do as he has made up his mind, not reluctantly or under compulsion, for God loves a cheerful giver" (2 Cor. 9:7). *What* we do is important, but *how* we do it may be even more important. If we do something with a bad attitude, it pleases God less than if we do it with enthusiasm and affection. It is essential for us to serve God and others cheerfully, even when we may not feel like it. This is a type of interior mortification. To do something we dislike out of love for God and others is meritorious, especially when we force ourselves to do it with love and joy.

Meister Eckhart reminds us, "Holiness is doing the next thing that has to be done with your whole heart and finding *delight* in it." My parents used to tell me that if I choose to do something, I must either do it well or not at all. Doing something well in the eyes of God, and sometimes in the eyes of others, means doing it cheerfully. If we want to please the Lord and glorify Him by our actions, then we must make an effort to do everything with joy. When we try to do something with a smile and find delight in it, we usually will discover a certain enjoyment in that task. Our desire to please the Lord and glorify Him through cheerful service turns our actions into gifts of love for the Lord.

When we work joyfully, besides glorifying God and sanctifying our actions, we lift up others and bear witness to Christ. Being around a cheerful person can have a very positive effect on our own emotions and well-being. On the other hand, being around a grim person can bring us down. Therefore, out of charity to our neighbor, we should try to be positive and uplifting. Further, if they know that we are Catholic, we will bear witness to Christ and His Church. As Christians, we must constantly be aware of how others perceive us and whether we are helping or hurting the Body of Christ. We have been commissioned to share the good news with others and bring them to Jesus. The vocation of every Christian is to share the message of the gospel, and a most powerful way to do that is to be joyful.

Cardinal Timothy Dolan of New York wrote that once, when he was visiting a hospice for AIDS patients operated by the Missionaries of Charity, a man there told him that he wanted to be baptized. When asked why, the man told Cardinal Dolan that he was moved by the joy of the sisters. He wanted to possess that same contentment. Evangelization is accomplished not with a frown but a smile. Mother Teresa writes: "Joy is a net by which we catch souls. God loves a cheerful giver: We give most when we give with joy. If you have difficulties in your daily life, accept them with joy, with a big smile. In this, others will see your good works and glorify the Father."[78] I have celebrated the sacraments and served with the Missionaries of Charity, and I am very impressed with their sacrificial love. It comes as no surprise that *cheerfulness* is included in their constitutions, which state that "the Spirit of the Society is one of Loving Trust, Total Surrender and Cheerfulness as lived by Jesus and Mary in the Gospel." Mother Teresa would be proud that members of her community continue to bring glory to God and build His kingdom on earth by their presence, service, and joy.

Similarly, the Carmelite Sisters of the Sacred Heart of Los Angeles express great joy. That is why I go to their Sacred Heart Retreat House to do my yearly personal retreat and to give retreats. It is personally edifying just to be in their presence and see their holiness and joy. Their chaplain, Fr. Donald Kinney, O.C.D., tells me that their founder, Venerable Mother Luisita, would ask a sister who was sad and gloomy whether she had a visitor recently, referring to the enemy. St. Ignatius of Loyola tells us that one way to discern whether an influence is from the good spirit or the evil spirit is that sadness and agitation usually come from the bad spirit, while calmness and fervor come from the good spirit. We do need to be aware of our disposition and demeanor and know that they have a powerful effect on our lives and ministry. We also need to cultivate cheerfulness, not only for our sake but for the sake of God and those around us.

We are naturally drawn to joy because we are naturally drawn to God, the source of all bliss. Happiness attracts, and joy is contagious. In his Apostolic Exhortation on the Proclamation of the Gospel *Evangelii Gaudium*, Pope Francis advises: "An evangelizer must never look like someone who has just come back from a funeral! Let us

[78] Mother Teresa, *Thirsting for God: A Yearbook of Prayers, Meditations, and Anecdotes* (Cincinnati: St. Anthony Messenger Press, 2000), 29.

recover and deepen our enthusiasm, that 'delightful and comforting joy of evangelizing.'"[79] It is true that oftentimes, Catholics do not appear or act in ways that edify others and bring them to Christ. We are reminded that we are temples of the Holy Spirit, and our love of God should cause His joy to overflow in us.

Truth be told, I am not a naturally cheerful person. I have taken the four temperaments test, which revealed that I have a melancholic temperament. So I tend to be serious, introspective, and quiet, and this can be off-putting to others. Since I am a Catholic priest, I have a special duty to evangelize and to reveal God's love and joy. Therefore, I often must remind myself to be outwardly joyful and to have fun when ministering to others in order to share the good news, bear witness to Christ, and glorify the Father. It is not so much a "fake it till you make it" gimmick; it is more about reminding myself that I have many reasons to be joyful in the Lord and that my actions and demeanor speak louder than words. The following quote has been attributed to St. Francis of Assisi: "Preach the Gospel at all times; use words when necessary." Truly, sharing the joy we have in God is a key component of spreading the gospel message and building up the Body of Christ. Joy comes from God and brings people to Him.

Joy in Hope

As Christians, we have every reason to be the happiest people in the world. Truly, we should call to mind more often and celebrate the abundant gifts that we have received from the Lord. The greatest of these is the gift and hope of eternal life. The more we hope in

[79] Pope Francis, Apostolic Exhortation on the Proclamation of the Gospel in Today's World *Evangelii Gaudium* (November 24, 2013), no. 10.

the Lord and His promise of eternal joy in heaven, the more everything falls into perspective and the burdens of this world become lighter. Specifically, there is cause for rejoicing in the Incarnation, the Paschal Mystery, and especially the Resurrection.

The Resurrection of Jesus at Easter should pervade our lives and imbue us with optimism. St. John Paul II reminds us, "We are the Easter people and Alleluia is our song!"[80] The pope explains: "Because man has been redeemed by God ... the redemption pervades all human history.... The power of Christ's cross and resurrection is greater than any evil which man could or should fear."[81] Christians are a people of faith, hope, and joy because Christ has conquered the world. We know that death and evil do not have the last word.

Comparably, Pope Emeritus Benedict XVI speaks of the transformative power of the Resurrection, which changes everything: "Jesus rises from the grave. Life is stronger than death. Good is stronger than evil. Love is stronger than hate. Truth is stronger than lies.... He draws all of us after him into the new light of the resurrection and he conquers all darkness."[82] With faith in Jesus and the Resurrection, we are confident and unafraid, knowing that, in the end, good will triumph over evil. This confidence should make us overflow with courage and enthusiasm, not just every Easter but every Sunday when we celebrate the Resurrection and

[80] Pope John Paul II, Angelus, Apostolic Journey to the Far East and Oceania, November 30, 1986, no. 3, http://www.vatican.va/content/john-paul-ii/en/angelus/1986/documents/hf_jp-ii_ang_19861130.html.

[81] Pope John Paul II, *Crossing the Threshold of Hope*, ed. Vittorio Messori (New York: Alfred A. Knopf, 1994), 219.

[82] Pope Benedict XVI, Homily for the Easter Vigil, April 7, 2012, http://www.vatican.va/content/benedict-xvi/en/homilies/2012/documents/hf_ben-xvi_hom_20120407_veglia-pasquale.html.

remember that we are all pilgrims on a journey, making our way back to our Father's house.

As Catholics, we fast at certain times and feast at others. During Lent and Advent and on Fridays, we fast and practice self-denial in communion with Jesus. But during Easter and Christmas and on solemnities, we feast. We are not puritans; we know how to have fun and enjoy the gifts that delight us. St. Thomas Aquinas says we should avail ourselves of the simple pleasures in life, such as a restful night's sleep and a hot bath.[83] St. Teresa of Avila enjoyed quail. I enjoy alternative music, Japanese food, and soft peanut butter cookies with milk. So take time out to enjoy the simple but good things in life. Listen to your favorite music, go to your favorite restaurant, or enjoy the latest blockbuster. Life is too short for us to be grumpy and miserable. We are meant to delight in Fr. Spitzer's first two levels of happiness, as long as we seek the higher joys of levels three and four. We do need balance: to be a saint is to enjoy all of God's gifts in a way that glorifies Him.

Moreover, take delight in all the little gifts that come from the Lord in our daily life: the serenity of the sunrise, the beauty of nature, the innocence of children, the creativity of artists, the companionship of pets, the support of family and friends, the goodness of neighbors, and more. Refer all these back to God. Let us learn to notice and appreciate the gifts of God in our lives. Wherever we are, regardless of our circumstances, we can ask ourselves, "What is good right now?" and then savor the moment as a grace from God. Ultimately, all contentment we experience comes from the Lord.

Lastly, as Christians, we can take ourselves too seriously sometimes. Therefore, implement some playfulness and levity in your life. Do not be a bore. It is okay to be silly, to laugh, and to have fun. Many saints were known for their humor and lightheartedness.

[83] Aquinas, *ST* I-II, q. 38, art. 5.

The Lord wants His children to laugh, breathe, make room for leisure, and let down their hair. I am sure that Mary, Jesus, and St. Joseph found delight in various aspects of life. Let us, therefore, imitate our Mother and be joyful in the Lord as we bear witness to Christ and glorify the Father.

Practical Suggestions

1. Enjoy the simple things in life, but refer or connect them to God. We do need the happiness of levels one and two, but try to live mostly on levels three and four.
2. Spend time seeking happiness on level four instead of spending too much time and energy pursuing happiness on levels one, two, and even three, which will prevent you from finding the joy of the transcendent God.
3. Pray and abide in God's love, allowing the Lord to fill you up with His Holy Spirit.
4. Recall that the more we lead a virtuous and holy life, the more peace we will have.
5. Meditate on the goodness and perfection of our beloved Lord and His Blessed Mother.
6. Pray and meditate on the Joyful and Glorious Mysteries of the Rosary with Mary. Imagine and share her joy in each mystery.
7. Celebrate the joy of the Resurrection every Sunday, even every morning.
8. Implement some playfulness and levity in your life.
9. In every situation, ask yourself, "What is good right now?"

7

Docility to God's Will

The more responsive we are to God's will, the more He will work in us.

Mary said, "Behold, I am the handmaid of the Lord; let it be to me according to your word." (Luke 1:38)

Similar to humility and the desire to serve and be united with the Lord is the ability to conform our will to God's will as much as possible. In this chapter, we will explore this concept, which, though multifaceted, ultimately boils down to seeking and then living out the will of God. An essential quality for doing God's will is *docility*, which is the willingness and readiness to be taught or guided. In other words, it is a disposition that helps us to be flexible and to cooperate with God and His inspirations.

As with humility, the secular world does not understand docility and thinks of it as a weakness. But it takes tremendous strength to die to self in order to live out God's will. Mary and the saints understand the importance of the virtue of docility and how pleasing it is to the Lord. They also understand the complementary dispositions of *responsiveness*, which is the ability to react quickly and positively to the inspirations of the Holy Spirit, and *obedience*, which means conforming one's will to the will of God. Applying these difficult yet saintly qualities to our lives always helps us to seek and align our will to God's will.

God's Will Is Always Best

Prideful and self-absorbed, we tend to think that our will is best, and most of us live in pursuit of it. But Mary and the saints know that God's will is always better than our will, and so they try to seek God's will in all things and live it out as perfectly as possible. When we are humble, we realize our limitations and weaknesses and are suspicious of our impulses and desires, as well as our ability to choose that which is most conducive to our happiness. At the same time, we know that God is all-knowing, all-powerful, and all-loving; hence, He knows exactly what will bring our greatest happiness, and He desires our greatest good. In short, God's will is always best for our sanctification and His glory. We tend to be shortsighted, but God sees the bigger picture, and if we follow His plan instead of ours, we will be much better off in the end.

Because of our limited capacities, we often cannot see or understand why God wills certain things. But especially during these times, we need to trust in the Lord and His love for us. God tells us in Scripture: "For my thoughts are not your thoughts, neither are your ways my ways, says the Lord. For as the heavens are higher than the earth, so are my ways higher than your ways and my thoughts than your thoughts" (Isa. 55:8–9). We cannot expect to know and understand all the ways of God. As adults, we know and do things that little children do not understand. No matter how much we may try to explain, they will never fully grasp everything because of their limited capacity. Greater still is the difference between God and us. If we understood everything that God does, then we would be on the same level as Him and would no longer be humans. Therefore, we must trust that the Lord knows and wants what is best for us.

The story of my vocation exemplifies this truth. Growing up, I never once turned to the Lord to ask Him what I should do with my life. I sought and followed the advice of my parents and others and followed the desires of my heart, but never did I think of asking God what He thought was best for me. I grew up in a lukewarm Catholic family: we went to church on most Sundays, and I received all the Sacraments of Initiation, but I was never taught to seek the will of God in my life. So I became an attorney. I thought this would be a good career for me and would bring me gainful employment, a relatively high income, and a certain status in society. Also, I never considered anything outside of married life. I went along with the expectation that I would find someone, get married, and have a family. The priesthood or religious life was never a consideration.

I had drifted away from God and His Church. When I went to college and then law school, I stopped attending Mass. Even as an attorney, I did not practice my faith. I was focused instead on the things of the world. I purchased a house and a BMW and had an active dating life. But the Lord was patient with me. He allowed me to pursue my own goals and follow my own will and the ways of the world. Then, He started to bring me back to Himself. It was through the women I dated that the Lord started my return to the Church. Around 2001, I was dating a devout Catholic woman who wanted me to go to church with her on Sundays. So, in order to make her happy, I started going to Mass with her on the weekends. Things did not work out between us, and we parted ways. However, I continued to go to Mass on the weekends by myself and started to practice my faith again.

But God was just getting started. The next woman I dated also happened to be a very devout Catholic. She introduced me to daily Mass, the Rosary, and Eucharistic Adoration. Because of her influence, I became a Eucharistic minister and a lector at my parish. I was learning so much about my faith and actively practicing it for the first time in my life. It was during this same time that I experienced some difficulties at work. I started to think about finding a new job or even a new career. I wanted to do something that I was passionate about. I explored different ideas, but nothing felt right. Then, I turned to the Lord in prayer and asked Him to help me find the right job and career path. Up to this point in my life, I had always pursued my own will, going after the things that I thought would make me happy. But for the first time in my life, I found myself at a dead end.

Shortly after my prayer, at least three different people asked me if I had ever thought about the priesthood. The woman I was dating asked me if I had ever thought about becoming a permanent deacon. I was thirty-six at the time, and until this point in my life, no one had ever asked me about the priesthood or diaconate. I had no idea what it took to become a priest or a permanent deacon. I started to search the Internet, and the more I read, the more I was attracted to the priesthood. This was both exciting and scary at the same time. I was not ready for a life of celibacy but was undeniably pulled and attracted to the priesthood. Somehow, I felt that this was what God wanted me to be, that I would be passionate in my work, and that I would find true fulfillment.

After much prayer and discernment of God's will for my vocation, I took a leave of absence from my employment, sold my house and BMW, and entered the seminary. Even while I was in the seminary, I continued to discern my vocation and tried to be completely open and docile to God's will, whatever it might be. In the end, God confirmed that He willed for me to become a priest, and in June 2011, I was ordained for the Diocese of Orange. Since then, I have received so many blessings, and I love being a priest!

It is not always easy, but I know that this is God's will for me, and I am truly happy and fulfilled. More and more, I understand that in everything, not just my vocation, God's will is always better than mine. I have learned not to trust my own will but to seek and follow God's will in all things. He knows better than I what will bring me the greatest happiness in this life and in the life to come. Truly, "in His will is our peace."[84]

To Love God Is to Do His Will

Those who are close to the Lord embrace, love, and adore His will. Jesus gives us an example when He openly praises God the Father for His precious will: "In that same hour he rejoiced in the Holy Spirit and said, 'I thank you, Father, Lord of heaven and earth, that you have hidden these things from the wise and understanding and revealed them to infants; yes, Father, for such was your gracious will'" (Luke 10:21). Jesus, Mary, and the saints marvel at God's holy will, which is often contrary to the ways of the world. St. Paul tells us: "God chose what is foolish in the world to shame the wise, God chose the weak in the world to shame the strong, God chose what is low and despised in the world, even things that are not, to bring to nothing things are, so that no flesh might boast in the presence of God" (1 Cor. 1:27–29).

Those who love the Lord not only delight in His precious will but also do everything they can to make it come to fruition. They volunteer to carry out God's plan because of their eagerness to be His instruments. In the prophets, the Psalms, Jesus, Mary, and the saints, we see that the Lord is most pleased by the desire and

[84] Dante Alighieri, *Paradiso*, in *The Divine Comedy: Inferno, Purgatorio, Paradiso*, trans. Allen Mandelbaum (New York: Alfred A. Knopf, 1995), canto 3, line 85.

willingness to do His will: "Here I am, Lord; I come to do Your will."[85] When we love, we want to please and never contradict our beloved, and so it is with the Lord. Those who love Him seek to please Him in all that they do. They never want to disappoint or offend or oppose His desires. Those who love the Lord find joy in doing His will: "I delight to do your will, O my God" (Ps. 40:8).

All parents are pleased when their children quickly and joyfully do as they are asked. On the other hand, how many parents are disappointed when their children are slow to obey, or ignore or otherwise do not do what they are asked? It is thus with the Lord: He especially delights in those who quickly and joyfully seek to carry out His will. Those who love God immensely have given their entire will, being, and life back to the Lord. St. Ignatius's *Suscipe* prayer reflects this sentiment: "Take, Lord, and receive all my liberty, my memory, my understanding, and my entire will, all I have and call my own.... Everything is yours; do with it what you will." Those who love the Lord desire that His will be accomplished in them and through them.

We are in good company when we seek to live out God's will. We imitate Jesus, Mary, and the saints, who live to do God's holy will. Jesus says, "My food is to do the will of him who sent me, and to accomplish his work" (John 4:34). Doing the Father's will is what sustains Jesus. It gives Him strength and energy and fulfills His hunger. It is most pleasing to the Lord when we conform our free will to His will out of faith, hope, and love, especially when it is difficult for us. Such was the case when Jesus was in the Garden of Gethsemane, about to undergo His Passion. He prayed, "Abba, Father, all things are possible to you; remove this chalice from me; yet not what I will, but what you will" (Mark 14:36). In the Our Father, Jesus taught us to desire the fulfillment of God's will always

[85] See Heb. 10:9; Ps. 40:7–8; 1 Sam. 3.

and everywhere: "Thy will be done on earth as it is in heaven." Those who do the will of the Father are indeed closest to Jesus and resemble Him the most: "For whoever does the will of my Father in heaven is my brother, and sister, and mother" (Matt. 12:50).

Like her Son, Mary is completely docile to the Holy Spirit, conforming her will to God's will at all times. At the Annunciation, when Mary learned from the angel Gabriel that God wanted her to be the Mother of His Son, she gave her unreserved *fiat*: "Mary said, 'Behold, I am the handmaid of the Lord; let it be to me according to your word'" (Luke 1:38). This was not a one-time yes but the beginning of many yeses. Immediately after the Annunciation, at the prompting of the Holy Spirit, Mary left in haste for the hill country to visit her cousin Elizabeth and stayed there for three months to help her. When Herod sought to kill the baby Jesus, God willed that the Holy Family flee by night to Egypt, and Joseph and Mary did so immediately. When God willed that Jesus undergo His Passion and death, Mary accepted all the suffering involved in God's plan of salvation. Mary's last statement in the Bible is her exhortation to the servers at the wedding at Cana: "Do whatever he tells you" (John 2:5). Mary tells all of us to imitate her by always doing the will of God.

Living Out God's Will

How, then, do we go about doing God's will? How do we even know what God's will is? God has already revealed His will to us through His Word, which has been handed down to us in Sacred Scripture and Sacred Tradition. The most basic way of doing God's will is to keep the commandments and obey His Word according to the teachings of the Church. Jesus told His disciples, "If you love me, you will keep my commandments" (John 14:15). Jesus spoke repeatedly about the importance of being faithful to the Word of God:

> Every one then who hears these words of mine and does them will be like a wise man who built his house upon the rock; and the rain fell, and the floods came, and the winds blew and beat upon that house, but it did not fall, because it had been founded on rock. And every one who hears these words of mine and does not do them will be like a foolish man who built his house upon the sand; and the rain fell, and the floods came, and the winds blew and beat against that house, and it fell; and great was the fall of it. (Matt. 7:24–27)

But Scripture can be difficult to understand and open to different interpretations. That is why Jesus established His Church on the rock of Peter and gave her the authority to teach, govern, and sanctify: "And I tell you, you are Peter, and on this rock I will build my Church, and the gates of Hades shall not prevail against it. I will give you the keys of the kingdom of heaven, and whatever you bind on earth shall be bound in heaven; and whatever you loose on earth shall be loosed in heaven" (Matt. 16:18–19). In the Psalms, God is often referred to as the *rock*, our only source of trustworthiness. Likewise, God's eternal Word, Jesus, is perfectly trustworthy. And Christ is the cornerstone and the head of the Church.

By changing Simon's name to *Peter*, which means "rock," Jesus gives him a share in this divine trustworthiness for his unique role in God's plan of salvation as the foundation of the Church. Hence, the Church participates in this quality of unconditional trustworthiness. Here, Jesus uses the term *my Church* for the first time. Peter may be the rock, but the Church belongs to Christ. Jesus established and sustains His Church, through which He communicates truth and grace to the world. Therefore, "the gates of the netherworld," that is, the powers of darkness, can never overcome her.

Peter is also entrusted with the keys to the kingdom of heaven. In the Old Testament, the king would entrust the keys of the kingdom to his most powerful senior official, who would pass them down to his successor. Entrusted with the keys, Peter becomes the first pope of the Church, and this line of succession has continued to the present day. With the keys comes the authority. Jesus tells Peter, "Whatever you bind on earth shall be bound in heaven; and whatever you loose on earth shall be loosed in heaven." According to Jewish traditions, *binding and loosing* refers to three types of power. The first is teaching authority: the power to decide what constitutes acceptable and unacceptable behavior. The second is juridical authority: the power to receive (or deny) a person into the faith community. And the third is spiritual authority: the power to forgive or retain sins. Hence, Peter and the apostles are given the office of teaching, governing, and sanctifying the new people of God. And this power has been passed down in an unbroken line of apostolic succession to the bishops of the Church. Jesus promised to remain with His Church and send the Holy Spirit to safeguard the truth of her teaching: "When the Spirit of truth comes, he will guide you into all the truth" (John 16:13). Through the Bishop of Rome and the Holy Spirit, Jesus is always present and actively protecting, leading, and guiding His Church.

In the 1960s and 1970s, some misinterpretations of the Second Vatican Council were promulgated, and amid the confusion, some men and women left the priesthood and religious life. Some even left the Church. Yet many did remain faithful. Cardinal Ratzinger gave a speech entitled "Why I am still in the Church," in which he compared the Church to the moon. As the moon receives light from the sun, so the Church receives light from the Son, allowing her to shine in the dark. Travelers to the moon explore the dirt and rocks on its surface but fail to appreciate the light that it reflects; they see details but miss a deeper truth. Likewise, many people focus on the Church's dirt and blemishes but fail to see the beauty of her radiance. In the night of our estrangement from God, the Church shines with the light radiated from Christ.[86] It is Jesus Himself who is present and active in His Church, giving her the light and beauty of truth, grace, and salvation.

Catholic theology is almost always a matter of *both-and* rather than *either-or*, and this holds true for the Church, which is *both* human *and* divine; she is made up both of saints *and* sinners. The Bride of Christ is imperfect and yet constantly renewed by the Holy Spirit. Christ tells us that His Church will be brought to glorious perfection at the end of time. Despite human weaknesses, the Church has not only survived but thrived for over two thousand years. This demonstrates that Jesus is truly present in His Church, perpetually guiding, protecting, and purifying her until "the Church is the spotless bride of the spotless Lamb."[87]

Besides observing the Word of God and the teachings of the Church, another way we may know that we are doing God's will is by being faithful to the duties of our state in life. If you are married and have a family, then you do God's will by being the best spouse and parent you can. If you are a priest or religious, then you do God's will by being faithful to your vocation, which includes being faithful to your vows and promises. In other words, we are to grow and flourish where we are planted. Do not wish or daydream about a different state in life than the one to which you are committed. Do not wish to be somewhere else, thinking the grass will be greener on the other side. God means for us to grow and leave our mark where we are. Mother Teresa writes, "You have to be holy where you are—wherever God has put you."[88] To the fullest extent

[86] Joseph Ratzinger (Pope Benedict XVI), *Fundamental Speeches from Five Decades*, ed. Florian Schuller, trans. Adrian Walker (San Francisco: Ignatius Press, 2012), 142–143.

[87] CCC 796.

[88] *Mother Teresa: Her Essential Wisdom*, ed. Carol Kelly-Gangi (New York: Fall River Press, 2006), 59.

possible in the here and now, be true to your vocation, with all the opportunities and circumstances that life presents.

At the same time, we must be attentive to all that is happening in our lives. God is constantly revealing His will to us from moment to moment in the people and circumstances of our lives. For example, Mother Teresa writes: "The very fact that God has placed a certain soul in our way is a sign that God wants us to do something for him or her. It is not chance; it has been planned by God. We are bound by conscience to help him or her."[89] We should try to see our lives as a book, movie, or play, with God as the author and director and us as the actors or characters. God is in charge of the script, direction, and casting. The more closely our performance follows God's will, the better the story will turn out. As actors, we have the freedom and luxury to improvise, be creative, and let our personality shine through as we put our own stamp on the story. But we can also be difficult and unreasonable and demand that the story be rewritten to suit our own tastes and preferences. This means the performance will not turn out as well as it could have, had we allowed God's will, vision, and plan to prevail. In union and cooperation with the Lord, together, we create the work of art that is our life.

Discerning God's Will in Important Matters

There are times when we have to make an important decision and we want to know God's will for us. We know that God's will is always best, and so we want to choose that which God would have us choose. Those who are close to the Lord have already started thinking like Him. They are filled with grace and are growing in the virtues and the gifts of the Holy Spirit. In particular, they are

[89] Ibid., 23.

developing the virtue of prudence and receiving the gifts of counsel, knowledge, wisdom, and understanding while practicing the theological virtues of faith, hope, and love. All these traits help them make a good and wise decision.

But sometimes, we need more clarity and more help from above to discern correctly that which is best—that which is God's will. St. Ignatius of Loyola, in his *Spiritual Exercises*, has given us ways to discern God's will when we have two good choices before us. (If one choice is evil, sinful, or contrary to the teachings of the Church, then it can be immediately eliminated. God would never ask us to make any such choice.) This principle can be applied to major life decisions, including but not limited to one's vocation to marriage, the priesthood, or consecrated life. St. Ignatius tells us that if a decision as to one's vocation has already been made, then that decision is permanent and unchangeable and should not be made again but lived out in the best way possible.[90] If a person is married, unless the marriage is found invalid, he or she has made an unchangeable choice, and there is no reason to reconsider. Likewise, if one is ordained a priest or has taken final vows as a religious, the choice is final, and there is no reason to entertain thoughts of changing one's vocation. Even if the decision was made without proper discernment, the commitment has been made and must be lived out as well as possible, with the knowledge that God will supply the necessary graces.[91]

Besides our vocation, there are other major life decisions in which we should seek to correctly discern God's will—for instance, going back to school, marrying a certain person, relocating, or

[90] *The Spiritual Exercises of St. Ignatius: Based on Studies in the Language of the Autograph*, trans. Louis J. Puhl, S.J. (Chicago: Loyola Press, 1951), 72.

[91] Ibid. In reality, there are circumstances that allow for spouses to be separated and for priests and religious to be released from their clerical state and religious vows.

changing jobs or careers. St. Ignatius tells us that if such a decision has already been properly made, there is no reason that it should be reconsidered. But if the decision has not been properly made, one should discern God's will by following certain guidelines.

St. Ignatius tells us that there are three times when a correction in life may be made. The first time is when God so moves a person's will that he or she must follow without hesitation.[92] Examples of this include the conversion of St. Paul and the calling of St. Matthew. Both men were so moved that they were certain of their calling. Usually, the person who experiences this gift is devout, meaning his or her heart is open and receptive, and he or she already possesses the virtues and the gifts of the Holy Spirit. Though rare, this first example does happen, and the person receives the gift of clarity beyond doubt and experiences a sense of certitude, peace, joy, and freedom. Nevertheless, it is always prudent to test out this call, if possible, and to seek confirmation from a spiritually wise person. For example, when I read about the priesthood for the first time, I sensed a powerful pull, a supernatural attraction, and an understanding that I had found what I had been searching for and what God wanted me to pursue. Nevertheless, I had to test it out to confirm that it was the will of God for me.

The second time when a correction in life may be made is when much light is derived from consolations and the discernment of spirits.[93] In times of spiritual consolation, we sense that God is near; we are filled with peace, joy, and love and are drawn toward a certain choice. On the other hand, in times of spiritual desolation, we are influenced by bad spirits. We feel agitated and disturbed, and we experience doubt and fear about the same choices that attracted us in times of consolation. This is because when we experience

[92] Ibid., 74.

[93] *Spiritual Exercises*, 74.

consolation, the Holy Spirit is at work in us and is leading us to find peace and joy in God's will. When we experience desolation, the evil spirits are at work creating doubts and fears to lead us away from God's will for us. This second opportunity for correction in life involves a process that, over weeks or months, may reveal a pattern that gives us clarity.

If we do receive clarity about a certain decision, we may use a third way to confirm our choice (or to gain clarity if we have not received it). This third time when a correction in life may be made is when we are not agitated by the different spirits and have a free and peaceful use of our natural powers. We place before our mind the matter about which we wish to make a choice, and we consider the end for which we are created: the service and glory of God, our salvation, and our sanctity. Then, we should be completely indifferent with no inordinate attachments, ready to follow whichever choice is most pleasing to God. Finally, we should ask God to reveal His will and help us choose as He desires.

Regarding this third time of making a correction or decision in life, there are four ways of placing the matter before our mind. The first way of discerning is to make a list of advantages and disadvantages for each good choice, taking into account the possible results of each scenario—namely, the results that contribute, or do not contribute, to the service and glory of God (rather than the results that offer worldly or selfish advantages or disadvantages). Then, we must select the weightiest and most reasonable choice. This method is very practical and helps us to see clearly which choice best serves the glory of God.

As an example, I once planned to apply to a spiritual direction program that would have involved going to another state for three weeks out of the year for three years. I thought this was what I wanted to do and what God wanted for me. But neither had I gone through the proper discernment nor did I receive clarity. A friend of mine said that when she prayed for me, she seemed to hear God saying that I had not asked Him, only other people. I did not know what she meant. I thought that I had asked God in prayer about the spiritual direction program, but the truth was, I did not receive clarity. Instead, I had asked a couple of other people who recommended the program. So then, I decided to use the method of listing the pros and cons. When I did this, it became clear to me that God did not want me to attend the program at that time. The advantages of attending the spiritual direction program included gaining more knowledge about spiritual direction, leading retreats, and obtaining a certificate in this area. The disadvantages, however, included taking a lot of valuable time away from ministering at my parish and giving retreats. I would not have been able to develop my Fullness of Grace ministry, including this book, or take necessary vacation time. In the end, it was clear that God did not want me to take the spiritual direction program but to focus on my parish responsibilities, give retreats, and expand the Fullness of Grace ministry.

The *second* way to discern by placing the matter before my mind is to consider a person whom I have never seen or known, who faces the same choice as I, and for whom I desire all perfection. What advice would I give him or her to obtain the greater glory of God and his or her personal perfection? Then, I would follow this advice. This way allows me to take a step back and be more objective. Since I do not know this person and his or her decision does not concern me, I can see the big picture from a different point of view. In this way, I can discern more clearly how best to glorify God and grow in sanctity.

The *third* way to discern is to imagine myself at the point of death and ask, looking back, which choice I wish I had made. When we are about to die, all that truly matters is that we have loved God and done His will. Everything else is passing and meaningless. This exercise gives us clarity and helps us to focus on what really matters in life. Transient things lose their luster, worldly attractions reveal their emptiness, and selfish motives become repugnant. Again, at the time of death, and with that clarity, what choice do I wish I had made? Then, make that choice now. Often, we hear that when a person is on his or her deathbed, he or she will not wish to have worked longer hours at the office but to have spent more time with family and friends and in service of society. Our priorities change when we are confronted with the ephemerality of this life and the endlessness of eternity.

The *fourth* way to discern is similar to the deathbed scenario. I can picture myself on the Day of Judgment and consider which choice I wish I had made. Which would have promoted the greater glory of God? Did this choice allow me to love God fully, or with reservation? As I stand before Jesus and give an account of how I have used my time, gifts, and opportunities in this life, I ask whether I loved God with all my heart and soul and strength. Did I use my gifts for selfish motives or for the glory of God? Which choice would have helped me love, serve, and glorify God more fully? That is the choice I want to make. My desire to love God as best I can will help me identify this choice.

Lastly, whatever choice I make based on the above methods, I ask the Lord to confirm it by speaking to me in my heart or through the people and circumstances of my life. Also, I should seek confirmation from an experienced and knowledgeable spiritual guide. If possible, I can test the waters and try out my decision. Then, I will know for sure if I have made the right choice, the one that God wills for my sanctification and for His greater glory.

Holiness Is Conformity to God's Will

Jesus, Mary, and the saints teach us that holiness means conforming our will to God's. Receiving an inner light from God, St. Faustina explained that holiness consists in uniting ourselves to God and His will at all times:

> Today during meditation, God gave me inner light and the understanding as to what sanctity is and of what it consists.... Neither graces, nor revelations, nor raptures, nor gifts granted to a soul make it perfect, but rather the intimate union of the soul with God.... My sanctity and perfection consist in the close union of my will with the will of God. God never violates our free will. It is up to us whether we want to receive God's grace or not. It is up to us whether we will cooperate with it or waste it.[94]

In this statement, St. Faustina also explains that God gives us the grace to desire and to conform our will to His, and if we do, we cooperate with His grace and benefit from it rather than wasting it. God is always inviting us to conform our will to His, and the saints respond positively by striving to do God's will in all things. In her Morning Offering, St. Thérèse of Lisieux prays for the grace to fulfill God's will perfectly: "O my God, I ask you for myself and those dear to me the grace to fulfill perfectly your holy will."[95] We, too, should pray for the grace to fulfill God's will perfectly in our lives. Jesus told St. Faustina to write the words "From today on my will does not exist" on a clean sheet of paper and then draw a large X on that page. On the other side, He told her to write these words: "From today on, I do the Will of God everywhere, always, and in everything."[96] It is most pleasing to the Lord when we die

94 *Diary*, no. 1107.

95 *The Prayers of Saint Thérèse of Lisieux: The Act of Oblation*, trans. Aletheia Kane, O.C.D (Washington, DC: ICS Publications, 1997), 86.

96 *Diary*, no. 372.

to our own will and instead seek to do His will. In this way, Jesus truly lives in us and can accomplish incredible things through us.

The greatest suffering for the souls in purgatory is their separation from God, and this is the result of their sins and attachments caused by the pursuit of their own will instead of the will of God while on earth. Oh, how they wish they had loved God more and done His will while they had the chance in this life! Through the saints and mystics of the Church, the souls in purgatory implore us to learn from them and avoid purgatory, as much as possible, by loving God and doing His will in this life.

It is never too late to start doing God's will. Jesus tells the chief priests and the elders the following parable:

> "What do you think? A man had two sons; and he went to the first and said, 'Son, go and work in the vineyard today.' And he answered, 'I will not'; but afterward he repented and went. And he went to the second and said the same; and he answered, 'I go, sir,' but did not go. Which of the two did the will of his father?" They said, "The first." Jesus said to them, "Truly, I say to you, the tax collectors and the harlots go into the kingdom of God before you." (Matt. 21:28–31)

Tax collectors and other sinners did not live according to the laws of God, but at the preaching of Jesus, they converted and conformed their way of life to the ways of God. And so, they will enter heaven before the chief priests and elders, who say they do the will of God but in fact do not. Jesus wants everyone to be converted to following the will of God, which means to believe in Jesus and follow His ways.

It is important that we get into the habit of seeing and seeking God's will in all things and then embracing and living it out as perfectly as possible. God will give us the grace if we are open and docile and desire to do His will in everything. Docility can be particularly challenging for some people who are striving for holiness because we often want to be in control. But if we want to make progress in the spiritual life, we need to be flexible, open to the inspirations and the guidance of the Holy Spirit, and comfortable with change and unpredictability. Mother Teresa writes: "I must give myself completely to Him. I must not attempt to control God's actions. I must not desire a clear perception of my advance along the road, nor know precisely where I am on the way of holiness. I ask Him to make a saint of me, yet I must leave to Him the choice of that saintliness itself and still more the choice of the means to lead to it."[97] Oftentimes, God gives us just enough light to take that next step. But we tend to want to know the future, to jump ahead, and to see the ending. Nonetheless, God tells us to trust and follow His will as He reveals it to us. Remember that the Holy Spirit is the wind that blows where and how He wills as He leads us to our beatitude. Our job is to be attentive and responsive by adjusting our sails accordingly.

To allow ourselves to be led by the Holy Spirit is to have the true freedom of the children of God: freedom from worries, impulses, sin, the world, and ourselves. In this way, we are able to forget ourselves and live for God in the here and now. Cooperating with grace is like accepting the Holy Spirit's invitation to dance and letting Him lead as we follow along. Insofar as we are in sync with the movements of the Holy Spirit, grace and beauty will abound. God wants to transform us by His grace, and the more docile, cooperative, and responsive we are, the more graces God pours forth to perfect each of us as His instrument and masterpiece. St. Faustina writes, "I understood that we should take great heed of our interior inspirations and follow them faithfully, and

[97] Mother Teresa, *Her Essential Wisdom*, 60.

that faithfulness to one grace draws down others."[98] The more we imitate Mary and the saints and are attentive and faithful to the promptings of the Holy Spirit, the more we will conform to Christ and be filled with His graces.

Practical Suggestions

1. Pray over and over the line from the breviary "Incline my heart according to your will O God" (Ps. 119:36, Grail translation), or the words "Speak, for your servant hears" (1 Sam. 3:10).
2. Get to know and speak often to your guardian angel, whom God has given you to protect you and help you to know and do His will.
3. Try to be attuned to the Holy Spirit at all times. Imagine that you have a Holy Spirit app on your phone. Make sure to turn on notifications, so that when God has something to tell you, you will get the message immediately and respond promptly.
4. Recall that the more time we spend with Jesus in prayer, the more we will know His will.
5. Be thoroughly familiar with the Word of God. This way, you will come to know the Lord and His will more and more.
6. Try to be more observant of the people and circumstances of your life to discern the guiding hand of God.
7. Be familiar with St. Ignatius of Loyola's method for the discernment of spirits.
8. Use the ways St. Ignatius shows us to discern God's will in important life matters.

[98] *Diary*, no. 756.

9. Try to be less attached to sin, the world, and yourself, so that you are available to do God's will.
10. Pray the Daily Consecration to the Holy Spirit (by Blessed Concepción Cabrera de Armida): "Holy Spirit, receive the perfect and total consecration of my entire being. From now deign to be in every instant of my life and in my every action my Director, my Light, my Guide, my Strength and all the Love of my heart. I abandon myself without reserve to your divine actions and want to be ever docile to your inspirations. Holy Spirit, transform me with Mary and in Mary into Jesus Christ for the glory of the Father and the salvation of the world. Amen."

8

Love of Neighbor

The more we love and serve our neighbor
out of love for God, the more He will reward us.

In those days Mary arose and went with haste into the hill country, to a city of Judah, and she entered the house of Zechariah and greeted Elizabeth. . . . And Mary remained with her about three months, and returned to her home. (Luke 1:39–40, 56)

To Love God Is to Love Our Neighbor

As mentioned in the previous chapter, which focused on the love of God, the virtue of charity has two components: "Charity is the theological virtue by which we love God above all things for his own sake, and our neighbor as ourselves for the love of God."[99] In this chapter, we will focus on the second part of charity—that is, the love of neighbor, which is based on our love for the Lord. Indeed, the two go hand in hand. We cannot truly love God unless

[99] CCC 1822.

we love our neighbor. St. John tells us: "If any one says, 'I love God,' and hates his brother, he is a liar; for he who does not love his brother whom he has seen, cannot love God whom he has not seen. And this commandment we have from him, that he who loves God should love his brother also" (1 John 4:20–21).

Let us face it, the second part of charity can be much more demanding than the first for many of us. Loving God may not be as difficult once we understand that He loves us infinitely and that He is perfect in every way and, therefore, worthy of all our love. But loving our neighbor is a different story: our neighbor may hate us, hurt us, or be just plain difficult and unpleasant to be around. But God has placed us among other people precisely to give us the means by which we can demonstrate our love for Him and learn to love as He loves. God the Father told St. Catherine of Siena:

> I ask you to love me with the same love with which I love you. But for me you cannot do this, for I loved you without being loved. Whatever love you have for me you owe me, so you love me not gratuitously but out of duty, while I love you not out of duty but gratuitously. So, you cannot give me the kind of love I ask of you. This is why I have put you among your neighbors: so that you can do for them what you cannot do for me — that is, love them without any concern for thanks and without looking for any profit for yourself. And whatever you do for them I will consider done for me.[100]

It is easy to tell God that we love Him, but He wants us to show our love for Him by loving our brothers and sisters, including those who may be especially difficult. Jesus repeats this truth when He tells us, "Truly, I say to you, as you did it to one of the least of these my brethren, you did it to me" (Matt. 25:40).

[100] Catherine of Siena, *The Dialogue*, 121.

It is true that God has no need of us, for He is sufficient and complete in and of Himself. But He created us out of pure love so that we may share in His life, love, and joy. So our love for God is reciprocal, because He loved us first. But God wants us to learn to love as He loves, that is, with a completely self-giving love for the good of the other with no self-interest.

Our culture is confused about the meaning of love. Love is not an attraction, a warm feeling, or a personal satisfaction in being with another. St. Thomas Aquinas tells us that the true meaning of love is to will the good of the other.[101] When we love someone, we desire and choose what is best for him or her; we want his or her good and happiness. Love is not about how the other person makes us feel; rather, it is about desiring that which is most beneficial to the other. The focus is not on us and what we can get out of this relationship but on the other person and his or her good. God has placed us among our neighbors so that we may show our love for Him by giving ourselves purely for the benefit of others without any expectation of personal gain.

To love God is to love all His children too. When we love someone, we must love what he or she loves and what is dear to him or her. We cannot love someone and despise his or her family. So it is with the Lord. When we love Him, we must love His children because He loves them. Every human person, regardless of who he or she is, is a child of God. God created all people in His image and likeness, and they are redeemed by Christ and destined for eternal happiness with God. Every person is precious to the Lord, and He wants his or her greatest good. Therefore, if we truly love God, we take on His mind and heart; we love what He loves and in the way He loves. C.S. Lewis tells us, "Next to the Blessed Sacrament itself, your neighbor is the holiest object

[101] ST I-II, q. 26, art. 4.

presented to your senses."[102] We need to learn to look at everything and everyone with the supernatural eyes of God, to see beyond the rough exterior and the sins and see the soul within that reflects the image of the Father.

Every time we look at the crucifix, we see the love of God, which is revealed by the sacrifice of Jesus for our salvation. The vertical beam represents our relationship with God, and the horizontal beam represents our relationship with one another. One cannot exist without the other; the two go hand in hand, and therefore, love of God and love of neighbor are one. Because of their burning love for God, the saints have a passionate desire for the salvation of souls. To love our neighbor is to desire his or her greatest good, which is eternal life. God desires that every person be saved, and if we are to love God, we must desire the same. Therefore, the saints all live with great zeal for the glory of God and the salvation of souls. The word *enthusiasm*, which is another way to say *zeal*, comes from the Greek root *en theos*, which means "God is within." The zeal of the saints for the salvation of souls comes from the Holy Spirit living and acting in them and their knowledge that the Most High dwells within each person.

That is why the Church's mission is evangelization. Christ commissioned His disciples with these words: "Go therefore and make disciples of all nations, baptizing them in the name of the Father and of the Son and of the Holy Spirit, teaching them to observe all that I have commanded you" (Matt. 28:19–20). Every Christian has been called to love and lead others to Christ. We are not meant to strive for holiness alone but to help each other fulfill our universal vocation to intimacy with God, holiness of life, and service to God and others. We are not meant to be lone stars in

[102] C. S. Lewis, *The Weight of Glory and Other Addresses* (New York: HarperCollins, 2001), 46.

the sky but to lead a cluster of stars, together forming a beautiful constellation for God.

Using Our Gifts

To love our neighbor, then, is to use our gifts for the good of others and the glory of God. God has entrusted each person with certain gifts, talents, and abilities to be used not for selfish or sinful purposes but to help others. St. Peter tells us, "As each has received a gift, employ it for one another, as good stewards of God's varied grace" (1 Pet. 4:10). If we use our gifts rightly, they will grow and flourish, but if we do not, they will fade away. Jesus tells the parable of the talents to drive home this point:

> For it will be as when a man going on a journey called his servants and entrusted to them his property; to one he gave five talents, to another two, to another one, to each according to his ability. Then he went away. He who had received the five talents went at once and traded with them; and he made five talents more. So also, he who had the two talents made two talents more. But he who had received the one talent went and dug in the ground and hid his master's money. Now after a long time the master of those servants came and settled accounts with them. And he who had received the five talents came forward, bringing five talents more, saying, "Master, you delivered to me five talents; here I have made five talents more." His master said to him, "Well done, good and faithful servant; you have been faithful over a little, I will set you over much; enter into the joy of your master." And he also who had the two talents came forward, saying, "Master, you delivered to me two talents; here I have made two talents more." His master said to him, "Well done, good

> and faithful servant; you have been faithful over a little, I will set you over much; enter into the joy of your master." He also who had received the one talent came forward, saying, "Master, I knew you to be a hard man, reaping where you did not sow, and gathering where you did not winnow; so I was afraid, and I went and hid your talent in the ground. Here you have what is yours." But his master answered him, "You wicked and slothful servant! You knew that I reap where I have not sowed, and gather where I have not winnowed? Then you ought to have invested my money with the bankers, and at my coming I should have received what was my own with interest. So take the talent from him, and give it to him who has the ten talents. For to every one who has will more be given, and he will have abundance; but from him who has not, even what he has will be taken away." (Matt. 25:14–29)

St. Paul tells us that each of us has been given special gifts, sometimes referred to as *charisms*, to be used for building up the Church. These charisms include wisdom, knowledge, faith, healing, prophecy, teaching, administration, and speaking or interpreting tongues (see 1 Cor. 12:4–11; Eph. 4:11). Therefore, it is important that each of us knows our gifts and puts them to use. Here is a quick way to discern our special gifts: first, it is something we do especially well, much better than the average person. Second, we enjoy doing it. Third, others benefit from it. We will need to test it out to confirm that it is indeed a gift. Then, we must put it to use so that it will develop and increase; otherwise, it will fade away.

I know a priest who is naturally very shy and quiet. Even in the seminary, he was told that he needed to speak and interact more with others. Then, after ordination, he received the gift of preaching, which he developed through prayer, meditating on Scripture, and preparing and delivering homilies that are anointed by the Holy Spirit to touch, move, and inspire his listeners. His gift of preaching has grown because he has put in the time and effort to develop and use it for the good of others and for the glory of God. Conversely, I know of another priest who received the gift of praying in tongues. But over the years, he has not used it, and now he can no longer pray in tongues. He has lost the gift. We must use our gifts well if they are to grow.

Prayer is another gift that is meant to be used not only for our personal benefit but for the good of others and the glory of God. Praying is an act of charity. In fact, prayer can do more good for someone, and for the world, than we can on our own. Some people have a special charism of intercessory prayer, and if they use and develop it, it can become a powerful means of charity. There are cloistered and monastic religious communities that uphold the world and the mission of the Church by their prayers. Only in heaven will we come to know and fully appreciate all those who have helped us by their prayers and all whom we have helped by ours.

Know that the more generously we exercise our God-given talents for the good of others, the more we will be rewarded: "Give, and it will be given to you; good measure, pressed down, shaken together, running over, will be put into your lap. For the measure you give will be the measure you get back" (Luke 6:38). Truly, God can never be outdone in generosity. How sad it would be if we never discerned and lived out our unique gifts. Each one us will have to give an accounting of how we used our time, energy, and gifts on the Day of Judgment. Did we use what was entrusted to us for the good of others and the glory of God or for selfish reasons? We will be judged accordingly. The opposite of love is not hate but selfishness; it is love turned inward. Mother Teresa writes, "To love, it is necessary to give: to give it is necessary to be free from selfishness."[103] When we take care of others, God takes care of us: "And God is able to provide you with every blessing in abundance, so that you may always have enough of everything and may provide in abundance for every good work" (2 Cor. 9:8).

Created in the image and likeness of God, we are made to love and to be loved. The Holy Trinity is a relationship of self-giving love: the Father gives Himself and everything He has completely to the Son. The Son receives the Father's love and gives Himself back to the Father completely. This love is so intense, so real, that it is the Person of the Holy Spirit, the bond of love between the Father and the Son. Made in God's image, we are created for this self-giving love. It is in loving that we become more fully human and more like God. Vatican II tells us that "man ... cannot truly find himself except through a sincere gift of himself."[104] Unless we make a sacrificial gift of self to serve others out of love for God, we will never become the person that God made us to be. St. John Paul II adds, "Life has meaning to the extent that it becomes a free gift for others."[105] We are not meant to live for ourselves but to follow the examples of Jesus, Mary, and the saints, and to give ourselves freely to the service of God and others. It is only in giving that we find meaning, fulfillment, and true happiness in this life and the next.

Levels of Love

In addition to the four levels of happiness, Fr. Spitzer speaks about four levels of love. The first level, which is the lowest and the most basic, is love based on the pleasure of the senses and physical

[103] Mother Teresa, *Thirsting for God*, 153.

[104] Vatican Council II, *Gaudium et Spes*, no. 24.

[105] Pope John Paul II, *Crossing the Threshold of Hope*, 121.

gratification. I may say, "I love you," but what I really love is how pleasing you are to my senses: you are attractive to the eyes. Your smell is intoxicating. Your touch drives me wild. This love is superficial and selfish and based mostly on physical chemistry and attraction. What I love most is your body and how you make me feel. Many people confuse lust with love, and in this type of relationship, both parties, in an unspoken way, agree to use and be used by each other for sensual gratification.

The second level of love is based on the ego. People like to feel good about themselves, and this type of relationship is more about status and utility. I love the other person because he or she increases my self-esteem. For example, I love a person because he or she looks good on paper; this person is wealthy, powerful, and successful. Also, he or she treats me like a prince or princess. Because of this person's status and how he or she treats me, I feel like a million bucks when I am with him or her. This kind of love, like the first, is superficial and self-centered. Although unspoken or even unconscious, the focus is mostly on what the other person can do for my ego. Unfortunately, many people in our world live and love on these first two levels.

The third level of love is based on a commitment to the other person. I love the other person for who he or she is. I truly care for the other person and want his or her good, and I am willing to sacrifice for his or her happiness. This type of love is tested, for example, when one person becomes debilitated. Does the other person leave or stay in this relationship and sacrifice for the good of the other? This type of love requires empathy, conscience, and grace. Sometimes, one person is on level three while the other person is on levels one and two. But the third level is still not enough. Even non-Christians and atheists can love on this level.

The fourth level of love is based on the transcendent or the supernatural. This love desires the *greatest* good of the other, which is holiness and eternal life. This love imitates the love of God, who desires that each person attain his or her greatest good and happiness by fulfilling his or her vocation in this life and sharing in the fullness of God's life, love, and joy in the life to come. This love requires sacrifice, self-forgetfulness, and acceptance. Imitating Christ, we sacrifice for the other, forget ourselves to serve the other person's greatest good, and accept whatever happens. For instance, this love requires speaking the truth when the other person does something that is not conducive to his or her salvation, even though this may adversely affect the relationship. I must forget myself and consider and desire the other person's greatest good, even though he or she may get upset with me. True love requires not going along with what the other person wants if it is not conducive to his or her greatest good. Like God, we love the person but hate the sin, or to put it another way, we hate the sin because we love the person.

Not Judging, but Forgiving

A big part of loving our neighbor is not judging but forgiving him or her. Jesus tells us, "Judge not, and you will not be judged; condemn not, and you will not be condemned; forgive, and you will be forgiven" (Luke 6:37). Many of us have a tendency to judge others and find it difficult to forgive, especially when someone has hurt us deeply. Such cases, rather than instances when someone has caused us minor or trivial harm that is easy to let go of, will be our focus here.

People are often confused about forgiveness. It is probably easier to say first what forgiveness is *not*. Forgiveness is not ignoring, condoning, excusing, or justifying the action of the one who hurt us. It is also not forgetting, which takes time. We have all heard the phrase "Forgive and forget," but forgetting is not easy, especially when someone has truly hurt us. Only in time can we really forget, but we can forgive nevertheless. Forgiveness also does not require the other person to say, "I am sorry." Many people are not sorry for hurting us, but our forgiveness is not dependent on their apology. Along the same lines, we do not need to contact the other person and tell him or her, "I forgive you." Reconciliation is generally desirable, but in some cases, it is not wise to go back to a situation that is harmful. Some relationships can never be restored to how they were before the hurt. We do not have to trust the offender again, but we can still forgive him or her.

Forgiveness *does* come into play when another person has unjustly hurt us. We have the right to be angry, but we choose to overcome the anger. We choose to offer the wrongdoer compassion, mercy, and love, which is a gracious gift to the offender, a canceling of the debt.

Why should we forgive? One reason is because God has forgiven us much and continues to forgive us. In Scripture, we read:

> Then Peter came up and said to him, "Lord, how often shall my brother sin against me, and I forgive him? As many as seven times?" Jesus said to him, "I do not say to you seven times, but seventy times seven.
>
> "Therefore the kingdom of heaven may be compared to a king who wished to settle accounts with his servants. When he began the reckoning, one was brought to him who owed him ten thousand talents; and as he could not pay, his lord ordered him to be sold, with his wife and children and all that he had, and payment to be made. So the servant fell on his knees, imploring him, 'Lord, have patience with me, and I will pay you everything.' And out of pity for him the lord of that servant released him and forgave him the debt. But that same servant, as he went out, came upon one of his fellow servants who owed him a hundred denarii; and

> seizing him by the throat he said, 'Pay what you owe.' So his fellow servant fell down and pleaded with him, 'Have patience with me, and I will pay you.' He refused and went and put him in prison till he should pay the debt. When his fellow servants saw what had taken place, they were greatly distressed, and they went and reported to their lord all that had taken place. Then his lord summoned him and said to him, 'You wicked servant! I forgave you all that debt because you pleaded with me; and should not you have had mercy on your fellow servant, as I had mercy on you?' And in anger his lord delivered him to the jailers, till he should pay all his debt. So also my heavenly Father will do to every one of you, if you do not forgive your brother from your heart." (Matt. 18:21–35)

God the Trinity is infinite. When we finite beings commit sins, our debt is infinite, because we have offended the infinite Divine Persons. We can never make up for it. Therefore, God sent His Son to become one of us, to suffer and die and rise again to atone for our sins and to reconcile us with the Father. Since God has forgiven us, we can surely forgive one another.

God wants us to forgive one another because doing so is best for us, while not doing so is destructive. The Lord never asks that we do anything unless it is for our benefit and the common good. In this case, forgiveness also helps us to resemble the Lord. "To err is human, but to forgive is divine," as Alexander Pope said. Forgiveness is a God-like quality, and our vocation is to resemble the Lord more and more. Jesus tells us, "Be merciful, even as your Father is merciful" (Luke 6:36), and teaches us in the Our Father to pray, "Forgive us our trespasses as we forgive those who trespass against us." The key word here is *as*. We are asking the Father to forgive us *as* we forgive others. In other words, we are asking God not to forgive us if we do not forgive others. Jesus wants us to know that our forgiveness is dependent upon our forgiving others.

By not forgiving, we give in to the influence of the threefold enemy: the flesh, the world, and the devil. St. Paul reminds us to live by the Spirit and not by the flesh because the two are opposed (Gal. 5:17). The works of the flesh include "enmity, strife, jealousy, anger, selfishness, dissensions, party spirit, [and] envy" (Gal. 5:20–21), all of which directly oppose the forgiveness, peace, and unity of the Spirit.

The world also encourages us to stand up, strike back, get even, and make the other person pay for what he or she did to us. But Jesus warned against retaliation:

> You have heard that it was said, "An eye for an eye and a tooth for a tooth." But I say to you, Do not resist one who is evil. But if any one strikes you on the right cheek, turn to him the other also; and if any one would sue you and take your coat, let him have your cloak as well; and if any one forces you to go one mile, go with him two miles. Give to him who begs from you, and do not refuse him who would borrow from you.
>
> You have heard that it was said, "You shall love your neighbor and hate your enemy." But I say to you, Love your enemies and pray for those who persecute you, so that you may be sons of your Father who is in heaven; for he makes his sun rise on the evil and on the good, and sends rain on the just and on the unjust. For if you love those who love you, what reward have you? Do not even the tax collectors do the same? And if you salute only your brethren, what more are you doing than others? Do not even the Gentiles do the same? You, therefore, must be perfect, as your heavenly Father is perfect. (Matt. 5:38–48)

As disciples of Jesus, we are called to live by a higher standard and to break the cycle of escalating vengeance. Without forgiveness, suffering and injuries will only proliferate.

The third enemy is the devil. The word for *devil* in Greek is *diabolos*, which means "one who scatters." The "father of lies" (John 8:44) loves to sow discord, dissent, and division. He loves to incite conflict, misunderstanding, and aggression within families, among friends, and in communities. On the other hand, God is about compassion, gentleness, understanding, self-control, charity, and unity. When we do not forgive, the enemy wins.

Lastly, the consequences of not forgiving are detrimental. By not forgiving, we actually hurt ourselves more than we hurt the offender. We suffer psychologically, emotionally, physically, and spiritually. We also waste a lot of valuable time and energy thinking about and replaying the offense and reliving the pain. Not forgiving brings out the worst in us; it hardens our hearts and turns us into someone we are not. When we do not forgive, we sever relationships that could be mended, and we damage our other relationships by being in a bad mood and taking out our frustrations on those who are closest to us. Not forgiving can also be passed down to future generations, ruining additional lives.

Consequently, not forgiving damages our relationship with God, as our refusal to let go creates obstacles to grace. We cannot rightly love God if our heart is burdened with anger, resentment, or hatred. Jesus reminds us to prioritize reconciliation: "So if you are offering your gift at the altar, and there remember that your brother has something against you, leave your gift there before the altar and go; first be reconciled to your brother, and then come and offer your gift" (Matt. 5:23–24). We do not have the proper disposition to worship God rightly and receive all the graces that He wants to give us unless our heart is free of hostility toward another. Not forgiving prevents us from loving as we should and becoming holy as God created us to be.

How, then, do we forgive? Forgiveness usually does not happen overnight but is a process that takes grace, time, effort, and perseverance. God gives us the grace, but we need to do our part.

First, ask the Lord to help you *identify* and uncover the source and depth of your anger. It may be something obvious, but it might also be something that has been building up over time and has many hidden layers. Second, *accept the pain*; share it with the Lord, and ask Him for healing. If we deny the pain or anger, we block our own healing. Partaking frequently in the Sacrament of Reconciliation is helpful in the healing process. Third, *decide* to forgive, because forgiveness is a *choice*, not a feeling or an emotion. Bring God into the process, and pray for the desire and ability to forgive, heal, and let go. Put aside any thoughts of revenge. Try not to say anything negative about the offender to people who do not need to know. Fourth, work toward understanding, *empathy*, and compassion for the other person. Give people the benefit of doubt, because sometimes the incident is not intentional. People often act the way they do for a reason. When we put ourselves in the other person's shoes, his or her actions become easier to understand. What was life like for him or her when he or she was growing up? The problem may be a product of genes or environment or a combination of these or many other factors. For instance, if a person is quick to anger, it could be that he or she was exposed to violent outbursts while growing up. Also, what was life like for the other person at the time he or she offended you? Maybe the person was struggling with his or her own problems. Also, try to think of the other person's positive qualities. When we are angry, we can demonize the other person, but we must remember that everyone has some redeeming qualities. Empathy requires looking for the good in others, because if we do not, we will only see their faults and shortcomings. Try to see the other person with the eyes of God—as His son or daughter made in His image and likeness and destined for eternal life.

Furthermore, acknowledge that we are all human. We are broken, weak, and in need of God's grace. St. Thérèse writes, "I understand now that charity consists in bearing with the faults of others, in not being surprised at their weakness; in being edified by the smallest acts of virtue we see them practice."[106] We can relate to and identify with others because we, too, have made mistakes, hurt others, sinned, and needed forgiveness. And so, we imitate God in being generous and giving them a break. Mercy is empathy plus generosity. Frequent reception of the Eucharist, which is the sacrament of love and unity, conforms us to Christ, who prayed, "Father, forgive them; for they know not what they do" (Luke 23:34), as He was being crucified. God the Father tells St. Catherine of Siena: "Where the human will is concerned you must consider my will rather than people's evil intentions; for I am their judge, not you, but I."[107] We tend to attribute bad motives to people's actions when we really do not know all that is involved. Only God knows. In the Creed, we express our belief that Jesus will come to judge the living and the dead. We leave judging to the Lord.

We also discover that our suffering has meaning and value (we will explore this further in the next chapter) and that we can unite our pain to that of Jesus during His Passion and Crucifixion. Pray the Rosary (especially the Sorrowful Mysteries), meditate on the Seven Sorrows of Mary, and pray the Divine Mercy Chaplet, which includes the prayer "For the sake of His sorrowful passion, have mercy on us and on the whole world." With time, God's grace, and our efforts, we will discover the liberation of forgiveness and experience the peace and freedom of the children of God.

Our Blessed Mother is a model of charity and forgiveness, and she loves others with the heart of God. Immediately after the

[106] *Story of a Soul*, 220.

[107] Catherine of Siena, *The Dialogue*, 191–192.

Annunciation, Mary set out in haste to visit her elderly cousin, Elizabeth, who was six months pregnant. Mary is not concerned about herself or her well-being but is always thinking of how she can serve others and glorify God. At the wedding at Cana, the Mother of God was the first to notice that the wine was running low, and she brought it to the attention of Jesus. Mary is attentive to the needs of others and eager to help. Like God, Our Lady cares for the well-being of others and desires their greatest good and happiness.

In addition, Mary does not get angry or hold a grudge but forgives generously. I believe that when Peter denied Jesus three times, Mary did not hold that against him. She knew he was weak and scared. I also do not think Mary was angry with the other apostles who deserted Jesus—she understands human weakness. When the crowd demanded that Jesus be crucified, Mary was devastated, yet she accepted the pain. I believe that as the soldiers scourged, mocked, and crucified her own flesh and blood, she forgave them from her heart. Like God the Father, Mary so loved the world that she freely gave us her only begotten Son. Mary's love is sacrificial, self-forgetful, and accepting. Our Mother is empathetic, generous, and forgiving and wants her children to be the same.[108]

Love according to St. Paul

If you have been to a Catholic wedding, chances are you have heard the reading about love from chapter 13 of St. Paul's First Letter to the Corinthians. This is a beautiful reading with which many people are familiar, yet we may not fully understand and appreciate the deeper meaning that St. Paul intended. The love

[108] There are times when righteous anger is appropriate. An example of this is when Jesus drove out the money-changers in the temple area (Matt. 21:12; John 2:15).

he describes is not just beautiful; it is demanding: "Love is patient and kind; love is not jealous or boastful; it is not arrogant or rude. Love does not insist on its own way; it is not irritable or resentful; it does not rejoice at wrong, but rejoices in the right. Love bears all things, believes all things, hopes all things, endures all things" (vv. 4–7). This passage complements or confirms the way we have understood thus far the love of neighbor.

Love is patient in that it is slow to anger and not impulsive. It exercises the type of restraint that Jesus and Mary demonstrated in their lives, especially during the Passion. At some point, we need to realize that no person or relationship is perfect, and we cannot expect things to go our way all the time. Love does not demand that other people behave and act according to our preferences. Each person is unique and has his or her way of doing things, and we need to accept and respect that fact. Love does not immediately react with harshness to the weaknesses and faults of others but knows that everyone is human. Love is meek, gentle, and patient. This description of love reminds me of my grandmother, with whom I was very close while growing up. My grandfather was very demanding and difficult, yet I never once saw my grandmother react harshly. She was indeed very patient and loving—qualities that are greatly lacking in our world. Those who are patient reflect the love of God. Let us pray that we can be like Jesus and Mary: meek, gentle, and patient.

Love is kind and is eager to act for the benefit of others. It is warm, benevolent, and magnanimous. One who loves is generous with his or her time and service, without any expectation of payment. I see this love at my parish in the volunteers who give their time and energy to serve the good of the Church without expecting anything in return. We also see this love in Mother Teresa and in her sisters, who dedicate their lives to helping the poorest of the poor. They love with the generous heart of God. May we, too, give of our time and talents to serve the good of others and build up the Church.

Love is not jealous when it values and rejoices in the achievements of another. It does not see the other person as a threat but recognizes that everyone has different gifts and a unique path in life and reflects a certain attribute of God. Love makes us one with the beloved, whose gifts become our own. This love celebrates all the different gifts and accomplishments that contribute to the common good and bring glory to God. There is no room for envy when the focus is not on oneself but on the good of the other and the kingdom of God. When God and others rejoice, we celebrate with them.

Love is not boastful: those who love refrain from talking about themselves and are focused on others. They do not need to be the center of attention and prefer not to be noticed. Their love is humble and does not admit pride or vanity, which diminish the capacity for love. Similarly, *love is not arrogant*; it has no false or exaggerated sense of self-importance. Love understands, embraces, and shows concern for the weak. In its empathy and solidarity, this love gladly associates with the lowly. When one member suffers, we all suffer.

Love is not rude: love is never belligerent or abrasive. As much as possible, it avoids giving offense. It is tactful and considerate and is never obscene or disrespectful. This love is graceful and thoughtful, and its actions, words, and gestures are pleasing and not abrasive. Love does not like to make others suffer but is gracious and polite. Looking out for the other, *love does not insist on its own way*: love sacrifices for the good of the other without expecting anything in return. Self-giving love transcends the demands of justice. This love is easily observed in parents, who readily make sacrifices to care for their children at a great cost to themselves.

Love is not irritable and is not quick-tempered. It does not give in to hostility, anger, or indignation; rather, it seeks peace and harmony. Love is mild and tranquil. *Love is not resentful* in that it does not take account of evil done to it. It is not discouraged when wronged. Love does not ponder the evil it observes in others and does not gossip. It excuses and seeks to understand the weaknesses of others. Love forgives. Similarly, *love does not rejoice at wrong, but rejoices in the right*: it is highly sensitive to harm done to others and to all forms of injustice. Love rejoices in good and truthful conduct, morally upright behavior, and beautiful and exemplary deeds. Love is righteous.

Love bears all things and resists making negative comments about others. It accepts their faults and imitations refrains from passing judgment. *Love believes all things*: one who loves is inclined to believe the best about others and to trust their motives and actions. Love sets free; it does not try to control, possess, or dominate.

Love hopes all things because even if evil is evident in someone, love does not despair of the future. It trusts in the basic goodness and potential of the person. Love knows that people can change, mature, and surprise us and that God can make crooked lines straight. *Love endures all things* in that it bears every trial with a positive attitude. Christian love stands firm in hostile surroundings and does not give up but counts on the final triumph of the good. This is the love of Mary and the saints and the martyrs.

No Regrets

When we have God's love in our heart and soul, we strive to share it with others and to love God by loving our neighbor. This life is short, and we do not know when we will be called from this world; therefore, let us try to love, give, and serve at every occasion. The Lord gives us many opportunities to love Him through others. But we need to be attentive and take advantage of these occasions when we have the chance. When I was in the seminary, I went to do a retreat in Lourdes. One morning, while out walking, I saw a beggar and his family. But I walked past them without giving them anything. As I continued walking, I started to feel bad and decided to turn around and go back to give them some money. But they were no longer there, and I did not see where they went. I felt a deep regret for not helping them when I had the chance. This experience affected me so profoundly that I made a promise always to give to a beggar if I had the chance.

Growing up, I was very close to my grandfather. After he passed away, I thought about writing a book about his fascinating life. I learned a lot from him, I wanted to document his life and share it with others. And so, I started interviewing members of my family. During one conversation, an aunt told me about the time she gave my grandfather an expensive bottle of wine for his birthday. He wanted to open it right away, but she told him to save it for another special occasion. But that occasion never came: shortly after his birthday, he passed away unexpectedly. My aunt deeply regretted not letting him open and enjoy the expensive wine. Life is short and fragile. We really do not know when someone we love will be taken from us. Therefore, we should savor every moment and bring peace and joy to others whenever we can.

Sometimes, we take life and family and friends for granted and mistreat each other instead of loving as we should. A survivor of the Auschwitz concentration camp told the following story: when she was fifteen and her brother was eight, they were brought to the camp by train. During the trip, she noticed that her brother did not have any shoes on his feet. She suddenly snapped at him, saying something like "Why are you so stupid? Why can't you keep your things together, for goodness' sake?" Unfortunately, those were the last words she ever said to her brother, who did not survive. Once she was freed from Auschwitz, she made a promise to herself never to say anything to anyone that she could not accept as the very last words she said to that person. Sometimes, we simply cannot take back what we have said.

Life is short and unpredictable, and our opportunity to love is limited; therefore, we should not pass up an opportunity to practice charity. When I was a transitional deacon and helping out at a parish for the summer, I brought Communion to the sick and homebound. One day, I brought Communion to a lady named Barbara. After receiving Communion, she wanted to give me a couple of books. As I was waiting for her to get them, I noticed a plaque on the wall with the following quote from Stephen Grellet: "I expect to pass through this world but once. Any good, therefore, that I can do, or any kindness I can show to any human being, let me do it now. Let me not defer it or neglect it, for I shall not pass this way again." Just a month later, Barbara passed away, and I preached at her funeral. I am blessed to have met Barbara and brought her Communion. I still have her books and remember the quote that I saw at her home.

Made in the image and likeness of God, we are created to love and to be loved. This is manifested in how we treat those around us. The more we love, the more God infuses our soul with His love and sanctifying grace, which we reveal to and share with others through our loving service. Like Jesus, Mary, and the saints, who understood the preeminence of love, we are meant to be channels of God's grace to the world.

Practical Suggestions

1. Try to see Jesus in each person and know that by loving and serving others, we love and serve Jesus Himself.
2. Pray St. Ignatius of Loyola's prayer for generosity: "Lord Jesus, teach me to be generous; teach me to serve You as You deserve, to give and not to count the cost, to fight and

not to heed the wounds, to toil and not to seek for rest, to labor and not to seek reward, except that of knowing that I do Your will. Amen."

3. Pray for the sanctity and happiness of those who hurt you.
4. Be attentive to your thoughts. When you find yourself thinking critical, envious, or uncharitable thoughts about someone, let these thoughts go, and instead think about his or her positive qualities.
5. Try to see each person with the eyes of Jesus and to love them with His heart.
6. Discern your gifts and charisms and put them to use for the good of others and the glory of God.
7. Try to live and love on levels three and four.
8. Always be on the lookout for opportunities to practice charity. Do not let them pass by, but take the chance to do some good for others.
9. Practice charity, and it will get easier. Look forward to the day it becomes second nature.
10. Pray the Prayer of St. Francis: "Lord, make me an instrument of Your peace. Where there is hatred, let me sow love; where there is injury, pardon; where there is doubt, faith; where there is despair, hope; where there is darkness, light; where there is sadness, joy. O, Divine Master, grant that I may not so much seek to be consoled as to console; to be understood as to understand; to be loved as to love. For it is in giving that we receive, it is in pardoning that we are pardoned, and it is in dying that we are born again to eternal life."
11. Recall that desires, prayers, words, teachings, examples, and deeds—great or small—are acts of charity that we owe to others and to God.

9

Abandonment to Divine Providence

The more we accept and trust that God is in control of all things and that He wills the best for us, the more God will manifest His goodness and wisdom.

But standing by the cross of Jesus were his mother, and his mother's sister, Mary the wife of Clopas, and Mary Magdalene. (John 19:25)

Faithfulness, Not Success

We are called to love our neighbor, which means sacrificing ourselves for his or her greatest good, while forgetting ourselves and accepting whatever happens. Often, when we sacrifice for the good of others, we expect acknowledgment and gratitude for our good deed, but we do not always get it. Even worse, sometimes, we may receive hostility and anger instead. Abandonment to divine providence means that we accept the responses of others and all the consequences of our act of love. Mother Teresa often said, "God does not require that we be successful, only that we be faithful." So we do our best to be faithful to the Lord and leave the results in His hands.

Of all the qualities of Mary, abandonment to divine providence may be the most difficult to imitate. Abandonment requires the use of all the qualities we have covered: humility, trust, love, union with God, gratitude, joy, and docility—all of which will be put to the test—as well as new virtues, such as mortification and perseverance. All twelve qualities will be called upon and put to work when we practice abandonment to divine providence, which is necessary if we are to advance in the spiritual life.

When I first discovered the concept of surrendering to divine providence, it changed my world completely. But to assimilate and grow in this vital component of holiness takes years of practice. Abandonment forces us to grow in holiness and mature in faith. It is not for the weak of heart; it separates the advanced from the beginners. According to Fr. Jean-Pierre de Caussade, S.J., who has written extensively on the topic, abandonment to divine providence is a way to perfection.

Providence refers to how God foresees, attends to, and provides for everything. He arranges all things for our greatest good, even to the smallest detail. We need to know that all matters are under God's control and that nothing happens without His knowledge and permission. Jesus reminds us to trust in God's knowledge, power, and goodness: "Are not two sparrows sold for a penny? And not one of them will fall to the ground without your Father's will. But even the hairs on your head are all numbered. Fear not, therefore; you are of more value than many sparrows" (Matt. 10:29–31). God sustains, protects, and directs His creation according to His wisdom and love. Therefore, Jesus encourages us to trust in God's providence:

> Therefore I tell you, do not be anxious about your life, what you shall eat or what you shall drink, nor about your body, what you shall put on. Is not life more than food, and the

> body more than clothing? Look at the birds of the air: they neither sow nor reap nor gather into barns, and yet your heavenly Father feeds them. Are you not of more value than they? And which of you by being anxious can add one cubit to his span of life? And why are you anxious about clothing? Consider the lilies of the field, how they grow; they neither toil nor spin; yet I tell you, even Solomon in all his glory was not clothed like one of these. But if God so clothes the grass of the field, which today is alive and tomorrow is thrown into the oven, will he not much more clothe you, O you of little faith? Therefore do not be anxious, saying, "What shall we eat?" or "What shall we drink?" or "What shall we wear?" For the Gentiles seek all these things; and your heavenly Father knows that you need them all. But seek first his kingdom and his righteousness, and all these things shall be yours as well. Therefore do not be anxious about tomorrow, for tomorrow will be anxious for itself. Let the day's own trouble be sufficient for the day. (Matt. 6:25–34)

God takes care of the birds, the flowers, and all of nature. How much more will He protect, provide, and care for His sons and daughters?

The Mystery of Suffering

Many people ask: If God is all-knowing, all-powerful, and all-loving, why is there so much evil in the world? The mystery of evil and suffering is perplexing. Neither do we comprehend fully nor can we explain sufficiently the reasons for and meaning of suffering. We know that God created everything good and that led by Lucifer, one-third of the angels rebelled against God and became evil by their own doing. They were cast out of heaven, and they incite people to sin (see Rev. 12:4, 8–10).

Out of love, God created man in His image and likeness and endowed him with free will, but Adam and Eve misused this gift and chose to rebel against God; hence, sin and death entered into the world. Consequently, although we still have free will, it has been diminished by concupiscence. Tragically, many of us misuse and abuse our free will by choosing evil rather than good. So, much of the suffering and evil in the world is the result of our own choices and the consequence of both Original Sin and personal sin.

Nothing happens to us without God's permissive will, including sin, suffering, and death. And if the Lord allows evil to happen, it is to bring about a greater good. St. Thomas Aquinas, quoting St. Augustine's *Enchiridion*, writes: "'Since God is the highest good, He would not allow any evil to exist in His works unless His omnipotence and goodness were such as to bring good even out of evil.' This is part of the infinite goodness of God, that He should allow evil to exist and out of it produce good."[109] This is most evident in the Paschal Mystery: through the unjust suffering and torturous death of God's only begotten Son, eternal life was made possible for all humanity.

Goodness comes from our own suffering as well, but this can be difficult to recognize in the moment. Only after the pain has subsided can we look back and realize that good did come out of evil. For example, consider a man who has been unfairly fired from his job. He searches diligently for work but is unable to find employment. Therefore, he decides to go back to school for a graduate degree. While in graduate school, he meets his future wife. After graduation, he is offered a better and more lucrative job. In retrospect, getting fired unjustly was a blessing in disguise. But for losing his job and being unable to find work, the man never would have gone back to school and, therefore, would not have met his wife or

[109] Aquinas, *ST* I, q.2. a.3.

discovered a new and much better career. But again, many times, we cannot recognize the benefit that comes from trials, especially when we are in the midst of them. It is during these times that we are called to trust the Lord and surrender to Him, knowing that everything is given to us out of love for our sanctity and salvation—our greatest happiness.

St. Paul tells us, "We know that in everything God works for good with those who love him, who are called according to his purpose" (Rom. 8:28). Everything, including suffering, is given to us for our benefit. All things work together for our good and for the glory of God if only we love and trust in the Lord, knowing that everything is part of the divine plan to make us saints. St. Catherine of Siena tells us: "Know in truth, that everything that God allows is for our salvation."[110] We have to trust that everything can work to our advantage and greatest good, even if the benefits are not readily apparent. God has a way of making use of everything for His glory and our ultimate happiness. Challenges in life are not meant to make us miserable but to bring out the best in us. Think of parents: they go against the wishes and preferences of their children not to make their lives difficult but because they want what is best for them. So it is with the Lord. Scripture tells us:

> "For the Lord disciplines him whom he loves, and chastises every son whom he receives." It is for discipline that you have to endure. God is treating you as sons; for what son is there whom his father does not discipline?... He disciplines us for our good, that we may share his holiness. For the moment all discipline seems painful rather than pleasant; later it yields the peaceful fruit of righteousness to those who have been trained by it. (Heb. 12: 6–7, 10b–11)

[110] *The Letters of St. Catherine of Siena,* vol. 1, trans. and ed. Suzanne Noffke, O.P. (Tempe, AZ: ACMRS Press, 2001), 75.

The Father trains His children in holiness not out of anger but out of love, so that we may resemble Him. We may not recognize the benefits of this training here on earth, but we will in heaven. Therefore, we should try to accept suffering with faith, patience, and love, knowing that God has allowed it to bring about our greatest good. Acceptance is not passive; it is an active, intentional, and courageous movement of the will to participate in God's plan for us.

Of course, suffering is not good in and of itself and should not be sought for its own sake. It should be avoided, minimized, and alleviated as much as possible. However, sometimes, there comes a point when circumstances are beyond our control and suffering is unavoidable. That is when we need to know how to suffer well by surrendering to divine providence. Even when we sin or make mistakes, we can offer our contrite and humble hearts to the Lord, asking Him to make things right. God has a way of writing straight with crooked lines and bringing good out of our faults, weaknesses, and sins.

How to Suffer Well

To suffer well requires the humility to accept that our intellect and understanding are limited and that we do not know everything. God's ways and His thoughts are beyond our capacity to understand or appreciate. Humility also helps us accept responsibility for everything that happens to us instead of blaming God and others. Perhaps we have contributed to our predicament by being negligent and imprudent. Through lack of foresight, we may have brought our problems on ourselves. Maybe our poor choices and sinful behavior have led us into difficulties and hardships.

At the same time, we trust that God knows and desires what is best for us, even though we may not fully comprehend it at the moment. When afflicted with unexpected challenges, we can say with Job, "Naked I came from my mother's womb, and naked shall I return; the LORD gave, and the LORD has taken away; blessed be the name of the LORD" (Job 1:21). We praise the Lord for everything, whether good or bad. The book of Job helps us to understand and accept that suffering remains a mystery and we cannot demand a full account of the workings of God. After Job and his friends argue and speculate about the reason for his suffering, God intervenes. He makes Job aware of the miracle of creation and thereby shows him that humanity is limited in time, power, knowledge, and ability in comparison with the infinitely superior and incomprehensible God who has been at work in all things since the beginning. By showing Job the majesty and beauty of creation, God reveals to him the greater context of his existence and reassures him that his Maker is unimaginably wise and infinitely powerful and good. In this way, God reminds Job that his misery is not the center of creation, but his existence is intertwined with that of innumerable others. Humility and trust in the Lord place our suffering in the context of a larger divine plan for humanity and all creation.

We trust that God not only loves us but also will give us the grace we need to handle any difficulties that come our way. God does not abandon us to our own devices but provides us with the strength we need to handle adversity. St. Paul writes: "And to keep me from being too elated by the abundance of revelations, a thorn was given me in the flesh, a messenger of Satan, to harass me, to keep me from being too elated. Three times I begged the Lord about this, that it should leave me; but he said to me, 'My grace is sufficient for you, for my power is made perfect in weakness'" (2 Cor. 12:7–9). It is God's power that sustains and strengthens us during trials. The more we must endure, the more graces we receive. Each of us has his or her own cross and the graces that come with it. Know that whatever the Lord allows us to endure, He gives the help to bear it.

When we suffer, we should unite ourselves to Christ, rely on His grace, and join our suffering to His for the ongoing work of redemption. This way, our suffering is not meaningless but takes on value and purpose. When our trials are united to Jesus, they become meritorious for us and for others. Never suffer alone but always in union with Christ and His Church for the love of God. Pain endured out of love is meritorious and pleasing to the Lord.

Suffering allows us to demonstrate not only our trust but also our love for the Lord. To love is to suffer for the good of the other. Suffering takes on value and meaning when endured with faith and love. St. Faustina says: "When we suffer much we have a great chance to show God that we love Him; but when we suffer little we have less occasion to show God our love; and when we do not suffer at all, our love is then neither great nor pure. By the grace of God, we can attain a point where suffering will become a delight to us, for love can work such things in pure souls."[111] Jesus underwent His Passion for love of us, and at the same time, He gave us an example of the value of suffering when embraced out of love. We imitate, participate, and conform to Jesus when we suffer for love.

Suffering with humility and trust and in union with Christ out of love for God, we bear trials patiently, knowing that they, too, shall pass. After St. Teresa of Avila passed away, her sisters found the following words written on a bookmark in her breviary: "Let nothing disturb you, let nothing frighten you. All things are passing; God never changes. Patience overcomes all things; He who possesses God lacks nothing; God alone is sufficient." This saint endured many trials in her lifetime and learned how to keep her difficulties in perspective by reminding herself to remain at peace, knowing that all things shall pass and that God alone remains constant. St. Teresa also reminds us that when we get to heaven,

[111] *Diary*, no. 303.

we will look back and see that all the suffering we endured on earth was nothing more than a bad night in a cheap motel.[112] Likewise, St. Paul tells us, "I consider that the sufferings of this present time are not worth comparing with the glory that is to be revealed to us" (Rom. 8:18). When we keep our eyes on the prize, we are able to deal calmly with temporary inconveniences and tribulations.

Another way to lighten the cross is to embrace it. When we are afraid of and run away from suffering, it becomes unbearable, but when we accept the cross courageously, its sting is lessened. Jesus embraced His Cross and carried it willingly to the end. He wants disciples who will imitate Him by taking up their crosses and following Him. Mary and the saints did not flee from the cross but faithfully embraced challenges head-on. St. Thérèse of Lisieux writes:

> I understood that to become a *saint* one had to suffer much, seek out always the most perfect things to do, and forget self. I understood, too, there are many degrees of perfection and each soul is free to respond to the advances of our Lord, to do little or much for Him, in a word, to *choose* among the sacrifices he was asking. Then, as in the days of my childhood, I cried out: "My God, '*I choose all.*' I don't want to be a *saint by halves*. I am not afraid to suffer for You."[113]

We do not go looking for trouble, but we do not run away from it either.

Lastly, the saints teach us not only to embrace difficulties but also to find gratitude and joy in them. We are grateful and joyful in knowing that trials are a means for our growth and holiness. St.

112 Teresa of Ávila, *The Way of Perfection*, trans. and ed. E. Allison Peers (New York: Random House, 2004), 265.

113 *Story of a Soul*, 27.

Peter tells us, "But rejoice in so far as you share Christ's sufferings, that you may also rejoice and be glad when his glory is revealed" (1 Pet. 4:13). Similarly, St. Paul rejoices in his suffering because he knows that it is not wasted but benefits the Church (see Col. 1:24). We practice abandonment to divine providence by relying on God's grace, uniting ourselves to Christ in love, and enduring difficulties with humility, trust, courage, gratitude, and joy. In this way, our suffering is not wasted, but has value, meaning, and purpose.

Value and Meaning of Suffering

Since the Son of God became human, suffered, and died to atone for our sins and reconcile us with the Father, suffering is no longer mere evil but takes on meaning and value. Suffering can merit expiation, which is atonement and reparation for sins. Divine justice requires reparation for sins. Serious sins that we commit after Baptism are forgiven in the Sacrament of Reconciliation, but the temporal punishment for sin remains. For example, say a lady does not like me and decides to slash the tires on my car. Thereafter, she feels bad and apologizes. I forgive her, but she still owes me four new tires. Likewise, our sins against God may be forgiven, but we still need to make reparation for our offenses, whether in this life or in purgatory. By enduring well the trials of life, we make reparations for our sins and even for those of others. St. Faustina states, "God often grants many and great graces out of regard for the souls who are suffering, and He withholds many punishments solely because of the suffering souls."[114] The saints also tell us that it is better to make reparation for our sins in this life than in purgatory.

Another value of suffering is purification. It sanctifies and conforms us to Jesus. Suffering has a way of making a person wiser

[114] *Diary*, no. 1268.

and more virtuous. One who has endured suffering usually grows in maturity, faith, patience, and compassion for others who suffer. People who have never suffered can be arrogant, superficial, and standoffish, but those who have endured difficulties in life tend to grow from their experience and become kinder, stronger, and more human. St. Paul writes, "We rejoice in our sufferings, knowing that suffering produces endurance, and endurance produces character, and character produces hope" (Rom. 5:3–4).

The purification process is not without pain. For example, gold is purified under extreme heat. As it melts, other metals float to the surface. These less precious metals are then skimmed off so that when the gold hardens, it becomes purer and more valuable. Similarly, growth requires trials. Jesus tells St. Faustina: "Those who are like Me in the pain and contempt they suffer will be like Me also in glory. And those who resemble Me less in pain and contempt will also bear less resemblance to Me in glory."[115] In order to conform to Jesus' perfection, we must also be conformed to His suffering. Suffering purifies us by helping us to become detached from sin, the world, and ourselves. We come to recognize the harm of sin, the worthlessness of worldly allurements, and the impediment of pride.

Some people who are faithful to the Lord and are growing in holiness experience a lot of trials. This is so that they may advance even higher in the spiritual life. Jesus warns us that pain will accompany growth in perfection: "I am the true vine, and my Father is the vinedresser. Every branch of mine that bears no fruit, he takes away, and every branch that does bear fruit he prunes, that it may bear more fruit" (John 15:1–2). The pruning may be painful yet necessary if we are to grow closer to the Lord. The Lord gives us trials not to make our lives difficult but to help us grow in virtue and be more conformed to Jesus. Every gardener knows that pruning

[115] *Diary*, no. 446.

at the right time and in the right area will accelerate growth and cause plants to flourish. Likewise, God is the master gardener who knows when, how, and where to prune each person so as to help him or her grow in perfection. Pruning *hurts*, yet it is necessary to maximize potential.

For a time, I was very interested in bonsai, a Japanese art form that uses cultivation techniques to produce, in small containers, small trees that mimic the shape and scale of fullsized trees. I had to learn to prune, twist the branches with wires, and use other shaping methods to create something beautiful. Similarly, God is an artist who prunes, twists, and forms us into His work of art. Indeed, being bent and clipped will cause pain and discomfort, but if we trust and cooperate with the Lord, we will become something beautiful and pleasing.

Alternatively, imagine that we are clay and God is a potter. If we are malleable, soft, and supple in His hands, He can more quickly and easily form us according to His will. But if we resist, fight, and become hard, we will experience more pain, and the Lord will take longer to perfect us. The saints are those who are pliable and cooperate with the Lord so as to reach perfection sooner.

Purification is necessary in order to advance through the stages of the spiritual life. It is widely agreed that there are three such stages. First, in the *purgative* stage, we have to take active steps to purify our senses and our spirit from sins and bad habits in order to grow in virtue and grace. Prior to entering into the *illuminative* stage, the Lord will further purify us by allowing us to undergo the *passive purification of the senses*, also known as the *dark night of the senses*, in which we experience dryness in prayer, anxiety, and temptations against faith, hope, and patience. As we proceed toward the *unitive* stage, we undergo the *passive purification of the spirit*, or the *night of the spirit*, in which we are stripped of light, knowledge, and sweetness. We experience distress and sadness because we feel abandoned by

God. These dark nights are necessary to purify and transform us into the likeness of Christ and unite us more closely to Him.

Lastly, suffering is valuable because it is redemptive. Jesus allows certain people to share in His redemptive suffering, especially those who are in the *unitive* stage and are closest to Him and do not need further expiation or purification. St. Paul writes, "Now I rejoice in my sufferings for your sake, and in my flesh I complete what is lacking in Christ's afflictions for the sake of his body, that is, the Church" (Col. 1:24). Christ's sufferings were, of course, sufficient for our redemption, but many are invited to participate in Christ's suffering for the benefit of the entire Church.

For example, many saints, such as Padre Pio, St. Francis of Assisi, and St. Faustina, experienced Christ's physical suffering in the form of the stigmata or other physical pains associated with His Passion. Others were given a share in Christ's interior suffering, including the sense of anguish and desolation that caused Him to cry out, "My God, my God, why have you forsaken me?" (Matt. 27:46). Saints who experienced this prolonged night of the spirit included Mother Teresa, St. Thérèse of Lisieux, and Blessed Maria Concepción Cabrera de Armida. Mother Teresa, in particular, experienced a sense of abandonment by God that lasted fifty years.[116] Leading lives of reparation, these saints were asked to be victim souls, that is, to suffer in union with Christ to atone for the sins of others, to obtain the grace of conversion for sinners, or to contribute in some other way to the merits of the communion of saints.

Jesus' profound suffering on the Cross in His humanity, which led Him to pray Psalm 22—a psalm of both suffering and triumph—is deeply mysterious. We know that even on the Cross, by virtue of the beatific vision, Jesus beheld Himself in God's embrace as the

[116] Paul Murray, O.P., *I Loved Jesus in the Night: Teresa of Calcutta—A Secret Revealed* (Brewster, MA: Paraclete Press, 2008).

eternal Son. This makes His unique experience of suffering entirely numinous. While we cannot suffer the same way Christ did because of His Hypostatic Union, we can nonetheless become sharers in His suffering to a lesser degree, and our suffering is meritorious when consecrated to Christ in grace.

The saints tell us not to waste our suffering but to unite it to Christ out of love, for our good and the good of the Church. They tell us that in heaven, we can no longer suffer. Therefore, we should take advantage of our limited time on earth as an opportunity to offer up suffering for the glory of God and the sanctification of souls. Suffering has value, meaning, and purpose. Through it, we can make reparation for our sins, purify and conform ourselves to Christ, and participate in His redemptive work. We should try to suffer well in imitation of Jesus, Mary, and the saints; that is, we should marshal all the qualities mentioned in this book in order to maximize the merits of suffering.

Our Lady of Sorrows

Mary had to practice surrendering to divine providence throughout her earthly life. From the moment of the Annunciation, when she was troubled by the angel Gabriel's greeting and wondered how she would conceive a child, Mary, nevertheless, gave her *fiat*: "Let it be to me according to your word" (Luke 1:38). Although Mary did not fully understand the workings of God, she abandoned herself to His holy will. As God's plans unfolded in Mary's life, she had to renew or repeat her *fiat* over and over, never saying no to the Lord but always proclaiming, "Let it be done to me according to your will."

We see that in Mary's life, joy was always mixed with suffering. Before she was to give birth to Jesus, she and Joseph had to travel to Bethlehem because of a decree from Caesar. And when Mary was about to give birth, there was no place for them in the inn. Jesus had to be wrapped in swaddling clothes and laid in a manger. At the Presentation of Jesus in the temple, Simeon said to Mary, "Behold, this child is set for the fall and rising of many in Israel, and for a sign that is spoken against (and a sword will pierce through your own soul also), that thoughts out of many hearts may be revealed" (Luke 2:34–35). Mary accepted all these hardships with resignation to the divine will. But this was just the beginning of the many sorrows that Mary would experience as the Mother of Jesus.

The Seven Sorrows of Mary also included the flight into Egypt to escape King Herod, who was trying to kill the infant Jesus. Then, when the Holy Family left Jerusalem after Passover, Jesus stayed behind in the temple, causing Mary and Joseph to search frantically for Him:

> After three days they found him in the temple, sitting among the teachers, listening to them and asking them questions.... And when they saw him they were astonished; and his mother said to him, "Son, why have you treated us so? Behold, your father and I have been looking for you anxiously." And he said to them, "How is it that you sought me? Did you not know that I must be in my Father's house?" And they did not understand the saying which he spoke to them. (Luke 2:46, 48–50)

Mary did not understand why Jesus had remained at the temple. Yet she surrendered to divine providence, knowing that Jesus was the Son of God sent to live out God's redemptive plan.

As the Mother of Jesus, Mary was united to her Son and shared fully in His mission of redemption. In a most acute way, she experienced all the physical and spiritual pain and agony that Jesus endured, including the sense of being abandoned by God on the Cross. Blessed Maria Concepción Cabrera de Armida wrote: "The Passion of Jesus was also Mary's passion. She alone was the one who understood this cry of Jesus in His abandonment. The measure is that of love, the measure of love is that of grace, and Mary was full of grace, of love, and of sorrow."[117] Mary's suffering was intensified because of her purity, perfection, and oneness with Jesus. No human person's suffering resembled that of Jesus as much as Mary's suffering did. She participated in Christ's life, mission, and redemptive suffering in the most radical way possible. Jesus told Blessed Maria Concepción Cabrera de Armida, "As co-redemptrix, Mary heard in her soul so wholly pure the echo of all my agonies, humiliations, outrages and tortures, felt the weight of the sins of the world which made my heart bleed, and the moving sorrow of the abandonment of heaven which obtains graces."[118] Because she shared in Christ's Passion and death to an unparalleled degree, Mary is sometimes given the title *Co-Redemptrix*.[119]

Just like Jesus, Mary embraced all the pain and humiliation destined for her. She abandoned herself to God's plan. Mary's suffering was intended neither in reparation for her sins nor for her purification, because she was sinless. But all her suffering was a share in Christ's work of redemption—her pain merited graces for us, her sons and daughters. We all suffer because we sin, but Mary never sinned and yet suffered more than all of us.

Not only did Mary suffer when Jesus suffered, but she experienced much pain after Jesus ascended into heaven because she had to continue her life on earth separated from her Son.[120] Since

[117] M. M. Philipon, O.P., ed., *Conchita: A Mother's Spiritual Diary*, trans. Aloysius J. Owen, S.J. (New York: Alba House, 2009), 213.

[118] Ibid., 223.

[119] The question of Mary's putative role as "co-redemptrix" is still open for theological debate.

[120] This position is open to theological debate. For this interpretation, I am relying on the private revelations of Blessed Maria Concepción Cabrera de Armida.

she enjoyed perfect love and union with Jesus, the physical and emotional separation during those years before her Assumption were agonizing. But God allowed Mary to experience a prolonged sense of being abandoned by God during her later years so she could merit more graces for the Church. Jesus said to Blessed Maria Concepción Cabrera de Armida: "The martyrdom of Mary after my Ascension was not caused solely by my material absence. She suffered terrible tests of abandonment like to that I Myself underwent on the Cross. My Father united her to Mine which gained so many graces."[121] Many people are not aware of the pain that Mary endured in the last years of her life or how perfectly she surrendered to divine providence. Jesus continued: "This abandonment of Mary, this vivid and palpitating martyrdom of her solitude, the desolating martyrdom of divine abandonment, which she suffered heroically, with loving resignation and sublime surrender to My will, is not honored."[122]

Not only are we to honor Mary for her heroic participation in Jesus' suffering, but we are to imitate all her virtues. Jesus told Blessed Maria Concepción Cabrera de Armida:

> In my spiritual life in souls, my Mother was never separated from Me, that is, the imitation of both our lives must be simultaneous on earth, Mary's life was modeled on Mine. Thus, just as I was the Redeemer, she was the co-redeemer. The souls who love her most and who are most like her, are the souls who are most like Me most perfectly. You must imitate her in the practice of virtues, I always told you, especially in her humility and her purity of heart.[123]

[121] *Conchita*, 223.
[122] Ibid., 224.
[123] Ibid., 173.

The Imitation of Mary

To imitate Mary is to imitate Jesus, because no other person is more perfectly conformed to Jesus than His Mother.

If we wish to resemble Jesus and Mary, we must practice abandonment to divine providence. Mother Teresa reminds us that this is the way to holiness: "Total surrender to God must come in small details as it comes in big details. It is nothing but a single word: *Yes*. 'I accept whatever you give, and I give whatever you take.' It doesn't mean to do extraordinary things, understanding big things—it is a simple acceptance, because I have given myself to God, because I belong to Him."[124] I keep a copy of this quote in my journal and refer to it when times are tough. We need to practice surrendering to divine providence in small, everyday situations, so that we may surrender to divine providence when we are truly tested.

Practical Suggestions

1. Pray the optional Collect for the Friday of the fifth week of Lent: "O God, Who in this season give your Church the grace to imitate devoutly the Blessed Virgin Mary in contemplating the Passion of Christ, grant, we pray, through her intercession, that we may cling more firmly each day to your Only Begotten Son and come at last to the fullness of His grace."
2. Remember and repeat what God said to St. Julian of Norwich: "All shall be well, and all shall be well, and all manner of thing shall be well."
3. Remember and repeat the prayer that Jesus taught the author of *In Sinu Jesu*: "Jesus, King of Love, I put my trust in your merciful goodness."

[124] Mother Teresa, *No Greater Love*, ed. Becky Benenate and Joseph Durepos (Novato, CA: New World Library, 1989), 148.

4. Practice saying the Serenity Prayer. "God, grant me the serenity to accept the things I cannot change, the courage to change the things I can, and the wisdom to know the difference. Living one day at a time, enjoying one moment at a time, accepting hardship as a pathway to peace, taking as Jesus did this sinful world as it is, not as I would have it; trusting that You will make all things right if I surrender to Your will, so that I may be reasonably happy in this life and supremely happy with You forever in the next. Amen."

10

Mortification

The more we die to self, the more God lives in us.

And when the time came for their purification
according to the law of Moses, they brought him
up to Jerusalem to present him to the Lord ...
and to offer a sacrifice according to what is said
in the law of the Lord, "a pair of turtledoves,
or two young pigeons." (Luke 2:22, 24)

Self-Control

In abandonment to divine providence, we learn to accept whatever comes our way, including suffering, knowing that God has allowed it so that He can bring about a greater good. But this alone is not enough. We are called actively to die to ourselves in order to live truly for the Lord. Mortification means dying to self through asceticism or self-denial so that we may have control over our lower desires and foster our spiritual desires. This is a foreign concept in our overindulgent world, where bodily pleasure is highly sought-after.

Mortification is necessary because we all suffer from an inclination to evil, including an inordinate desire for the pleasures of the flesh, excessive self-love, and disordered affections for created things. We all have a tendency to sin, which is to go against God, truth, and right reason. St. Paul speaks about this interior conflict between good and evil: "For I do not do the good I want, but the evil I do not want is what I do" (Rom. 7:19). Therefore, in order to gain control over our lower impulses and unruly desires and to choose that which is most pleasing to God, we have to practice self-denial. Asceticism puts a check on our sensual selfishness, which has no limits. Mortification allows us to attain the true freedom of the children of God, which is the ability to know and choose that which is best and reject that which is harmful.

We are rational beings made in the image and likeness of God and destined for eternal beatitude. Yet our souls are wounded by Original Sin, which causes us to think, speak, and act in ways that are irrational, impulsive, and harmful to ourselves and to others. The practice of self-denial allows us to say no to our lower desires and impulses in order to say yes to our higher calling. Mortification is necessary if we are to grow in purity and holiness. It cleanses, strengthens, and rightly orders our will so that it can conform to God's will. Mortification helps us to uproot selfish sensuality, which is the source of many sins and vices.

Jesus knows our fallen nature and encourages us to be vigilant and guard against the weaknesses of the flesh: "Watch and pray that you may not enter into temptation; the spirit indeed is willing, but the flesh is weak" (Matt. 26:41). The practice of self-denial strengthens the spirit and gives it control over the flesh. Without this self-mastery, we are enslaved to a distorted will and judgment. St. Paul tells us that we need to die to our sensual desires if we are to live for the Lord: "Those who belong to Christ Jesus have crucified the flesh with its passions and desires" (Gal. 5:24). Death to sin is necessary if we are to live in holiness.

Another way to look at this is that we need to empty ourselves of inordinate attachments and selfish desires in order to make room for the Lord. Being true disciples of Christ requires dying to our sinful nature so that Jesus can fill us up with Himself. If Jesus is truly to live and work in us, we need to die to sin, attachments, and self-will. We can learn much from Mary and the saints, who emptied themselves to reflect Christ more fully. St. John the Baptist puts it this way: "He must increase, but I must decrease" (John 3:30).

Paschal Mystery

The Paschal Mystery is the suffering, death, and Resurrection of Jesus, which brought forth new life for all humanity. The order of this mystery is essential: there must be suffering and death before there is to be new life. We see the stamp of the Paschal Mystery in all creation. For example, in autumn, leaves begin to turn yellow and brown and fall to the ground as they die. As winter arrives, the trees and plants are bare and dormant. In the spring, new life appears, and the plants and trees start to sprout new buds and flowers. By summer, they are bursting with life and abundance of fruit. In autumn, the cycle starts all over again. We see that it is necessary for trees and plants to undergo this process of loss and death in order to create new life and vibrantly bear much fruit. If there is a mild winter and plants do not go completely dormant, they will produce little fruit in the spring. Only after a harsh winter will they fully "come back to life" and bear an abundance of healthy, juicy, and flavorful fruit.

A similar process occurs when a woman is pregnant. For nine months, she has to suffer and die to herself through morning sickness, discomfort, and intense labor pains before giving birth to a new human life. Another example is a forest fire, which is destructive and deadly yet necessary to bring forth new growth. Forest fires are sometimes deliberately set so that the old vegetation may be burned away to make room for the new. Death comes before new life.

So it is with the spiritual life. We need to die to our old self and its sinful ways so that our new self in Christ may emerge. St. Paul writes, "Put off the old man that belongs to your former manner of life and is corrupt through deceitful lusts, and be renewed in the spirit of your minds, and put on the new man, created after the likeness of God in true righteousness and holiness" (Eph. 4:22–24). Dying to self is a lifelong struggle because of our fallen human nature. If we wish to be perfectly conformed to Christ and serve Him unreservedly, then we need to embrace mortification. Death to self is necessary if we are to find the fullness of life.

Jesus tells His disciples about the necessity of dying to self to attain eternal life:

> Truly, truly, I say to you, unless a grain of wheat falls into the earth and dies, it remains alone; but if it dies, it bears much fruit. He who loves his life loses it, and he who hates his life in this world will keep it for eternal life. If any one serves me, he must follow me; and where I am, there shall my servant be also; if any one serves me, the Father will honor him. (John 12:24–26)

Jesus was born into this world to die and rise to new life. As followers of Christ, we need to follow Him to Calvary before we can rise to newness of life. We will bear fruit to the extent that we die to ourselves and live for God. How much of our time and energy is focused on ourselves, and how much is focused on serving the Lord? We cannot serve two masters. Jesus tells us: "No one can serve two masters; for either he will hate the one and love the other, or he will be devoted to the one and despise the other. You cannot serve God and mammon" (Matt. 6:24). Mary and the saints heed these words; they love, serve, and are devoted to God and despise the things of the world.

Demands of Discipleship

True and faithful discipleship demands self-renunciation. Jesus does not mince words as He spells out the radical demands of discipleship: "If any man would come after me, let him deny himself and take up his cross daily and follow me. For whoever would save his life will lose it; and whoever loses his life for my sake, he will save it" (Luke 9:23–24). In the Gospel of Luke, Jesus tells us to deny ourselves and take up our cross—not once, or once in a while, or when circumstances demand, but *daily*. In order to grow in perfection and conformity with Jesus and participate more fully in His redemptive work, we must make self-denial a constant way of life. The Christian life is marked by the habitual spirit and practice of self-denial and sacrifice in union with Christ for the good of the Church.

The spiritual life demands a constant stripping away of all that weighs us down in the service of Our Lord. This includes sins, worldly comforts, and personal attachments. To follow Jesus faithfully is to conform ourselves to His spirit and way of life, which, in essence, is a life of self-emptying love. Jesus warned His followers of the cost of discipleship:

> As they were going along the road, a man said to him, "I will follow you wherever you go." And Jesus said to him, "Foxes have holes, and birds of the air have nests; but the Son of man has nowhere to lay his head." To another he said, "Follow me." But he said, "Lord, let me first go and bury my father." But he said to him, "Leave the dead to bury their own dead; but as for you, go and proclaim the kingdom of God." Another said, "I will follow you, Lord; but let me first say farewell to those at my home." Jesus said to him, "No one who puts his hand to the plow and looks back is fit for the kingdom of God." (Luke 9:57–62)

Poverty

If Jesus has nowhere to lay His head, then His disciples must likewise be prepared to give up all possessions and worldly comforts for the sake of the kingdom. To the rich young man who wanted to be perfect, Jesus said, "If you would be perfect, go, sell what you possess and give to the poor, and you will have treasure in heaven; and come, follow me" (Matt. 19:21). Indeed, perfection includes imitating Jesus in His simplicity and poverty. Material possessions weigh us down and cause us to rely on and become attached to them. When Jesus sent out the Twelve to preach and to heal, He said to them, "Take nothing for your journey, no staff, nor bag, nor bread, nor money; and do not have two tunics" (Luke 9:3). Disciples are not to rely on their own resources or abilities but on Jesus alone.

The spirit of humility and detachment is essential. But real poverty forces one to turn to the Lord and rely on Him completely. People who are truly poor tend to have more faith and devotion than those who are wealthy. Jesus warns against the danger of riches: "How hard it is for those who have riches to enter the kingdom of God! For it is easier for a camel to go through the eye of a needle than for a rich man to enter the kingdom of God" (Luke 18:24–25). That is why so many saints, such as St. Anthony of the Desert, St. Francis of Assisi, and St. Clare, gave up worldly goods for a life of poverty. These saints completely devoted themselves to imitating and relying on Jesus and bearing witness to the gospel.

Likewise, members of religious orders give up all their personal possessions and make vows of poverty in imitation of the life and perfection of Jesus. Worldly possessions and attachment to material wealth are obstacles to faithful discipleship because they encumber, distract, and burden us, keeping us from our one true goal, which is to love and serve the Lord. In contrast, those who can let go of material goods and wealth are liberated and free to focus on, love, and serve God alone.

Liberty

I can speak from personal experience. When I was an attorney, I had many possessions, and my heart was focused on acquiring the things of the world. I had a house, a nice car, and a good legal career. I thought that worldly goods and status would bring me happiness and fulfillment, yet I was stressed and not at all at peace because I was far from God, the only true source of our joy. I was not practicing my faith; rather, I was immersed in the world and pursued created things instead of the Creator. However, worldly riches did not give me satisfaction but constant tension, as well as feelings of discontent and emptiness.

But after my conversion and my decision to enter the seminary, with the help of careful discernment and God's grace, I freely gave up my job, sold my house and car, and paid off my law school loans. I felt liberated. A burden had been lifted from my shoulders, and I became free to focus on the Lord and His will for me. Jesus reminds us not to set our hearts on material goods, which are temporary, but on the eternal treasures of heaven: "Do not lay up for yourselves treasures on earth, where moth and rust consume and where thieves break in and steal, but lay up for yourselves treasures in heaven, where neither moth nor rust consumes and where thieves do not break in and steal. For where your treasure is, there will your heart be also" (Matt. 6:19–21). Self-denial helps us to order our priorities rightly. Then, we will not pursue worldly goods as ends in themselves but as the means by which we discover the Giver of all good gifts.

We know that the rich young man who approached Jesus wanted so much to inherit eternal life, yet he was attached to his wealth and could not break free from it: "When the young man heard this he went away sorrowful; for he had great possessions" (Matt. 19:22). How tragic it is that we allow earthy wealth to enslave us and prevent us from pursuing our true vocation to holiness and heaven. St. John of the Cross laments: "O souls, created for these grandeurs and called to them. What are you doing? How are you spending your time? Your aims are base and your possessions miseries. O wretched blindness of your eyes."[125] Mortification liberates us from disordered attachments so that we may pursue our greatest good. As children of God, we are to be free from disordered affections and to love as God loves.

The Holy Family

Mary and the Holy Family practiced mortification, moderation, and simplicity, and each of their hearts was free and rightly ordered. They had no unhealthy attachments because their hearts and wills were perfectly aligned with God's.

The Holy Family lived poorly and simply. We read that at the Presentation of Jesus in the temple, Mary and Joseph offered a pair of turtledoves or two young pigeons (Luke 2:24), which means that they were not wealthy enough to offer a lamb. Scripture tells us that St. Joseph worked as a carpenter to support the Holy Family, so they were most likely a family of moderate means. The Holy Family espoused self-denial in order to live a life of poverty and simplicity while practicing charity and generosity toward the needy and places of worship.[126]

The saints, especially those who belonged to religious orders, knew the value of voluntary poverty; it allowed them to sacrifice their desires and conform themselves to Christ for the glory of God and the sake of His kingdom. Voluntary poverty liberates us from

[125] *The Collected Works of St. John of the Cross*, trans. Kieran Kavanaugh, O.C.D., and Otilio Rodriguez, O.C.D. (Washington, DC: ICS Publications, 2017), 624.

[126] *Life of Mary*, 98.

attachment to worldly goods and forces us to rely on the Lord, who is always faithful and wants us to trust in Him. Voluntary poverty is pleasing to the Lord, yet many are not able to respond to this grace. They remain attached to their own resources, which give them a sense of security and afford them the comforts of life.

Our Blessed Mother told the mystics: "There is no more acceptable gift to God than voluntary poverty. There are few who use temporal riches well and offer them to the Lord with generosity. You can make such an offering of the things necessary for sustenance, giving a part to the poor."[127] Those who practice radical poverty are never abandoned but are blessed abundantly. St. Paul reminds us that our generosity will be rewarded: "You will be enriched in every way for great generosity, which through us will produce thanksgiving to God" (2 Cor. 9:11). There is a limited amount of resources in the world. Conscience and charity dictate that we be responsible stewards, not hoarding what we do not need but freely sharing what we have with others. Mother Teresa said, "Live simply so that others may simply live."

By living in poverty and simplicity, we imitate Jesus, Mary, and the saints and demonstrate that our treasure is not in this world but the next. At the same time, we help others and glorify the Father. We recognize that we are pilgrims in this world, and so we travel lightly. By living with minimal possessions, we free our hearts and minds to pursue the eternal. We also guard against the materialism, consumerism, and commercialism prevalent in society today and avoid the worldly traps of possessions, power, privilege, and pleasure. As Christians, we are called to be countercultural.

The mystics tell us that the Blessed Virgin Mary was very neat, clean, and orderly.[128] With minimal possessions, she was able to order

[127] Ibid., 127.
[128] *Life of Mary*, 97.

her environment in a simple way that would be most conducive to prayer and holiness. Having a clean, simplistic, and orderly environment helps to create a similar effect in our minds and hearts, purging us of sins, anxieties, and confusion, and establishing a pure, holy, and inviting environment for the Lord. I like to have my environment neat and orderly, free of clutter. This helps me free my mind and spirit so that I can focus and pray. Limiting our possessions helps us relax, rest, and focus on what is most essential: God Himself.

The practice of almsgiving makes it easier for us to live simply. By sharing our resources with the needy, we are liberated from the preoccupation with and attachment to material wealth, and we practice generosity and solidarity. Scripture warns us of the danger of greed and attachment to wealth: "For the love of money is the root of all evils; it is through this craving that some have wandered away from the faith and pierced their hearts with many pangs" (1 Tim. 6:10). We practice almsgiving (along with fasting and prayer) in a special way during Lent to purge ourselves of sin, conform our lives to Christ, and grow in grace and holiness. These practices, however, should not be limited to Lent but should be a way of life.

Temperance

Fasting is another way for us to practice mortification and grow in grace and freedom. We may limit the amount of food that we eat, or we may abstain from certain types of food. The mystics tell us that when Mary was a young girl living in the temple, she wanted to give up meat, fish, and milk.[129] The priests allowed Mary to abstain from meat and milk but said she could eat fish on special feast days.[130] Even though she did not suffer from concupiscence, Mary

[129] *The Life of Mary*, 43.
[130] Ibid.

practiced mortification out of love for God. Throughout her life, our Blessed Mother practiced moderation, fasting, and self-denial, eating mostly bread, vegetables, and fruit. St. Alphonsus Liguori, quoting St. Bonaventure, said, "Mary would never have found so much grace if she had not been moderate in her meals; for grace and gluttony do not go together."[131] In this way, Mary and the other members of the Holy Family practiced the virtues of temperance, simplicity, and poverty with regard to food.

How often these virtues are absent in today's world, where there is a tendency to "supersize" food portions. Even our soda containers are five times the normal size. The convenience store 7-Eleven sells the Big Gulp (30 ounces), the Super Big Gulp (40 ounces), and the Double Big Gulp (reduced from 64 to 50 ounces because it was too big to carry). These supersized drinks are advertised as "genetically engineered to quench even the most diabolical thirst." The word *diabolical* (which refers to the devil) is used to promote many products, including food items, because it gives the impression that something is extreme, daring, and exciting. Also, in today's culture, people who love food are fondly called "foodies." It is one thing to enjoy food and give thanks to the chef and glory to God, but it is quite another to engage in gluttony, a sensual vice that is characterized by excessive indulgence in the pleasures of food and drink.

The basic human drives for food and sexual gratification are in themselves wholesome because they aim at what is necessary for human life: sustenance and procreation. But the problem is that our attraction to these pleasures can easily become excessive in ways that undermine rather than promote the basic human good they are intended to serve. Abstinence and fasting are disciplines that

[131] Alphonsus Maria de Liguori, *The Glories of Mary: A New Translation from the Italian* (Liguori, MO: Liguori Publications, 2000), 348.

help curb our excessive appetites. These practices also heighten our sensitivity to others who do not have enough food, and to God, who provides, sustains, and blesses us.

Fasting is also a type of mortification that makes our prayers more efficacious. In Scripture, we read about a man whose son was tormented by a mute spirit. He brought his son to the disciples. They could not cast the spirit out, but Jesus could. The disciples asked Jesus why they were not able to cast it out, and He said to them, "This kind cannot be driven out by anything but prayer and fasting" (Mark 9:29). Sacrifices help us not only to grow in holiness but also to contribute to the good of the Church. We are called continuously to offer up sacrifices in union with Christ for the glory of God and the redemption of the world. Sacrifices, like all suffering, have the power to expiate sins, to purify, and to contribute to the redemptive work of Jesus. The saints constantly offer prayers, sacrifices, and good works for the sanctification of the world.

Eyes, Curiosity, and Imagination

St. Alphonsus Liguori said that although our Blessed Mother was filled with grace, she practiced mortification of the eyes; that is, she usually kept her eyes cast down, so as to avoid exposure to anything unwanted or harmful to her life of purity, which was reserved for God.[132] How much more necessary, then, it is for us to practice mortification of the eyes in our culture, where harmful and unwanted images are widespread. "The eye is the lamp of the body. So, if your eye is sound, your whole body will be full of light; but if your eye is not sound, your whole body will be full of darkness. If then the light in you is darkness, how great is the darkness!" (Matt. 6:22). We go to great lengths to prevent anything harmful

[132] Liguori, *Glories of Mary*, 347.

from entering our bodies, yet we are willing to look at anything, not realizing (or perhaps not caring) that what we see will remain in our mind, memory, and imagination.

We need to mortify not only our eyes but also our curiosity and imagination. I know people who initially looked at pornography out of curiosity. The images they saw stayed in their mind and affected their imagination, and they kept going back for more. Far too many people are addicted to pornography and other sexual sins, which can ruin marriages, families, relationships, careers, academic achievements, and spiritual lives. Remember that curiosity killed the cat. It can destroy our lives as well. Many forms of sin and addiction begin innocently enough but eventually lead to a life of destruction, misery, and bondage. Mortification of the senses, especially the eyes, as well as mortification of curiosity and imagination is vital for a healthy mind, heart, and spirit.

The practice of mortification helps us to gain control over our passions so we can love rightly and be at peace with ourselves, with others, and with God. Otherwise, our passions will control us, and we will be tormented. Self-denial helps us to have a spiritual sense of our sexuality, which then helps us to love and be in communion with God and others. The evangelical counsels of chastity, poverty, and obedience help us to conform ourselves to Jesus, Mary, and the saints; therefore, we should implement them in our lives so that we may fully serve Christ and His Church.

Relationships

In addition to our cravings for material wealth, food, and sex, we may have a disordered attachment to other people. In order to imitate Jesus, Mary, and the saints, we have to love others rightly: we must see and love each person with the supernatural eyes and heart of God and detach ourselves from personal relationships.

Only then will we be free to follow Jesus and fulfill our vocation as disciples. Going back to the Gospel passage about the radical demands of discipleship, we read: "To another [Jesus] said, 'Follow me.' But he said, 'Lord, let me first go and bury my father.' But he said to him, 'Leave the dead to bury their own dead; but as for you, go and proclaim the kingdom of God'" (Luke 9:59–60). To bury one's father is a family obligation, but Jesus must come first. No relationship or obligation should stand in the way of following Christ immediately and unreservedly. Even our family members and closest friends are given to us to help us live out our calling in life. If we become attached to any person, he or she can become an obstacle to our relationship with God.

The Holy Family teaches us how to put our relationships in their proper context, that is, God's plan for our sanctification and redemption. Mary loved Jesus, her own flesh and blood, with all her heart. Yet she knew that Jesus was the Son of God and that He had a mission. Mary's role was to help Jesus accomplish His mission of saving the world by His life, suffering, death, and Resurrection. Therefore, as the Mother of Jesus, Mary had to practice self-denial and accept that Jesus had to suffer and die in order to fulfill the Father's will. She constantly conformed her will to that of the Father and lived out her own vocation as Mother of Jesus and Mother of the Church.

I know of many parents who do not want their children to enter the priesthood or religious life and try to prevent them from doing so. But in this way, they work against the will of God. Parents need to realize that their children do not belong to them but to God. God has entrusted children to the care of their parents; therefore, parents need to encourage their children to discern and pursue their vocation. I also know of people who believed they had a vocation to the priesthood or religious life but did not pursue it because they were too attached to their family. Jesus made it clear, however:

"He who loves father or mother more than me is not worthy of me; and he who loves son or daughter more than me is not worthy of me; and he who does not take up his cross and follow me is not worthy of me" (Matt. 10:37–38). Jesus demands full, immediate, and unconditional commitment. He drives home the point that the kingdom of God must take priority over family relationships by using the following hyperbole: "If any one comes to me and does not hate his own father and mother and wife and children and brothers and sisters, yes, and even his own life, he cannot be my disciple" (Luke 14:26). Death to self includes detaching from our closest relationships and orienting our lives toward loving and serving the Lord.

Jesus must be our top priority. He demands total and undivided commitment: "Another said, 'I will follow you, Lord; but let me first say farewell to those at my home.' Jesus said to him, 'No one who puts his hand to the plow and looks back is fit for the kingdom of God'" (Luke 9:61–62). Once we commit ourselves to the Lord, there can be no looking back, no second-guessing, no flirting with temptations, and no entertaining distractions. Jesus wants followers who are loyal and faithful to the end. The practice of mortification frees us to give up everything and commit ourselves to the Lord: "So therefore, whoever of you does not renounce all that he has cannot be my disciple" (Luke 14:33). Mortification is necessary in order to detach ourselves from all things and persons and become the fully committed and faithful disciples that Jesus demands.

Our Lord promises explicitly that those who make sacrifices for His sake will be rewarded abundantly: "Truly, I say to you, there is no man who has left house or wife or brothers or parents or children for the sake of the kingdom of God, who will not receive manifold more in this time, and in the age to come eternal life" (Luke 18:29–30). Not a day goes by that I am not grateful for being a priest. I am exceedingly grateful for my vocation. I am blessed abundantly in every way, and I am joyful and feel fulfilled to be able to serve the Lord as a priest. Those who commit themselves to loving and serving the Lord faithfully will never be disappointed. But they, their ministries, and the people they serve will experience rewards and blessings many times over in this life and in the life to come. The more we give, the more we receive.

Prayer

Mortification is not limited to bodily senses or to relationships but includes the heart and the spiritual life. For example, we are called to be faithful to the Lord in worship and in prayer, even when it is inconvenient or when we do not feel like it. Many Catholics do not go to Mass on Sunday for a variety of reasons. They blame work, their families, and the busyness of life, all of which are not legitimate excuses. Many neglect prayer for the same reasons. Some complain that they do not feel anything during prayer or that they are too tired or distracted. God wants people who are faithful even when they do not feel like it or it is inconvenient. Some people say that they stopped going to Mass because it is boring, or they stopped praying because of dryness, but these are not valid reasons either.

Many people are still attached to their moods, feelings, and preferences. They place conditions on their spiritual lives. They will go to Mass only when there is time, or they will pray only when they are filled with zeal and fervor. Remember, we do not seek the consolation of God but the God of consolation. Oftentimes, God will give beginners in the spiritual life feelings of consolation and fervor to encourage them to seek Him in prayer and to change their lives for the better. But as they advance in the spiritual life, God will sometimes take away these consolations to test their loyalty and strengthen them in faith, hope, and love. Jesus does not want fair-weather friends who come to Him only when they need something or when it is convenient or to their advantage. He wants faithful friends who will be with Him in good times and in bad, in sickness and in health, and who will love Him for who He is, not for what He can do for them.

Mary and the saints were faithful to the Lord always, even during the most trying times. They trusted in God's love, fidelity, and presence, even when they did not *feel* His closeness or felt completely abandoned by Him. These are times of spiritual desolation, or the dark night of the senses or the spirit, in which we are tested in order to advance in conformity and intimacy with Christ. If we remain faithful, we receive many graces and grow in sanctity and union with the Lord. The practice of mortification detaches us from our senses, relationships, and self-will, and helps prepare us to make great progress in the spiritual life. Those who are reluctant to practice self-denial will not get very close to Christ. God gives us the grace to practice self-denial out of love for Him, but it is up to us to respond. To love truly is to die for the Beloved.

The Spirit of Mortification

The spirit of mortification is a gift. Mary and the saints learned to love the cross and to sacrifice out of love for God and His people. The spirit of mortification is a grace and requires a response. We must want to deny ourselves for the sake of the gospel, and we must ask for the gift to embrace and love the cross. In this way, we demonstrate our love for Christ and our desire to participate in His ongoing redemptive work. When we love Jesus, we want to unite ourselves to Him as we offer our bodies, our wills, and our entire lives to the Father for His glory and for the salvation of the world. Love necessitates union, suffering, and sacrifice for the service and the good of the Beloved.

A common theme in prayer and worship is offering ourselves in union with Christ to the Father for the salvation of the world. At every Mass, through the Holy Spirit and in union with the sacrifice of Jesus on the Cross, we offer ourselves to the Father for the redemption of the world. Christ is our head; we are His Body, and we come to share in His superabundant merits. On our own, we do not have much to offer to the Father. But what we do have, including our good intentions, prayers, and sacrifices, we can unite to the infinite merits of Jesus so that our works take on more meaning, power, and efficacy. Then, we can offer them to the Father, who is wholly pleased with the merits of His Son. To this end, through St. Faustina, Jesus taught us the prayers of the Divine Mercy Chaplet: "Eternal Father, I offer you the Body and Blood, Soul and Divinity of your dearly beloved Son, Our Lord Jesus Christ, in atonement for our sins and those of the whole world" and "For the sake of His sorrowful Passion, have mercy on us and on the whole world." Our works, when united to those of Jesus, become much more meritorious, efficacious, and pleasing to the Father. Why offer our works and sacrifices alone when we can unite them to the merits of Jesus, Mary, and the saints?

The spiritual life is one of constantly uniting ourselves to Jesus and continually offering ourselves and our works, prayers, and sacrifices in thanksgiving and praise to the Father through the Holy Spirit, in union with the merits of Christ, for the sanctification of the world. The theme of sacrifice is found throughout the Bible and in the liturgy. St. Paul tells us: "I appeal to you therefore, brethren, by the mercies of God, to present your bodies as a living sacrifice, holy and acceptable to God, which is your spiritual worship. Do not be conformed to this world but be transformed by the renewal of your mind, that you may prove what is the will of God, what is good and acceptable and perfect" (Rom. 12:1–2). At Mass, we pray, along with the priest, "May he make of us an eternal offering to you, so that we may obtain an inheritance with your elect."[133]

The "How" of Mortification

Like all things, mortification is less about *what* we do and more about *how* and *why* we do it. God looks at the motivation behind our every action. Our intentions must be pure; that is, we must practice self-denial not to prove something to ourselves or to impress others, but out of love for the Lord because it pleases Him and makes us one with Him in likeness and purity. At the same time, through self-denial, we contribute to the good of the Church and Christ's ongoing work of redemption.

Besides learning, appreciating, and asking for the spirit of mortification, we try to lead a life of self-denial, moderation, and simplicity by consciously trying to detach ourselves from sin, selfishness, and the things of the world: possessions, comfort, status, the opinions of others, and the pleasures of the senses, which include food and drink, sex, relationships, and self-will. We also surrender to divine providence and daily accept our cross with peace, trust, and resignation.

Additionally, we may wish to consider whether the Lord wants us to practice specific types of mortification. With the help of a spiritual director, we can discern in which areas of our lives the Lord is calling us to grow and how He wants us to die to ourselves. Often, in prayer, the Lord will speak to our hearts and inspire us to make certain acts of self-denial. Also, the people and circumstances of our lives will help us discern where and how God may be calling us to become detached, die to ourselves, and join our suffering with His.

[133] Roman Missal, Eucharistic Prayer III.

The Lord gives us the grace to do whatever He asks of us. So, when we practice any form of self-denial, we should be humble and rely not on our own strength but on God's grace. We need to ask the Lord for the grace to deny ourselves, because we are too weak on our own. We should also unite our intentions, sacrifices, and sufferings to those of Christ so that we may imitate Him, make reparation for sins, and participate in His work.

Lastly, we sacrifice with joy. Jesus reminds us:

> And when you fast, do not look dismal, like the hypocrites, for they disfigure their faces that their fasting may be seen by men. Truly, I say to you, they have their reward. But when you fast, anoint your head and wash your face, that your fasting may not be seen by men but by your Father who is in secret; and your Father who sees in secret will reward you. (Matt. 6:16–18)

We should even try to have fun and be creative and imaginative when practicing mortification. For example, during Lent, women may give up wearing makeup, men may give up hot water in the shower, and children may give up their toys. Others give up social media, coffee, shopping, TV, and many other pleasures. One girl I know gave up her bed and slept on the floor in a sleeping bag.

Jesus, Mary, and saints all lead lives of simplicity, moderation, and self-denial, and we are called to do the same. At Fatima, our Blessed Mother asked us to pray and do penance for world peace and the conversion of sinners. The message of prayer, self-denial, and acts of charity is not limited to Marian apparitions or Lent but must be a central theme for all Christians. St. Paul reminds us why we all have to practice asceticism: "Every athlete exercises self-control in all things. They do it to receive a perishable wreath, but we an imperishable. Well, I do not run aimlessly, I do not box as one beating the air; but I pommel my body and subdue it, lest after preaching to others I myself should be disqualified" (1 Cor. 9:25–26). By practicing mortification, we die to ourselves and to sin so that we may live in Christ. We want to be able to say one day with St. Paul, "I have been crucified with Christ; it is no longer I who live, but Christ who lives in me; and the life I now live in the flesh I live by faith in the Son of God, who loved me and gave himself for me" (Gal. 2:20). Self-denial is necessary for us to reject selfishness and love God with all our mind, heart, soul, and strength, and our neighbor as ourselves. We must also practice mortification to participate in Christ's ongoing work of redemption as His truly committed, faithful disciples, fully conformed to Him. Lastly, mortification is required if we are to live out our vocation according to God's will and experience the joy and peace of Christ in this life and the life to come.

Practical Suggestions

1. Practice moderation in eating and drinking.
2. Abstain from meat on Fridays and limit or give up certain types of food.
3. Try to live simply and give to charity.
4. Guard your eyes against impure and unhealthy images.
5. Practice abstinence, fasting, and other forms of self-denial
6. Pray the Divine Mercy Chaplet.
7. Pray the Sorrowful Mysteries of the Rosary in union with Mary and Jesus.
8. Prayerfully watch *The Passion of the Christ*, a film by Mel Gibson.
9. Pray the Stations of the Cross.

11

Desire and Efforts in Holiness

The more we desire and work to grow in holiness, the more God will assist us.

And he came to her and said, "Hail, full of grace, the Lord is with you!" (Luke 1:28)

Holy Desire

As we approach the end of this book, it is important to note that all of the qualities of Mary that we have covered so far will have no impact on your life, and the purpose of this book will not be realized, if you do not practice what you have learned. The benefit of this book would be limited to addressing purely academic concerns, satisfying your curiosity, or entertaining you. But I believe that if this book has kept you interested up until now, the Holy Spirit has placed in your heart a spark of desire to grow in holiness and strive for perfection. I do not think you would have picked up this book and read this far if you were not interested in advancing in your spiritual life.

Know that this holy desire itself did not come from you alone but from the Lord. St. Paul tells us, "God is at work in you, both to will and to work for his good pleasure" (Phil. 2:13). The desire for holiness is itself a grace, and like all graces, it will bear fruit only if we continue to respond to it. By reading this book, you have responded to grace. Eventually, either you can put this book away and never think about it again, or you can be motivated to put the things you have learned into practice. Know that the Lord is drawing you to the latter option: "You did not choose me, but I chose you and appointed you that you should go and bear fruit and that your fruit should abide" (John 15:16). The Lord respects our free will but also inspires us to desire the good and work toward perfection.

The Holy Spirit wants to purify our sinful inclinations and fill us with lofty desires, so that we may become holy and perfect. Desire marks the first step toward God: "For where your treasure is, there will your heart be also" (Matt. 6:21). We tend to resemble what we love. When we love the things of God, such as goodness, purity, and sanctity, we desire to become good, pure, and holy—we desire to become saints. We can exceed our current state of being by having holy desires that lift us beyond ourselves and our fallen human nature and allow us to participate in the divine nature. On the other hand, when we love the things of the world, we fall short of our potential; we become less human. We are capable of so much good and so much evil, but our path in life is directed by our love, our deepest desires. What are your desires? Are they lofty and spiritual or worldly and base? Choose carefully; you will become like what you love.

As we avoid sin, we seek the things that are above. We take to heart the words of St. Paul: "Finally, brethren, whatever is true, whatever is honorable, whatever is just, whatever is pure, whatever is lovely, whatever is gracious, if there is any excellence, if there is anything worthy of praise, think about these things" (Phil. 4:8). We tend to love the things that occupy our minds and hearts. In this way, we become what we think about. We can entertain the base desires of the flesh and become enslaved to lust, gluttony, and other sins, or we can meditate on the goodness and purity of God and His saints and become pure, chaste, and truly happy.

Desire is key because it stirs us to action and helps us to overcome obstacles to the good. But because of our fallen human nature, God must give us the desire for what is best for us. Jesus tells us, "No one can come to me unless the Father who sent me draws him" (John 6:44). In fact, God is constantly drawing us to Himself, but most of the time, we are not open or receptive. He waits until we are ready to respond to His promptings, and then He gives more graces to sustain and encourage us. God the Father told St. Catherine of Siena that Christ is like a bridge by which we ascend to heaven from earth. This bridge has three "steps" that signify the three states of the soul through which we progress in our journey to God. The first step signifies "the feet of the soul," which represent our affections: as the feet carry the body, so our desires carry our soul.[134]

Holy desires come from the Lord and are necessary if we are to advance toward Him. Many times, before performing a miracle for someone, Jesus would ask, "What do you want me to do for you?" (see Matt. 20:32; Mark 10:51). He wants us to desire and to choose what He intends to give us. God does not want to force anything upon us, not even that which He knows is good for us. We must want to be holy, to resemble Him, and to share in His eternal life. As St. Augustine says, "God created us without us, but He will not save us without us."[135]

God desires our holiness because we are made to share in His nature, life, and happiness. In the Old Testament, God instructs

[134] Catherine of Siena, *Dialogue*, 65.

[135] Augustine, "Sermon 169," 11.

Moses to say to His people, "You shall be holy; for I the LORD your God am holy" (Lev. 19:2). As God's people, made in His image and likeness, we are called to be like our Father, that is, to be holy. To be holy means to be set apart for the Lord, to be consecrated to Him, and to be separated from what is worldly and profane. St. Paul reveals, "He chose us in him before the foundation of the world, that we should be holy and blameless before him" (Eph. 1:4). Just like the early disciples of Jesus, you and I were specifically selected by God, out of all humanity and before the creation of the universe, to be holy and conformed to His Son. Jesus repeats the same idea when He tells His disciples that they do not belong to the world because He has chosen them out of the world (John 15:19). As disciples, we are set apart from the world in order to become holy like the Father. Jesus commands us, "Be perfect, as your heavenly Father is perfect" (Matt. 5:48). Children should take after their father and mother. God wills our sanctification and gives us the means to achieve it, but whether we do depends on our desire and efforts.

The saints became saints because they had a burning desire for sanctification. St. Thérèse of Lisieux desired to be a great saint and to love Jesus more than He had ever been loved before. St. Catherine of Siena asked God the Father how she could grow in purity and perfection. Mother Teresa made a promise to God never to refuse Him anything. Sanctity does not happen by accident, but only by a persistent and growing desire to be holy, perfect, and pleasing to God in all things and at all times.

Efforts

Although holy desire comes from God, pleases Him, and leads us to Him, desire alone is not enough. We must take active steps in conformity with our holy desires if we wish to achieve results.

Some people dream of becoming saints but lack the determination and courage needed to implement their desire to lead a saintly life. Holiness is not easy, but the struggle for sanctity is meritorious and pleasing to the Lord. He rewards us with more graces and strengthens us to keep pursuing the good and to persevere until the end, but we must continue to do our part to respond to God's gifts in order to advance in the spiritual life.

Fortitude is a supernatural strength given by the Holy Spirit to help us overcome difficulties, avoid dangers, and persevere in virtue and faithfulness to our duties in life. Like all the gifts of the Holy Spirit, fortitude is given to us at Baptism and strengthened in us at Confirmation. But the graces may lie dormant until we activate them by responding to God's inspirations and making efforts to grow in holiness. The more we respond, the more the gifts will grow and mature in us, and the more we will progress in perfection.

The Scriptures tell us that the road to holiness is not easy. Jesus Himself reminds us that desire and effort are required if we are to achieve the fullness of life. He says: "Enter through the narrow gate; for the gate is wide and the way is easy, that leads to destruction, and those who enter by it are many. For the gate is narrow and the way is hard, that leads to life, and those who find it are few" (Matt. 7:13–14). There is no easy way out. There are two paths in life, and most people choose the path of least resistance, that is, the path of worldly pursuits and fleeting pleasures, which ultimately lead to sin and misery. But we know better. We know that where there is no pain, there is no gain. Anything worthwhile requires commitment and sustained effort. This applies to everything in life. If we want to do well in school, we have to study. If we want to be successful, we have to work hard. If want to be healthy, we have to exercise and watch what we eat. Every time I go to the gym, regardless of the day or hour, I see the same people working out. These people are very disciplined: they avoid carbohydrates, eat lean protein, and hit the gym religiously. They are committed to having a healthy and gorgeous body. If these same people were on fire with love of God and committed to a life of holiness and virtue, they would become super-saints. St. Paul points out: "Every athlete exercises self-control in all things. They do it to receive a perishable wreath, but we an imperishable" (1 Cor. 9:25). People exercise much discipline, self-control, and sweat for an attractive body and admiration from others. How much more, then, should we struggle for holiness and eternal happiness with God?

Struggle is necessary to be strong, to grow, and to flourish. When we want to build more muscles and strength, we go to the gym and lift weights. Similarly, the more we make spiritual efforts, the stronger we become. There is a story about a boy who sees a young butterfly struggling to break out of its chrysalis. He wants to help the butterfly, and so he cuts open the chrysalis to let it out. But the butterfly is neither completely formed nor strong enough to survive on its own, and so it dies. The process of struggling to break out of the chrysalis is necessary for the butterfly to become strong and mature enough to survive on its own in the world. Strength, maturity, and stamina are formed through repeated efforts. Holiness takes time, patience, desire, and persistent effort. There are no shortcuts in the spiritual life. Perfection comes with a price.

There is a saying in the spiritual life that if you are not progressing, then you are regressing; if you are not advancing, then you are backsliding. There is no plateau. We can never be complacent or satisfied with our level of prayer, virtue, and intimacy with God. Holiness is an ongoing process, a lifelong pursuit, until we reach heaven. We can compare the spiritual life to swimming upstream: you have to exert continuous energy in order to get ahead. But as soon as you relax, you drift backward. Jesus reminds us of the necessity to be vigilant in avoiding the myriad of temptations and evil in this life, and He assures us that our continued efforts will be rewarded: "He who endures to the end will be saved" (Matt. 24:13). Perseverance in goodness and sanctity is not optional.

On the same note, St. Paul reminds us, "Work out your own salvation with fear and trembling" (Phil. 2:12). Salvation, holiness, and perfection can never be taken for granted. Nevertheless, many Christians are under the mistaken assumption that heaven is automatic. They nonchalantly think something like "If I don't kill anybody, then I have nothing to worry about." But in order to go to heaven, we must be perfectly purified. Nothing impure can be in God's presence in the heavenly kingdom.

I cringe every time I attend a funeral and hear the priest give the impression that the deceased is already in heaven. No matter how wonderful or exemplary a person may have been, we cannot know the status of his or her soul. To assume that he or she is in heaven is presumptuous and reckless. It is one thing to give the family comfort and hope, but it is quite another to canonize the deceased, that is, to make him or her a saint. If all the deceased's family and friends believe that their loved one is already in heaven, then no one will pray or offer Masses for him or her. Meanwhile, the soul of the deceased is likely suffering in purgatory, with no family or friends to help him or her reach heaven more quickly.

We are meant to go straight to heaven after this earthly life, and we should strive to do so. But that lofty goal requires that we be completely purified in this life. The reality is that most people do not put in the effort and are not completely ready to enter heaven upon death. Therefore, God in His mercy has given us purgatory as a safety net, if you will, to purify us completely so that we may enter into the beatific vision. My sense is that many people are not aiming straight for heaven but are content to go to purgatory. However, the saints tell us that purgatory is not fun, and it is so much better to be purified here on earth. Therefore, we should aim for heaven, and if we do not make it, we still have purgatory to fall back on. But what happens if we aim for purgatory and do not quite make it? That result is surely not fun.

The struggle for sanctity is necessary, meritorious, and pleasing to the Lord. To the extent that we put in the effort, God will supply us with the necessary graces so that we may reach our true home. But we tend to sell ourselves short, to settle for less. Often, our prayers are unanswered not because we ask for too much but because we ask for too little. God wants to make us great saints, but we would rather settle for mediocrity. Know that the desire and effort to grow in holiness will give us the graces we need to advance in the way of perfection.

Purity

Holiness requires that we be pure, that is, free from the defilement of lust and sexual immorality. It is imperative that we be vigilant in trying to be and remain pure. This challenge requires the desire and effort to avoid images and other temptations that lead us to impure and lustful thoughts and actions. No matter where we are—on the Internet, driving down the street, or walking through the mall—we are likely to encounter racy images or people dressed in a revealing manner.

Jesus warns us about the harmfulness of lust:

> You have heard that it was said, "You shall not commit adultery." But I say to you that every one who looks at a woman lustfully has already committed adultery with her in his heart. If your right eye causes you to sin, pluck it out and throw it away; it is better that you lose one of your members than that your whole body be thrown into hell. And if your right hand causes you to sin, cut it off and throw it away; it is better that you lose one of your members than that your whole body go into hell. (Matt. 5:27–30)

We should go to great lengths to avoid falling into temptations of impurity. Our Blessed Mother revealed to the children of Fatima that "the sins which cause most souls to go to hell are the sins of the flesh," or sins against chastity.[136]

As sexual and spiritual beings, we are all called to chastity, which is the peaceful integration of sexual thoughts, feelings, and desires. In general, our sexuality gives us the capacity to love and enter bonds of communion with others. This is expressed in a bodily and biological way through a lifelong commitment between a man and a woman in marriage. Their complementarity unites them as one flesh, and their lifelong mutual act of self-gift is open to new life. Chastity necessarily involves the ability to control our desires and impulses and the freedom to choose the good that is in conformity with our state in life and God's plan for our holiness.

Purity of mind, heart, and action is necessary if we are to become like God, who is purity itself. Furthermore, purity is necessary if we are to contemplate and grow closer to the Lord. Jesus said, "Blessed are the pure in heart, for they shall see God" (Matt. 5:8). There is a direct correlation between purity and the gift of contemplation. Accordingly, there is an inverse correlation between impurity or lust and contemplative prayer. If we want to be able to advance in prayer and to contemplate and understand God, we must rid ourselves of all sins, especially the sin of lust.

Recent advances in our understanding of the human brain explain why people who indulge in lust, gluttony, and rage have a hard time thinking clearly and praying. The amygdala, a primitive part of the brain, is responsible for animalistic instincts, such as our drives for food and sex and our fight-or-flight response. In contrast, the prefrontal cortex, the most advanced part of the brain, is

[136] John C. Preiss, *The Miracle and the Message: 100 Years of Fatima* (Huntington, IN: Our Sunday Visitor, 2017), 77.

responsible for reasoning, deep thinking, and prayer—in other words, the faculties that most resemble God's. An overactive amygdala can hijack the prefrontal cortex, making it difficult for us to think clearly and pray. In other words, those who indulge in lust, gluttony, anger, and fear have a hard time advancing intellectually and spiritually. Conversely, by practicing chastity, temperance, and self-control, we are better able to grow in our knowledge of and communion with God.

The virtue of chastity helps unite us to the Lord in prayer, knowledge, and friendship. Jesus demands that we be pure and chaste if He is to dwell in us and make us one with Him. St. Faustina records Jesus' words about the connection between purity and intimacy with Him: "I heard these words in my soul: You are My spouse forever; your chastity should be greater than that of the angels, for I call no angel to such intimacy as I do you. The smallest act of My spouse is of infinite value. A pure soul has inconceivable power before God."[137] Purity attracts God, while sin and lust repel Him.

Truly, sin and God do not mix. The more we empty ourselves of all that is not of God, the more He can fill us up with Himself; but the more we are filled with sin, self, and the world, the less room there is for the Lord. Imagine that God is chrism, or holy oil for anointing, and sin is filthy polluted water. Oil and water do not mix. The more we fill our lives with sin, the more the polluted water will push out the sacred chrism of God. Therefore, empty yourself of the polluted water of sin, and watch the Holy Spirit fill you up with His sacred chrism.

Impurity, in particular, is the greatest obstacle to contemplation and union with God. Many men, women, and even children struggle with lust and impurity. At a very young age, many children discover or are shown impure images and videos, which have

[137] *Diary*, no. 534.

addictive power. This is how many people become enslaved to pornography. Impure images tend to stay in the memory and imagination for a long time and become a constant source of agitation and temptation. The Internet makes pornography easily accessible, anonymous, and affordable — it is free. But pornography enslaves its viewers to a life of sin, temptation, and distress, and keeps them from fulfilling their call to holiness and union with God. We really need to protect ourselves, and our families, from the dangers of lust, pornography, and all forms of impurity.

St. Paul reminds us that in order to become holy, we must flee from every kind of sexual immorality and be able to exercise self-control over our sensual desires: "For this is the will of God, your sanctification: that you abstain from immorality; that each one of you know how to control his own body in holiness and honor, not in the passion of lust like heathens who do not know God" (1 Thess. 4:3–5). Purity of mind, heart, and body prepares us for union with God and gives us the freedom and direction to flourish in holiness.

Immaculate Conception

Mary, being our model of perfection, is immaculate — conceived without sin — and remained sinless throughout her whole life. Mary's many titles include "Holy Virgin of Virgins," "Mother Most Pure," "Mother Most Chaste," "Mother Inviolate," and "Mother Undefiled." Because of her purity, Mary is full of grace, close to God, and pleasing to Him. Although sinless, Mary practiced mortification of the eyes by gazing downward.[138] Furthermore, Mary was a woman of prayer, practiced the virtues, and fulfilled the duties of her state in life.

[138] Liguori, *Glories of Mary*, 347.

As sons and daughters of Mary, we are called to purity, chastity, and holiness of life. We also need to make efforts not to fall into sin, including taking custody of our eyes; avoiding near occasions of sin; practicing the virtues of prudence, fortitude, and temperance; and being faithful to our duties in life. Purity is beautiful and yet rare in our overindulgent, overstimulated, over-sensualized world. But purity is essential for living in union with the Lord.

Mary tells St. Faustina that after humility, purity is the virtue that is most pleasing to God and dearest to our Blessed Mother: "I desire, My dearly beloved daughter, that you practice the three virtues that are dearest to Me—and most pleasing to God. The first is humility, humility, and once again humility; the second virtue, purity; the third virtue, love of God. As My daughter, you must especially radiate with these virtues."[139] Since Mary is wholly pure and wants her children to be pure, she can also help us achieve purity if we turn to her in trusting, persistent prayer.

St. Faustina was given the gift of purity through the intercession of the Blessed Virgin Mary. The saint shares a powerful moment of grace:

> When we had left our kneelers and had started to recite the formula for the vows, Jesus appeared suddenly at my side clad in a white garment with a golden girdle around His waist, and He said to me, "I give you eternal love that your purity may be untarnished and as a sign that you will never be subject to temptations against purity." Jesus took off His golden cincture and tied it around my waist. Since then I have never experienced any attacks against this virtue, either in my heart or in my mind. I later understood that this was one of the greatest graces which the Most Holy Virgin Mary

[139] *Diary*, no. 1415.

> had obtained for me, as for many years I had been asking this grace of Her. Since that time, I have experienced an increasing devotion to the Mother of God."[140]

We, too, need to ask our Blessed Mother to give us the gift of purity so that we may ascend to great heights.

Seven Deadly Sins

Since we are talking about the sin of lust, let us also take a quick look at the other deadly sins, some of which we have covered already. This should help us to examine ourselves and know where we are weakest and most vulnerable, so that we can avoid succumbing to that particular temptation. At the same time, we should practice the remedies and opposite virtues to grow where we are most lacking, resist the downward spiral of sin, and start an upward spiral of grace.

The seven deadly sins, or the seven capital vices, as they are also called, are pride, greed, envy, sloth, gluttony, lust, and anger. They are called the capital sins or vices because they tend to generate other sins and vices, which can be considered their offspring. We will look at the remedies for these vices and their opposite virtues. As you read about these vices, try to identify which ones apply most to you, and then try to practice the remedies and opposite virtues until you are strengthened, healed, and formed in good habits.

The first deadly sin is pride, which, as we have discussed, is excessive self-esteem, meaning we have an inflated sense of our own excellence. Similar to pride is vanity: a strong desire to be noticed and honored by others, and a preoccupation with showing off our talents and making a good impression. Vain people are overly

[140] Ibid., no. 40.

concerned with what others think of them. The offspring of pride include bragging, hypocrisy, stubbornness, and contentiousness. Its opposite virtue is humility, which is acknowledging our humanity, limitations, and complete dependence on God.

The second deadly sin is greed, which is an inordinate love of money and material wealth. In the New Testament, we read that the love of money is the root of all evil (1 Tim. 6:10). Greed is the extreme, individualistic idea that I am entitled to amass as much wealth as possible and to do whatever I want with it, unhindered by any social responsibility. The offspring include petty thefts and the exaggerated notion of my rights and what belongs to me—a notion that ultimately violates justice. The remedies include solidarity with fellow human beings, simplicity in life, and a sense of stewardship—knowing that everything I have has been entrusted to me to be used in a way that will glorify God and help others. The opposite virtues are generosity, which is the disposition to give freely of what is mine for the benefit of others, and detachment from worldly things.

Next is envy, which is sadness or distress because someone else has something that I lack, and this somehow diminishes my self-worth. Envy is an inordinate desire for the possessions of others, even to the point of wishing them harm or rejoicing in their misfortunes. The offspring of envy include gossip, defamation, and sowing discord. The remedies include accepting ourselves, not comparing ourselves to others, and practicing the opposite virtues of charity and kindness. We all have different gifts, and when we see that others have something good, we should rejoice for them. With charity, we will the good of others, not their harm.

Then, there is sloth, or apathy, which is a lack of affection—a failure of love—and a type of sadness. It is laziness in matters of faith and opposes charity by negating the love of God Himself. For the slothful, God's own goodness is a turnoff, and the call to share in the divine goodness is unappealing. There is defiant sorrow in the face of God's good intentions. A person who is slothful neither desires holiness nor wants to make the efforts to grow in perfection. This is similar to but different from depression, which, in large part, is due to unavoidable factors. Sloth is sinful to the extent that it is voluntary. The offspring of sloth include faintheartedness, which is declining to pursue excellence of which we are capable and despairing at finding meaning in life and at the prospect of salvation. The remedies include any legitimate pleasure that brings joy, and the virtues of hope and gratitude for blessings received.

The fifth deadly sin, traditionally considered the least serious, is gluttony, which is a carnal vice characterized by excessive appetite for and inordinate preoccupation with the pleasures of food and drink. Gluttony is an absence of the restraint that dignifies the human condition. It includes partaking in food or drink beyond what is proper and necessary for physical, mental, social, or spiritual health. The offspring of gluttony include dull-wittedness, buffoonery (inappropriate playfulness), loquaciousness (being overly talkative), and drunkenness (not including alcoholism, which is a disease). The remedies include the virtues of temperance and moderation, as well as a spiritual outlook on food—seeing it as a gift from God to be consumed and enjoyed in a way that benefits us and brings Him glory.

The sixth deadly sin is lust, another sensual vice. It is an inordinate desire for sexual pleasure. The Ten Commandments prohibit not only adultery but also lustful desire for our neighbor's wife. Jesus condemns lustful desires as adultery of the heart (Matt. 5:28). Hunger for sexual gratification can be much more vehement than hunger for food; furthermore, the consequences of satisfying this hunger often extend directly to other persons and even to the next generation. Lust treats persons as objects to be used and exploited for selfish pleasure. The offspring of lust include imprudence—because nothing clouds the mind like uncontrolled lust—blindness to true human value, self-absorption, and rejection of God. The remedies include the virtue of chastity, which is a peaceful integration of sexual thoughts, feelings, and desires that allows us to use our freedom well, recognizing that we are more than our sexual urges. Either we control our passions and are at peace, or they control us and make us miserable.

The last deadly sin is anger, which is a passion that leads one to harm or want to harm another out of vengeance. It arises when we feel injured in some way and have the impulse to strike back. When this feeling is unreasonable or retaliation is disproportionate, anger becomes sinful. In short, anger is overreacting to a perceived injury. Anger can be entrenched in individuals, marriages, families, and workplaces. Its offspring include indignation, thoughts of revenge, incoherent expletives, insults, blasphemy, and violence. The remedies of anger include cooling off; addressing deeper emotions, such as wounded pride, grief, or fear; and cultivating the virtues of patience, gentleness, forgiveness, and love.

Conversion is a lifelong process. I hope that going over the seven capital vices helps you identify where you may need to focus your efforts. The remedies and opposite virtues will give you direction and encouragement as you strive to heal and prosper. To the extent that you desire and struggle for holiness, the Lord will supply the grace to liberate you from sin, bring you true freedom, and bless you with peace and joy.

The Whole Church

Our desire for and efforts in holiness are not just about us and our relationship with God; they also affect our family, friends, and community. Jesus told St. Faustina: "Know this, my daughter: if you strive for perfection you will sanctify many souls; and if you do not strive for sanctity, by the same token, many souls will remain imperfect. Know that their perfection will depend on your perfection, and the greater part of the responsibility for these souls will fall on you."[141] We are responsible for not only our own sanctification but also that of our parishes, our communities, and those closest to us. Jesus is counting on us to make a difference in the lives of others. Their perfection and eternal destiny are connected to our own longing and struggle for holiness.

Our impact can be exponential. By our own yearning and striving for holiness, we inspire our family, friends, and co-workers, who then inspire their family, friends, and communities. We become part of a chain reaction of holiness and goodness. We open the floodgates of grace as we cooperate with the Holy Spirit to renew the face of the world. The Lord wants to work in us and through us to build and establish His kingdom on earth. Like the disciples during the multiplication of the loaves, we just give Jesus all that we have, although it may not be much, and He multiplies our goods so that they become abundant and ultimately benefit more people than we can imagine. We do our part and let God's grace take care of the rest.

The communion of saints makes us part of a big family in heaven and gives us access to the treasury of the Church, which contains the merits of Jesus, Mary, and the saints. We are called not just to take from the treasury but to add to it our virtues, sacrifices, and prayers. By our desire and work for perfection, we contribute to the good of the whole Church for the glory of God and the salvation of souls. We do so by relying on God's grace and cooperating with the Holy Spirit, the Sanctifier, who knows how to conform us to Christ.

[141] *Diary*, no. 1165.

Finally, Leon Bloy writes, "The only real sadness, the only real failure, the only great tragedy in life is not to become a saint."[142] Nothing really matters except our sanctity and eternal life with God. Therefore, becoming a saint should be our focus, our obsession, and our life's mission. The more we desire and make efforts to grow in holiness, the more God will fill us with His graces, which overflow from us to others. The Lord does not simply want us to be filled with His gifts; He wants us to become channels of His grace for others and the entire Church.

Practical Suggestions

1. Our phones are a source of many temptations. Get a container that has a timer lock, such as a Kitchen Safe, or kSafe, and put your phone inside for a few hours when (or even before) temptation strikes.
2. Install accountability software, such as Covenant Eyes, on all devices that have access to the Internet.
3. Practice proper boundaries with everyone, especially persons whom you may find physically attractive and who may be a source of temptation.
4. Identify the capital sins you struggle with, practice the remedies and opposite virtues, and ask for the grace to grow where you are lacking.
5. Pray to Our Lady for the gifts of chastity and purity.
6. Get rid of temptations and avoid near occasions of sin.

[142] Leon Bloy, *The Pilgrim of the Absolute: A Selection of His Writings*, trans. John Coleman and Harry Lorin Binsse, ed. Raissa Maritain, with an introduction by Jacques Maritain (Tacoma, WA: Cluny Media, 2017), 251.

7. Surround yourself with holy and beautiful images for inspiration.
8. Read books that inspire you to grow in virtue and holiness.
9. Practice all the virtues.
10. Pray for the gifts of the Holy Spirit.
11. Get enough sleep, eat healthily, exercise, and practice taking deep breaths to cultivate energy and calm, think clearly, and increase your willpower.

12

Sacraments

The more we receive the sacraments with the proper disposition, the more they will give us grace.

And they held steadfastly to the apostles' teaching and fellowship, to the breaking of bread and to the prayers. (Acts 2:42)

Sacramental Grace

We cannot talk about growing in grace without talking about the sacraments, which were instituted by Jesus and entrusted to the Church in order to communicate grace. The *Catechism* tells us about the powerful graces we receive in the sacraments:

> [The sacraments] are *efficacious* because in them Christ himself is at work: it is he who baptizes, he who acts in his sacraments in order to communicate the grace that each sacrament signifies. The Father always hears the prayer of his Son's Church which, in the epiclesis of each sacrament, expresses her faith in the power of the Spirit. As fire transforms into itself everything it touches, so the Holy Spirit

> transforms into the divine life whatever is subjected to his power.[143]

The fullness of grace and truth is found in the Catholic Church. Christ established His Church to communicate grace and truth to all the world. The sacraments are the primary sources of grace of which we must avail ourselves if we are to receive all the blessings that God wants to give us.

Proper and frequent reception of the sacraments is indispensable for growing in the life of grace, truly becoming children of God, and conforming ourselves to Christ. The *Catechism* explains:

> The Church affirms that for believers the sacraments of the New Covenant are *necessary for salvation*. "Sacramental grace" is the grace of the Holy Spirit, given by Christ and proper to each sacrament. The Spirit heals and transforms those who receive him by conforming them to the Son of God. The fruit of the sacramental life is that the Spirit of adoption makes the faithful partakers in the divine nature by uniting them in a living union with the only Son, the Savior.[144]

Jesus has provided the means to sanctification through His Church. We do our part by availing ourselves of these channels of grace.

There are two sacraments that we can receive frequently: Eucharist and Confession, both of which are readily available. When I was going through my conversion and discernment of the priesthood, I was attending Mass daily, going to Confession monthly, and attending Eucharistic Adoration weekly. The graces from these practices accelerated my conversion and discernment. I therefore

[143] CCC 1127, emphasis original.
[144] Ibid., no. 1129, emphasis original.

highly recommend daily Mass, monthly Confession, and frequent visits to the Blessed Sacrament. These practices will jumpstart your spiritual life and transformation in Jesus.

Daily Mass is usually about a half-hour long. Daily Masses are offered in the mornings and evenings and sometimes even at lunchtime. You should be able to find a daily Mass near your home, workplace, or school that works with your schedule. You may have to wake up earlier or make time to attend after work or during lunch. At the very least, you should be able to go on Saturday morning. Also, most parishes offer Confession on Saturdays and other times during the week. You can also make an appointment for Confession. As for spending time with Jesus in the Blessed Sacrament, just go to your nearest Catholic church, and you should find the tabernacle in the church or the Blessed Sacrament chapel. Some places even have perpetual Adoration, or open access to the Blessed Sacrament at all times. You just have to recognize the incredible gift of the sacraments, especially the Blessed Sacrament, and avail yourself of them frequently.

It is essential that we receive the sacraments not only frequently but also rightly, that is, with the proper disposition. We must have faith that the sacraments are efficacious means of dispensing grace. The *Catechism* tells us that "celebrated worthily in faith, the sacraments confer the grace that they signify"[145] and that "the fruits of the sacraments also depend on the disposition of the one who receives them."[146] Faith, preparation, and right disposition are the keys to truly getting as much grace from the sacraments as possible.

Many people, however, do not come to Mass prepared. They become distracted during Mass, do not pay attention to the word of God, and receive Communion in a haphazard manner, without

[145] Ibid., no. 1127.

[146] Ibid., no. 1128.

faith in the Real Presence of Jesus. Finally, they leave the church in a hurry right after Communion, without praying or giving thanks to God. The lack of proper disposition deprives many people of the graces they would receive if only they were properly prepared, recollected, focused, and filled with faith, love, and gratitude.

The Holy Sacrifice of the Mass

Let us explore the Mass so that we can understand it better, enter into it more fully, and cultivate the proper disposition toward the liturgy, in imitation of Mary, so as to benefit from it more and more. The Mass is the source and summit of the Christian life. This means the Christian life revolves around the Mass. The Eucharist is the summit, meaning it is the highest form of worship and prayer, and there is no substitute for it. The Eucharist glorifies the Father, sanctifies the world, and gives us a share in God's life, love, and nature. This is the sacrament that Jesus instituted at the Last Supper with the command "Do this in remembrance of me" (Luke 22:19).

After the Ascension of Jesus, the Christian community was faithful in "breaking bread," that is, celebrating the Eucharist, as commanded by Our Lord. We read in the Acts of the Apostles that the early Christians "held steadfastly to the apostles' teaching and fellowship, to the breaking of the bread and to the prayers" (4:42). This is the same Eucharist that has been handed down to us from the apostles. The writings of the early Church show that the form of the Eucharist has remained essentially the same: first, we read the Word of God, and then we share the Body of Christ in communion with each other.

We know that Mary must have celebrated the Eucharist as well. Before Jesus died on the Cross, He entrusted Mary to St. John the Apostle as his mother and gave St. John to Mary to be her son. Tradition has it that St. John took care of Mary for many years until her Assumption into heaven. We know that Mary participated in the breaking of bread, probably on a frequent basis, because she lived with St. John and was close to the other apostles, who celebrated the Eucharist in fidelity to the instructions of Jesus. As we go through the parts of the Mass, think about how Mary must have participated in the liturgy, and try to emulate her perfect disposition.

First, we need to understand the supernatural aspect of the Mass. The Holy Trinity and the angels and saints are present at each Mass. What takes place in the Mass is beyond space and time—it extends beyond the building of the church, reaches back into history, and anticipates and prepares the world for the future heavenly banquet. As we worship, we enter into the heavenly liturgy and are joined by the angels and saints in praising God through Jesus and the Holy Spirit for the sake of the world's salvation. The Mass is historical, cosmic, and eternal. Most of all, the Mass is about love and an encounter with God—a relationship.

There are two general movements within the Mass. The first is the Father's giving of Himself, through the Son and the Holy Spirit, to the world by way of the Church. The Son is the mediator between God and man: "No one comes to the Father, but by me" (John 14:6). At Pentecost, He sent the Holy Spirit to sanctify the Church, which, in the second movement of the Mass, joins Christ and the Holy Spirit in praying to the Father for the world. It is through the Church that the world is saved. The Church is the sacrament of salvation—the vessel through which Christ communicates grace and truth to all.

As the Mother of God, Mary is keenly aware of the spiritual and heavenly dimensions of the sacred liturgy. Comfortable speaking with angels and familiar with the heavenly realm, Mary is caught up in the mystical and transcendent dimension of the Mass. She is completely absorbed in the celebration of the Eucharist. We, too, are called to be fully present, active, and absorbed in the heavenly liturgy.

Mary knows the necessity, value, and grandeur of the Mass. Like her, we need to understand and appreciate fully the gift of the Mass and never take it for granted. I celebrate Mass every day; even on my day off, I celebrate a private Mass. When I am on vacation, I attend daily Mass, and when I am on a cruise with my mother, I celebrate Mass in our cabin. No matter what you do for a living, the Mass is the most valuable way you can spend your time and the most important thing you do all day. Daily Mass is the most precious half-hour of your day. It is through the Eucharist that your salvation is accomplished.

We know that our Blessed Mother was always recollected and in union with God, but I think she would have prepared herself even more in prayer and recollection before the start of the Eucharist. Therefore, we also need to begin Mass with the proper disposition. We do this by arriving for Mass early. If we have an important meeting or event, we do not want to be late, and so we arrive in plenty of time to collect ourselves and get ready for what is to come. This goes all the more for the Mass, which is the most important meeting that you can participate in.

As you enter the church, be aware that you are in the house of God, a place of prayer, where God is truly present. When Jesus drove out the money-changers from the temple, He reminded us of His zeal that His Father's house be treated as a house of prayer (Matt. 21:12–13; John 2:14–17). Bless yourself with holy water as a reminder of your Baptism, which grafts you onto Jesus and makes you a son or daughter of the Father. Acknowledge God's presence in the tabernacle by genuflecting. If the tabernacle is not visible, bow to the sacred altar. Then, take some time to pray and prepare yourself to enter into the mystery of the Eucharist. Ask God for the grace to be truly present and attentive for His glory, your sanctification, and any special intentions you may have. Ask our Blessed Mother to help you take on her disposition, understanding, and manner of participation in the sacred liturgy.

At the entrance song, stand and sing joyfully with the congregation, knowing that the angels and saints are singing with us. As God's masterpiece, Mary probably has a beautiful voice for singing hymns of praise and worship. Even if you cannot sing well, try your best for the glory of God. We want to pray the entire Mass instead of simply observing. Vatican II called for full and active participation.[147] We do not want to be aloof, get distracted, or just go through the motions; rather, we must enter into and participate fully at Mass.

When we make the sign of the cross, do so reverently, remembering that by it, we are confessing our faith in Christ Crucified and the triune God. The words we say come from Jesus Himself. "In the name of Father and of the Son and of the Holy Spirit" (Matt. 28:19). When we say, "Amen," we say more than "I believe"; we affirm that what we have said is certain and firmly established.

Then, the priest greets the people as Christ, the head of the body, using the apostolic greeting of St. Paul: "The grace of Our Lord Jesus Christ, and the love of God, and the communion of the Holy Spirit be with you all." When we reply, "And with your spirit," we are saying, "May Christ be in the deepest part of your being, and may you be Christ for us now." Mary recognizes her Son in every priest, especially as he celebrates Mass. The ordained priest is another Christ—in Latin, *alter Christus*.

In the Penitential Rite, we take time to reflect upon and acknowledge our sins and ask God for forgiveness, so that we may be worthy to celebrate the sacred mysteries. The word *mystery* means

[147] Vatican Council II, Constitution on the Sacred Liturgy *Sacrosanctum Concilium* (December 4, 1963), no. 14.

that there is a hidden divine reality behind the human words, elements, and gestures. We also humbly confess to one another ("and to you, my brothers and sisters"). And we ask Mary and all the angels and saints "to pray for [us] to the Lord our God." The Mass is not a private form of worship but one that involves the whole Church.

During the Gloria, we join the angels in praising the Father, Son, and Holy Spirit. Praying the same words the angels sang when Christ was born, we thank God for sending us His Son. Finally, the Introductory Rite concludes with the opening prayer, or the Collect, which is addressed to God the Father. We remember what God has done for us, and with hope in the future, we ask for something in the present.

Liturgy of the Word

The Liturgy of the Word starts with a reading from the Old Testament, which prepares us for the New Testament. St. Augustine says that the New Testament is hidden in the Old and the Old Testament is revealed in the New.[148] From her Magnificat, which contained many lines from the Old Testament, we know that Mary was immersed in the Word of God. She was so familiar with Scripture that it became a part of her identity. Mary allowed the Word of God to penetrate her soul, enlighten her, and form her according to God's will. As we listen attentively to the Word of God, we, too, allow it to penetrate our heart, mind, and soul to illumine and to re-create us according to God's pleasure.

Silence then follows as we let God's Word sink in and take effect in us. Scripture tells us that "the word of God is living and

[148] Augustine, *Quaestiones in Heptateuchum* 2, 73: PL 34, 623; cf. Vatican Council II, Dogmatic Constitution on Divine Revelation *Dei Verbum* (November 18, 1965), no. 16; quoted in CCC 129.

active" (Heb. 4:12). The Word of God is unlike any other word; it has a supernatural quality that touches us, informs us, and changes us. If we are attentive and recollected, we will hear what God is trying to communicate to us in a universal as well as a personal and specific way.

In the Responsorial Psalm, we respond to God with the words of the Psalms, which are inspired by the Holy Spirit. When we pray the Psalms, we are using the same words that Jesus, Mary, and Joseph used to pray and sing to the Lord. We join Christ, Mary, the Holy Spirit, and the rest of the Church in praying to the Father. In the Second Reading, there is again a shift in movement as God speaks to His Church, this time through the letters of the apostles, who were eyewitnesses to the life, death, and Resurrection of Jesus.

In the Alleluia, which means "praise God," we stand and sing praise to God in preparation for the proclamation of the Gospel, at which the risen Lord intensifies His presence in the assembly. The Father's movement toward the world through the Son intensifies and climaxes. Appropriately, the proclamation of the Gospel is the center and climax of the Liturgy of the Word, and it is always about the life, death, and Resurrection of Jesus. Because the words of the Gospel are the words of Jesus, a deacon or priest always proclaims the Gospel reading. No matter how many times we have heard the same Gospel story, it will speak to us in a new and unexpected way if we are open and attentive.

Through the homily, the priest or deacon helps us to understand the readings better and to respond in a way that pleases the Father and builds up His kingdom. Even if the homilist is not engaging, God can still speak to us through him. Therefore, listen carefully to how God may be speaking to you. Remember that the Mass is not a form of entertainment and the preacher is not a performer. If you really enjoy the homily, give thanks to God in quiet prayer and meditate on the message, but do not applaud. Clapping is an expression of approval following a performance, which the homily is not; therefore, applause is inappropriate at Mass.

After the homily, take a moment to reflect quietly on God's message and how you can implement it into your life. Then, stand and proclaim the Creed with conviction—confirming and solidifying your belief in the essence of our Faith. Finally, join your prayers with those of the faithful in intercession for the Church and the world.

Liturgy of the Eucharist

Now, as we move to the Liturgy of the Eucharist, we prepare the altar and bring up the gifts to be offered to God. Offer your own sacrifices and burdens back to our Creator to be transformed. We offer up our lives through, with, and in Christ for our sanctification and the glory of God. St. Paul writes, "I appeal to you therefore, brethren, by the mercies of God, to present your bodies as a living sacrifice, holy and acceptable to God, which is your spiritual worship" (Rom. 12:1). This is not a time to be distracted, but to unite yourself to Christ and offer everything to the Father, who will sanctify and return it to you. Mary is always in union with Jesus and the Father, but particularly in this part of the Mass, the Blessed Mother gives completely to the Lord all that she is and all that she has, for her perfection and for His glory.

If you pay attention to the priest, you will notice that as he is preparing the gifts, he pours a drop of water into the wine. As he does so, the priest prays inaudibly, "By the mystery of this water and wine, may we come to share in the divinity of Christ, who humbled Himself to share in our humanity." The wine represents the divinity of Jesus, and the water represents our humanity. By mixing the water and the wine, we join ourselves with Christ as we offer both to the Father. Like Mary, we should ever desire and pray to share more fully in the divinity of Jesus.

Finally, after mixing the water and the wine, the priest washes his hands. He prays another inaudible prayer: "Lord, wash away my iniquity and cleanse me from my sins."[149] Now, Christ will make the hands of the priest His own hands.

In the Preface, the priest speaks first to the people, saying, "Lift up your hearts." Christ, the head, is telling His Body that we are going up to heaven. We respond, "We lift them up to the Lord." That is, we want to be there. We are in heaven now, and the priest reminds us of our purpose: "Let us give thanks to the Lord our God." And we assent, "It is right and just." Then, the priest speaks to God the Father on behalf of the Church. Succinctly, he expresses what Christ has done for us, and we ask that our voices blend with those of the angels and saints in singing God's praises. Mary is constantly singing God's praises and thanking the Lord. In the Eucharist, we join our Blessed Mother and all of heaven in praising God and giving Him thanks.

In the Sanctus, we join heaven in praising God with the heavenly hymn composed of the words sung to Jesus as He entered Jerusalem: "Holy, Holy, Holy, Lord God of hosts. Heaven and earth are full of your glory. Hosanna in the highest. Blessed is He who comes in the name of the Lord. Hosanna in the highest." Some mystics have told us that at the Sanctus, the angels descend from heaven and join us in singing their words. Isaiah had a vision of heaven with the angels singing these words: "I saw the Lord sitting upon a throne, high and lifted up; and his train filled the temple. Above him stood the seraphim; each had six wings: with two he covered his face, and with two he covered his feet, and with two he flew. And one called to another and said: 'Holy, holy, holy is the LORD of hosts; the whole earth is full of his glory'" (6:1–3).

[149] This prayer is taken from Psalm 51:2, which reads, "Wash me thoroughly from my iniquity and cleanse me from my sin."

St. John had a similar vision: "And the four living creatures, each of them with six wings, are full of eyes all round and within, and day and night they never cease to sing, 'Holy, holy, holy, is the Lord God Almighty, who was and is and is to come!'" (Rev. 4:8).

When you sing the Sanctus, know that Mary, the angels, and the saints are singing with you.

Eucharistic Prayer

At the start of the Eucharistic Prayer, we fall to our knees in adoration as Christ is about to come in a real, true, and substantial way. Kneeling is the proper posture before God. St. Paul writes, "Therefore God has highly exalted him and bestowed on him the name which is above every name, that at the name of Jesus every knee should bow, in heaven and on earth and under the earth, and every tongue confess that Jesus Christ is Lord, to the glory of God the Father" (Phil. 2:9–11). In *The Spirit of the Liturgy*, Pope Benedict XVI writes: "Worship is one of those fundamental acts that affect the whole man. That is why bending the knee before the presence of the living God is something we cannot abandon."[150] Kneeling is a natural posture for the Blessed Virgin Mary, because she always praying, worshipping, and adoring the Lord. We, too, take on this humble posture of worship as we acknowledge the true presence of Jesus in the Eucharist.

At one point during the Eucharistic Prayer, the priest extends his hands over the bread and wine, calling down the Holy Spirit to transform the species into the Body and Blood of Jesus. This part is called the *Epiclesis*. This is the same Holy Spirit who was

[150] Joseph Cardinal Ratzinger, *The Spirit of the Liturgy*, trans. John Saward (San Francisco: Ignatius Press, 2000), 191.

present at the creation of the world,[151] formed Jesus in the womb of the Blessed Virgin Mary, and raised Jesus from the dead. The priest then continues with the institution narrative, in which he uses the same words Jesus used at the Last Supper, and the past is made present.

God's Word has the power to create something even out of nothing. At the creation of the world, God said, "Let there be light," and there was light.[152] When Jesus says, "Be opened," the deaf hear;[153] when He says, "Arise," the dead are raised.[154] Therefore, when Jesus says, "This is my body,"[155] the bread becomes His Body; when He says, "This chalice … is the new covenant in my blood,"[156] the wine becomes His Blood. It is easier to change one thing into another than to create something out of nothing. And if God can create the whole universe out of nothing, He can surely change bread and wine into His Body and Blood.

Mary understands and knows that what appears to be bread and wine is the Body and Blood of her only begotten Son. She is filled with faith, love, and awe at this precious gift from Jesus, who keeps giving of Himself to us, even after He has ascended into heaven. At the elevation, the priest holds up the Body and Blood of Christ to the Father, and the people gaze in contemplation. At this sublime moment, everything stops as we join heaven in adoring and marveling at the true presence of Our Lord in the Eucharist. This is the time to love and be amazed in silent adoration, or to tell Jesus what is in your heart. He is looking at you with love and tenderness.

[151] Gen. 1:2.
[152] Gen. 1:3.
[153] Mark 7:34–35.
[154] Luke 7:14–15; Mark 5:41–42.
[155] Luke 22:19.
[156] Luke 22:20.

As we continue with the Eucharistic Prayer, we are joined with the whole Church across the world, across the centuries, in heaven and on earth. We name Mary, St. Joseph, the apostles, the martyrs, and the saints—all of whom are present. We pray for the pope, the bishops, and the entire world, and we remember our loved ones who have passed away. At the Doxology, the priest holds up the Body and Blood of Christ and presents them to the Father as an offering. He prays, "Through Him, and with Him, and in Him, O God, almighty Father, in the unity of the Holy Spirit, all glory and honor is yours, for ever and ever." And the people respond with the Great Amen. This is not a time to be shy: say or sing the "Amen," like you mean it, as if you are putting your life on the line in this offering of Jesus—Body, Blood, Soul, and Divinity—to the Father for the salvation of the world. Mary would say, "Amen," with every fiber of her being.

Communion Rite

As we begin the Communion Rite, we pray the Our Father, the prayer Jesus taught us. At the Agnus Dei, we acknowledge Jesus as the Passover Lamb sacrificed on our behalf to take away the sins of the world, and we ask for His mercy and peace. Then, the priest breaks a small piece of the large Host and drops it into the chalice, symbolically reuniting the Body and Blood of Christ—signifying the Resurrection—and praying quietly, "May this mingling of the Body and Blood of our Lord Jesus Christ bring eternal life to us who receive it." Then, the priest prays quietly, "Lord Jesus Christ, Son of the living God, who, by the will of the Father and the work of the Holy Spirit, through your death, gave life to the world, free me by this, your most holy Body and Blood, from all my sins and from every evil; keep me always faithful to your commandments, and never let me be parted from you."

The priest then genuflects, holds up the broken Body of Christ and His Blood, and then tells the people, "Behold the Lamb of God." The people respond with the words of humility and faith of the centurion in the Gospel: "Lord, I am not worthy that you should enter under my roof, but only say the word and my soul shall be healed." We acknowledge our unworthiness to receive Jesus and express confidence in His power to heal our sins and transform us into His likeness. When we eat food, it becomes a part of us. But when we receive Jesus, we become a part of Him. We are changed and participate more intimately in the divine life.

Mary must have been exceedingly grateful for the gift of the Eucharist and the opportunity to unite herself to her Son in this most profound way. She would have received Holy Communion with overflowing love and awe. We, too, should approach Communion with reverence, gratitude, and awe at such a gift. Let us not be distracted but focus on the gift of love and immortality. When the priest says, "The Body of Christ," say, "Amen," with faith that this really is the Body, Blood, Soul, and Divinity of Christ. Our gifts and lives brought to Christ are handed back to us transformed. We say, "Amen," ratifying the exchange and accepting our transformation into the Body of Christ.

Receive Jesus with much love and unite yourself to Him completely. Know that Jesus is truly in you and transforms you into Himself. Love Him, thank Him, and be one with Him in prayer. Kneel in adoration of Jesus, who is inside you, and speak to Him with gratitude and praise. Prolong this moment for as long as you can. Some people prefer to stand and sing, but I cannot help but fall to my knees in adoration of and union with the Beloved. Mary would have united herself completely to Jesus in love and adoration. Nothing would matter to her at this point but to love Jesus with all her heart, mind, and soul. This is the time of grace. Therefore, do not be distracted and irreverent but savor the moment of love and communion.

How disappointed Jesus is when we receive Him carelessly, without love and devotion. Jesus told St. Faustina: "My daughter, write that it pains Me very much when religious souls receive the Sacrament of Love merely out of habit, as if they did not distinguish this food. I find neither faith nor love in their hearts. I go to such souls with great reluctance. It would be better if they did not receive Me."[157] Love demands love in return. Love taken for granted is love spurned. Never take Holy Communion for granted. Always try to receive with faith, love, and gratitude, as would our Blessed Mother.

After receiving Communion is the time to speak to Jesus from your heart. Tell Him what is on your mind and heart. Let the Holy Spirit inspire you to ask Him to grant your deepest desires. Jesus is present in you, listening, loving, and healing. Do not waste this precious moment on anything else. Be present and one with your Lord.

At the Prayer after Communion, we thank God for the gift of Jesus in the Eucharist and pray that we remain faithful and bear much fruit from the sacrament. At the Concluding Rite, we receive the priest's blessing and are sent to be Christ in the world and to establish God's kingdom on earth. After the recessional hymn, we should spend some time in quiet thanksgiving.

When I attended Mass at the Franciscan University of Steubenville, everyone knelt in quiet prayer and thanksgiving after Mass. I was in the middle of the pew and could not have gotten out even if I wanted to. I was so surprised and impressed. I had never seen anything like it. After a few minutes, people started to get up and leave, but the whole congregation was in silent thanksgiving for several minutes. I think that Mary would have spent some time in silent adoration and thanksgiving at the end of the sacred liturgy. Let us learn from Mary and the students at Steubenville, and spend

[157] *Diary*, no. 1288.

some time in thanksgiving after Mass instead of rushing to get out of the church. Remember, the fruit of the sacrament depends in part on our disposition.

We miss out on so many graces when we do not receive Communion. Jesus told St. Faustina: "Oh, how painful it is to Me that souls so seldom unite themselves to Me in Holy Communion. I wait for souls, and they are indifferent toward Me. I love them tenderly and sincerely, and they distrust Me. I want to lavish My graces on them, and they do not want to accept them."[158] When something is readily available, we tend to take it for granted. If I said that I would give $1,000 to everyone who comes to church for half an hour, there would be a line out the door every day. Holy Communion is worth so much more, yet many do not come to receive it. This not only saddens Jesus but also causes us to miss out on the graces of the Eucharist.

Sacrament of Confession

Most Catholics go to Confession once or twice a year, which is the bare minimum for people in mortal sin. When it comes to our souls, our relationship with God, and eternal life, why would we do the bare minimum? Unfortunately, our culture has lost the sense of sin and appreciation for the Sacrament of Reconciliation. Most people do not even realize that they have sinned. Those who do recognize their sins think they can just confess directly to God. God does forgive less serious sins directly, but He wants us to confess our serious sins to a priest, who represents Christ and receives authority from Him to forgive sins.[159]

[158] *Diary*, no. 1447

[159] However, making an act of perfect contrition, which arises when God is loved above all else, "obtains forgiveness of mortal sins if

Jesus has given the Church the power to forgive sins. When Jesus appeared to the disciples in the upper room after His Resurrection, He said: "'Peace be with you. As the Father has sent me, even so I send you.' And when he said this, he breathed on them, and said to them, 'Receive the Holy Spirit. If you forgive the sins of any, they are forgiven; if you retain the sins of any, they are retained'" (John 20:21–23). Jesus *chose* to entrust the power to forgive sins to Peter and the apostles, the first bishops of the Church: "And I tell you, you are Peter, and on this rock I will build my Church, and the gates of Hades shall not prevail against it. I will give you the keys of the kingdom of heaven, and whatever you bind on earth shall be bound in heaven, and whatever you loose on earth shall be loosed in heaven" (Matt. 16:18–19). The power to bind and loose refers to the power to teach, govern, and sanctify.

Jesus has instituted the Sacrament of Reconciliation because He knows we need it. We tend to rationalize our sins away or sweep them under the rug. But God wants us to acknowledge our sins in a personal encounter. Because of our humanity, to receive total healing, we must verbally confess our sins to another person and hear the words of absolution: "I absolve you from your sins in the name of the Father, and of the Son, and of the Holy Spirit." This is reminiscent of why many people go to therapists: they need to talk to another person about what is troubling them and receive words of healing.

Mary, of course, is sinless and did not have to go to Confession. But we, on the other hand, are born with Original Sin and suffer from concupiscence. "Sin is an offense against reason, truth, and right conscience; it is failure in genuine love for God and neighbor caused by a perverse attachment to certain goods. It wounds the

---

it includes the firm resolution to have recourse to sacramental confession as soon as possible" (CCC 1452).

nature of man and injures human solidarity. It has been defined as 'an utterance, a deed, or a desire contrary to the eternal law.'"[160] Even if we have not committed a mortal or serious sin, we all have had thoughts and desires that are not consistent with the will of God.

When we commit a mortal sin—which occurs when something is serious, we know it is serious, and we do it anyway—we sever our relationship with God and are no longer in a state of grace. We then need to go to sacramental Confession in order to restore our relationship with God and receive His grace. Venial sins do not completely separate us from God but turn us away from and impair our relationship with Him. Therefore, we should go to Confession, tell God we are sorry, and ask His forgiveness to reconcile fully with the Lord. Sin severs or damages not only our relationship with God but also our relationship with others. We are all part of the Body of Christ, and sin hurts our dignity as children of God.

Sin also tends toward habit and proliferation. The *Catechism* tells us: "Sin creates a proclivity to sin; it engenders vice by repetition of the same acts. This results in perverse inclinations which cloud conscience and corrupt the concrete judgment of good and evil. Thus sin tends to reproduce itself and reinforce itself."[161] It is like a snowball effect. If we do not go to Confession to cleanse ourselves of venial sins, they will become more frequent and more serious. For example, if you have a small cut on your hand, you would want to clean the wound, put an ointment and bandage on it, and allow it to heal. On the other hand, if you just ignore the wound, it will become infected and the injury will get worse. Sin is like cancer in the soul: diagnose and remove it early and you will be restored to health, but if you wait too long, it will spread and ultimately lead to death.

[160] Ibid., no. 1849.
[161] Ibid., no. 1865.

Sin is also like filth in the soul. We change our clothes, brush our teeth, and shower every day because we care about our personal hygiene, as we should. But what about our spiritual hygiene? If we do not go to Confession, sin builds up in our soul, even though we may not be aware of it. Have you ever been around someone with bad breath or body odor? It is not pleasant. The same goes for our soul. If we do not go to Confession, our soul becomes foul and disgusting.

Sins can cloud our minds and hearts to the point that we get used to living in the dark. For example, if we are used to having a dirty window, we do not know what it looks like to see through a clean one. Or, if we wear brown or grey shirts, we do not readily notice little blemishes or stains. Going to Confession more and more often and forming our conscience accordingly is like starting to wear bright white shirts, on which little stains will be readily apparent. The closer we get to God, who is light itself, the more easily we can see our sins. The more we separate ourselves from sin, the more we can see our imperfections, and the more we want to grow in holiness. We spend so much time, attention, and money to make sure that we look good in front of others. If only we would pay the same attention and care to our souls to make sure we are pleasing in the sight of God.

Confession does not cost us anything, it is readily available, and its effects are literally life changing. It restores and strengthens our relationship with God, the Church, and our own dignity. It cleanses and purifies our souls to make them beautiful again. It heals the injuries caused by sin and restores us to health. Lastly, Confession empowers us to resist falling into sin. Yet many people are unaware of the destructiveness of sin and the powerful grace of Confession to undo the damage caused by sin.

God is the father in the parable of the prodigal son, waiting patiently for His wayward children to return to Him in the Sacrament of Confession so that they may be forgiven and restored to their full status as His sons and daughters. Jesus is the Good Shepherd who leaves behind the ninety-nine sheep to go searching for the one who is lost. But the Lord will not force reconciliation upon us. We have to want to return to the Father. We have to want to be found. We have to want to go to the Sacrament of Reconciliation.

To have a proper disposition when going to Confession, we should start by making a thorough examination of conscience, which is essential to making a good Confession. You can find many apps, websites, and printed materials to help you examine your conscience, or you might use the Ten Commandments or the seven deadly sins and their offspring as a guide. It is also a good practice to make an examination of conscience daily before going to bed, so that you become used to recognizing your sins and asking God for forgiveness.

An essential element of Confession is having true contrition, or sorrow, for our sins because they offend God, who is all-good and deserving of all our love. We arrive at contrition when we see the contradiction between God's love and our sins. From contrition flows the purpose of amendment, which is the resolution not to commit those sins again in the future. We resolve to change our life and place all our hope in God's help. With trust in God's mercy, we need to confess our sins to a priest, do the prescribed penance, and receive absolution.

Many people have experienced much relief, healing, and peace from the Sacrament of Confession. Many burst into tears of compunction, joy, and love as they are overpowered by the abundance of grace they receive in the sacrament. Personally, I can sometimes feel the outpouring of grace as the priest gives me absolution. I feel lighter, more joyful, and more peaceful after going to Confession. I feel closer to the Lord, and my ministry tends to be more fruitful. Grace flows more freely and abundantly after we have gone to Confession. We feel more alive, energized, and inspired to lead lives of holiness and work for the glory of God.

Eucharistic Adoration

I want to end this chapter by talking about Eucharistic Adoration, which is really an extension of the Mass. Many people do not understand this practice, its benefits, or what they should do during Adoration. Eucharistic Adoration was not practiced during Mary's earthly life, but the Blessed Mother adored Jesus during Mass, in her heart, and in her soul. We are privileged to have the opportunity to spend time with Jesus in the Blessed Sacrament, whether He is exposed in a monstrance or reserved in the tabernacle.

Jesus instituted the Eucharist for three purposes: to perpetuate His holy sacrifice on the Cross, to give us spiritual food for the journey to heaven, and to remain with us always in a concrete and tangible way. Imagine if Jesus were still on earth. Would we not go out of our way to be with Him? Yet that is what we have in the Blessed Sacrament, which is the real Body, Blood, Soul, and Divinity of Jesus. Many people walk past the tabernacle without even stopping or acknowledging His presence. If we truly believe in the Real Presence of Jesus in the Blessed Sacrament, would we not want to spend time near Him?

In the book *In Sinu Jesu*, Jesus tells a Benedictine monk, among other things, that He wants to start a springtime of holiness in the Church and the world, and Eucharistic Adoration is to be the primary means of this renewal.[162] In fact, much of the discussion in this chapter is based upon *In Sinu Jesu*.

[162] Benedictine Monk, *In Sinu Jesu: When Heart Speaks to Heart—The Journal of a Priest at Prayer* (Kettering, OH: Angelico Press, 2016), 131, 149.

Adoration entails many of the dispositions of Mary that we have discussed, especially in the chapters on union with God and love of God and during our discussion of the Holy Sacrifice of the Mass. So I will try not to repeat but to build on what has already been covered.

Often, I am asked, "What does one do during Adoration?" The first thing is to be truly present. When we come to Jesus in the Blessed Sacrament, He wants us to have faith in His Real Presence and to be recollected and attentive to Him in the here and now. Like Mary, the sister of Martha, we sit at the feet of Jesus completely absorbed by and focused on Him alone, oblivious to everything else. Adoration requires the gift of faith, which we receive in contemplation. We must ask for the grace to practice this high form of prayer.

Jesus wants us to take our time seeking, desiring, and beholding Him in the Blessed Sacrament. The Old Testament tells us to "seek the face of the God of Jacob" (Ps. 24:6). And Jesus assures us, "Ask, and it will be given you; seek, and you will find; knock and it will be opened to you" (Matt. 7:7). Good things come to those who patiently persevere in love. Jesus wants us to seek Him as did Mary Magdalene on the morning of the Resurrection (see John 20:1–18), or as the bride sought the bridegroom in the Song of Solomon:

> Upon my bed by night I sought him whom my soul loves; I sought him, but found him not; I called him, but he gave no answer. "I will rise now and go about the city, in the streets and in the squares; I will seek him whom my soul loves." I sought him, but found him not. The watchmen found me, as they went about in the city. "Have you seen him whom my soul loves?" Scarcely had I passed them, when I found him whom my soul loves. I held him, and would not let him go. (Song of Sol. 3:1–4)

Be patient and persistent in seeking your Beloved in the Blessed Sacrament, and you will find Him.

Jesus wants us not only to desire and seek Him but also to remain with Him and abide in Him, keeping Him company. Jesus desires intimacy with us more than we desire it with Him. He wants to be one with us as He is one with the Father. Be His friend, His confidant; spend time gazing at Him who is gazing lovingly at you. When you find yourself distracted, bring your attention back to the one you love. Place your heart inside His heart and remain resting there as did St. John, the Beloved Disciple. Friends grow closer only by spending time together, getting to know each other, sharing secrets, and learning to trust one another.

Truly, love is paramount. Learn to perceive and receive Jesus' love for you. Know that He loves you even when you do not feel it. Our hearts are too small and our love too fickle to take in His enormous love. Only by spending time with Him, letting Him love us, and loving Him in return can our hearts be enlarged to receive His infinite love. Practice loving Jesus with all your being—leaving no room for anything else.

Moreover, be filled with gratitude and praise for this incomprehensible gift of love—a gift that is rejected by so many people. Console your Beloved and make reparation for those who wound the heart of Jesus by their indifference, doubt, coldness, and contempt. The Father is grieved to see His Son so profoundly mistreated. Mary's heart is pierced anew with sorrow, and the angels weep but can do nothing, for only humans can make reparations for the acts and omissions of other humans. Therefore, join Jesus as a victim, and make up for His love that is spurned.

Jesus is not only the friend but also the physician of our souls. Therefore, we should come to Jesus as if to a doctor or a counselor. Knowing that we need help, we humbly allow Jesus to work in us. He knows what we need more than we do. Give Jesus permission to heal, repair, purify—whatever He needs to do to perfect you. Be contrite and repentant, as this is the first step toward conversion. Empty yourself before Our Lord, revealing everything to Him and letting Him fill you with Himself. Let down your guard and surrender to love. Trust that Jesus' desires for you are fulfilled to the extent that you submit to His love in the Blessed Sacrament.

Speak to Jesus simply and confidently. Surrender all your sins, inabilities, and weaknesses through Mary. And give to Jesus, as to an intimate friend, all your worries, anxieties, fears. Trust that He will take care of them. As Jesus says to the Benedictine monk and to us:

> Come to me with your questions, your perplexities, your needs. Nothing is too small for me and nothing is too great. I am here for you. I wait for you to share with me all that occupies you and all the questions that arise in your heart. Worrying and daydreaming are useless. What I ask of you is dialogue with me in the Sacrament of my Love, and a boundless confidence in my loving friendship.[163]

Pour out your heart to the Lord and let him comfort your soul.

Adoration is also a time to pray for ourselves and for others. Always pray with humility, childlike trust, and boldness. Have confidence in Jesus' love for you and for others. We do not need to tell Jesus what to do or to give Him solutions—it is enough to say, "So-and-so needs your help"—and trust that He knows best what to do. Remember Mary at the wedding at Cana: all she said to Jesus was "They have no wine" (John 2:3), and He did the rest. We can ask for specific things, but we should give Christ the freedom to do what is best in His wisdom and love. Let God surprise you, and abandon yourself to divine providence.

[163] Benedictine Monk, *In Sinu Jesu*, 136.

Know that God blesses all those whom we offer up in prayer and that Adoration is the most efficacious and fruitful way to obtain graces for others.

As with any conversation or friendship, there is a time to talk to Jesus and a time to listen to Him. Be comfortable with silence: it is in the silence of our heart that Jesus speaks. It is in silence that the Holy Spirit descends and works in us. It is in stillness that we come to know God. Become one with Jesus in silence. Lovers can simply abide in each other's presence without the need for words. Imitate St. John in resting in the heart of Jesus. Ask St. John to show you how to rest in the bosom of Jesus and say, "Speak Lord, for your servant is listening" (see 1 Sam. 3:10).

We have freedom to pray in a variety of ways in the presence of the Blessed Sacrament. We can pray the Rosary or read Scriptures or spiritual books, but we should try to have our heart fixed on Jesus. We can also rest if we are tired. Even our sleepiness does not impede the working of grace. In sum, Jesus says to us, "No need to fill up your time with thoughts and words, it is sufficient to speak as the Holy Spirit inspires, listen with the ear of your heart and abide for those who do not abide."[164]

Grace Abounds

What happens during Adoration? An abundance of grace is given to us. First, there is healing. We all have spiritual, emotional, and physical ailments, some of which we may not even be aware of, that need healing. Jesus, the healer of souls, knows what we need, and He goes to work on us when we present ourselves to Him. An important type of healing is detachment from sin. As we spend time in the company of Jesus, we become liberated from our enslavement

[164] Ibid., 181.

to sin, so that we may be free to fulfill our vocation as God's sons and daughters.

Along the same lines, we are slowly being purified while we are in the presence of Jesus. We all have some degree of disordered affection, inordinate self-love, and attachment. We have a divided heart, which Jesus wants to purify, make whole, and set on fire with the love of God. In other words, in Adoration, we are sanctified, that is, made holy, and conformed to Christ, who teaches and forms us in the virtues. Our faith in the Eucharist grows in proportion to our time in Adoration, and we are strengthened by grace and the gifts of the Holy Spirit.

The Eucharist is analogous to the sun. When we are exposed to the sun, we generate vitamin D and develop a tan. But the change is imperceptible. So it is when we are exposed to the Blessed Sacrament: we receive graces and are changed inwardly and outwardly in a way that is imperceptible but nonetheless real. In Adoration, we absorb the light of Jesus' countenance and the fire of His heart, and then we reflect His light and the warmth of His love to a world that is sometimes dark and cold. In short, we are transformed and perfected as God's instruments.

In Adoration, we grow in our union and friendship with Christ and come to know the desires of His heart. United to Jesus, we come to know, love, and trust the Father, and we receive the love of the Holy Spirit. We are united more closely to Mary and the saints. We also receive enlightenment from the Lord. I always try to prepare my talks and homilies in the presence of the Blessed Sacrament. There, Jesus teaches us, answers our questions, and gives us supernatural insights.

Lastly, we are consoled in His presence. Jesus says, "Come to me, all who labor and are heavy laden, and I will give you rest" (Matt. 11:28). When troubled by temptations, doubts, fears, sadness, or loneliness, come to Jesus, and you will find rest, peace, joy, and strength that the world cannot give. Jesus restores our energy and health and renews our soul and body.

How much time should we spend in Eucharistic Adoration? The answer depends on our duties in life. But whenever we have a chance, we should visit Jesus in the Blessed Sacrament. Even a little time set aside out of love is precious to the Lord. Archbishop Fulton Sheen said that all priests should make a holy hour each day. Depending on where you live, you may be able to find a church that offers perpetual Adoration and is not too far away.

Jesus also has a way of multiplying our time. You may think you are too busy to go to Adoration. But if you try to make the time, even if you have only a few minutes, Jesus will bless you with enough time to do everything that is necessary. Jesus promises us, "Seek first [your heavenly Father's] kingdom and his righteousness, and all these things shall be yours as well" (Matt. 6:33). Truly, Jesus rewards us for the faithful, loving sacrifices we make to be with Him.

The effects and benefits of Eucharistic Adoration are expansive, pervasive, and enduring. Adoration brings graces beyond the confines of the chapel or church. It increases vocations to the priesthood and religious life. Places where frequent or perpetual Adoration is offered tend to flourish spiritually, and people are drawn to them.

Try to make Eucharistic Adoration a priority. To the monk of *In Sinu Jesu*, Jesus revealed; "Nothing in your life is more important than the time you spend in adoration before my Eucharistic Face. Your energy and your capacity to do other things efficiently and in due order will grow in proportion to the time you consecrate to me alone."[165] It is the one thing necessary—everything else will be given to us. For the salvation of souls and the good of the Church, Jesus desires that we visit Him and come to know, love, and adore

[165] Benedictine Monk, *In Sinu Jesu*, 178–179.

Him in the Blessed Sacrament. It is a mystery that Jesus begs for our love, time, and friendship. He says to us:

> I yearn for the gift of your love in response to my love and for your presence to my sacramental presence. How long must I beg you for your time, your love, and your companionship? I am here for you; be here for me. Allow me to fill you even as you empty yourself before me. I am all yours; be all mine. Prefer nothing whatsoever to my Eucharistic love. Come before me giving thanks.[166]

Jesus has made Himself available through the sacraments in order to love us and shower us with graces. May we respond to His love by frequently availing ourselves of the Holy Sacrifice of the Mass, Confession, and Adoration, which we approach with the disposition necessary to flourish in holiness for the glory of God and the sanctification of souls.

Practical Suggestions

1. Make sure that you and your loved ones receive all the Sacraments of Initiation: Baptism, First Communion, and Confirmation.
2. Go to daily Mass with recollection, faith, and love.
3. Go to monthly Confession, preparing yourself with a thorough examination of conscience, true contrition, and gratitude for God's mercy.
4. Go to Eucharistic Adoration as often as possible and stay for as long as is practical.
5. Cultivate the proper dispositions of faith, love, gratitude, and recollection when participating in the sacraments.

[166] Benedictine Monk, *In Sinu Jesu*, 179.

6. Enter into the supernatural aspects of the Mass and the other sacraments.
7. Ask Mary and the saints to help you receive the sacraments frequently and with the best disposition.

Conclusion

The more we cultivate the attributes of Mary,
the more we flourish in grace.

And from his fulness have we all received,
grace upon grace. (John 1:16)

Recap

Now, following our discussion, we understand better the workings of grace — in particular, that it is a gift from God that requires a response on our part in order to make it fruitful; and that the more keenly we respond, the more we grow in God's gifts and advance in the spiritual life. Our Blessed Mother fully cooperated with God's grace; hence, she is God's masterpiece and our model of perfection.

We have examined in depth each of Mary's twelve qualities so that we may fully comprehend and put them into practice. It is only by integrating these qualities into our lives that we will be transformed into the likeness of Jesus, which is the ultimate goal of the Christian life. We should have these qualities ever present before our eyes, in our mind, and in our heart. We can use bookmarks or prayer cards that list the twelve qualities or create our own list to have with us always.[167] These reminders will help us think about and cultivate these virtues in our everyday lives. Many people tell me that they have posted the list of the twelve qualities in a prominent place where they can refer to it often. They subsequently find that they are making progress in their spiritual life. A person named Jennifer wrote: "I love your take on the 12 steps to becoming holy with Mary. It helps me a lot. I still apply them in my daily life."

God will give us plenty of opportunities to recall and implement one or more of these Marian qualities throughout the day. For example, when we get up in the morning, we can practice *gratitude* by thanking God for the gift of rest and the start of a brand-new day. During our morning prayer, we are reminded of the importance of being in *union with* God in prayer and throughout our day. As we make breakfast for our children, we are reminded to use quality ingredients out of *love for neighbor*, and we do our best to serve our family out of *love for God*.

Driving to work, we notice the beauty of the sunrise in the morning sky, and we *rejoice in the Lord*, who created all things. As we start to tackle our work, we accept our inabilities with *humility* while having *confidence in God*, knowing that He will assist us. When other people interrupt our work, we can practice *abandonment to divine providence*. For lunch, we can order a salad and water as a form of *mortification*. Before returning home from work, we can attend daily Mass to receive the *Sacrament* of the Eucharist. As we are driving home, we see a homeless man. We are inspired to give him some money, and so we practice *docility to God's will*. Before going to bed, we spend some time in prayer as we *desire and make efforts to grow in holiness*.

[167] Bookmarks and prayer cards listing the twelve qualities of Mary are available at www.fullnessofgrace.org.

These are just a few examples of how we can implement these qualities into our everyday life. The more conscientiously we do this, the more the qualities will be ingrained in us, and the more graces will be showered upon us. As you keep these qualities in mind, be aware of the times when you deviate from them, and then turn back toward them with God's help. Here is a succinct recap of each of the qualities of Mary that are most pleasing to the Lord:

1. *Humility*. This is the first and most important virtue to have if we are to grow in the other virtues. To be humble is to recognize our weaknesses and limitations and to depend completely on the Lord for everything. A humble person is not focused on himself or herself but on serving God and others.
2. *Confidence in God*. By nature, God is present and active in His creation. He works in our lives to the extent that we have faith in Him. Therefore, try to prevent and eliminate potential obstacles to faith, such as pride, attachments, apathy, and fear. Know that our faith will be tested if we are to advance, but always remember that the Father is pleased to give His children the kingdom of heaven.
3. *Love of God*. The greatest commandment is to love God with all our heart, soul, mind, and strength. We strive to do this by purifying our hearts and our intentions and doing everything well for the glory of God. Life is too short, and we can never love God enough; therefore, we must always seek to do that which is most pleasing to God.
4. *Union with God*. Cultivate recollection and oneness with the Lord at all times. Be attentive to the indwelling of the Holy Trinity in your soul, and spend time growing in relationship with each of the three Divine Persons. Live

in the present moment of God's love, and do everything in union with Him.

5. *Gratitude and praise.* Keeping in mind that God is the source of all that is good, we reflect often on our blessings and give the Lord thanks and praise for His boundless generosity and infinite goodness.
6. *Joy in the Lord.* We are joyful in the Lord because we know Him and His love for us. We strive to live in the peace of Christ and share it with others. In this way, we become pleasing to God, bear witness to Christ, and lift up others.
7. *Docility to God's will.* Knowing that God desires what is best for us, we seek to discern and follow God's will for our lives. To love God is to do His will in all things. We discern His will in important matters and follow the inspirations of the Holy Spirit.
8. *Love of neighbor.* We love everyone because of our love for God and because we are all His children. To love our neighbor is to desire his or her greatest good, which is to live out his or her vocation to holiness, service, and intimacy with the Lord. We love God and our neighbor by using our gifts and talents for the Lord's glory and for the benefit of others. We do not judge others but forgive them, knowing that we are all human.
9. *Abandonment to divine providence.* Know that nothing happens without God's permission and that He allows only what will bring about a greater good. Therefore, we surrender to all that happens, knowing that even suffering is given to us out of love. Uniting our trials with those of Jesus, we rely on His grace and share in His work of redemption for the expiation of sins and our purification.

10. *Mortification.* Cultivate a spirit of asceticism and practice regular self-denial to develop self-control over the desires of the flesh. This is necessary for us to achieve true freedom to know and choose that which is most pleasing to God. In practicing mortification, we further unite and conform ourselves to the Lord.
11. *Desire and efforts to grow in holiness.* We cultivate holy desires and make efforts to grow in holiness, knowing that sanctity is a lifelong process and that there are no shortcuts. We rely on God's grace and respond generously for our good, the glory of God, and the good of the Church.
12. *Sacraments.* Knowing that the sacraments are given to us by Jesus to communicate His grace, we receive the Holy Eucharist and attend Confession frequently and with the best possible disposition. We also spend time with Our Lord in the Blessed Sacrament, with faith in His presence, love, and power.

It is important to know ourselves in light of these qualities, especially those that we most lack, so that we may focus on and strengthen our weaknesses with God's help. Only by keen desire and persistent practice will these dispositions become more automatic. Our goal is to embody these universal qualities of Mary and the saints to the point that they become second nature, a permanent habit and disposition. But know that this is a lifelong process and that we will fall. Nevertheless, we get right back up, trusting in the Lord's mercy and relying on His love.

Unique Role of Mary

Hopefully, you now understand better the role of Mary in God's plan of salvation. In His infinite wisdom, God has included a feminine role in His work of redemption. He has entrusted this role to Mary. The Church tells us, "Just as a woman had a share in bringing about death, so also a woman should contribute to life."[168] At the Annunciation, the angel Gabriel announced to Mary that she had been selected by God to be the Mother of Jesus, the Messiah and the Son of God.

As the Mother of God, Mary must have been preserved from all sin from the moment of her conception. This was due to the grace that Christ obtained by His suffering, death, and Resurrection. This grace is called a *prevenient grace* because it was applied beforehand to Mary to keep her pure and sinless. Indeed, the Mother of God needed to be without stain or defilement because the Son of God was to live in her womb for nine months and receive His entire humanity from her: His flesh, bones, and DNA. Without Mary, there would be no Jesus. There would be the Word who is from the Father from the beginning, but without Mary's *fiat*, there would be no Incarnation of the Word. Additionally, just as Mary contributed to the Incarnation, as *Lumen Gentium* tells us, so too did she contribute to Christ's work of redemption by participating in His suffering in a radical way. We suffer because we have sinned. Mary never sinned, and yet she suffered more than most of us will ever suffer.

Mary is not only the Mother of Jesus but also our Mother. Mary was Jesus' last gift to us while He was on earth. Before He died on the Cross, Jesus gave Mary to St. John to be his mother, and St. John to Mary to be her son. St. John represents all of us; therefore, Jesus' last command to all of us is "Behold, your mother!" (John 19:27). Jesus knows how much we need Mary to help us, to intercede for us, and to be a model for us. By not accepting Mary, we are rejecting Jesus' gift and His command to take Mary as our Mother.

[168] Vatican Council II, Dogmatic Constitution on the Church *Lumen Gentium* (November 21, 1964), no. 56.

Why would we prefer to go it alone when Jesus has given us His own Mother to help us? Unfortunately, many Christians do not fully understand the role that God has intended for Mary in the work of salvation, and many do not have a devotion to our Blessed Mother. Some people see Mary as unnecessary or even as an obstacle to our relationship with Christ. But nothing could be further from the truth.

Devotion to Our Blessed Mother

Below are some of the many reasons we should have a devotion to our Blessed Mother.

God the Father wants us to contemplate Mary, who is His most perfect creature, His masterpiece. Therefore, God wants us to honor Mary and marvel at her qualities, which reflect God's own goodness, wisdom, and generosity. The Father wants us to see Mary as the creature that most closely resembles His Son, and to take her as our model. Mary does not want attention for herself but ultimately directs our attention to the Lord, who has done great things for her. She does not lead us away from God but brings us closer to Him by revealing God's goodness to her and all of creation. Mary takes nothing from God but lives to praise and glorify the Father in all that she does. When we venerate, honor, and love Mary, we praise, honor, and love God Himself in His wondrous creation of our Blessed Mother.

Jesus wants us to imitate Him in loving and honoring His Mother. To love Jesus is to love His Mother too. While on earth, Jesus loved, obeyed, and honored Mary (see Luke 2:51), and He wants us to do the same. Indeed, we are called to conform ourselves to Jesus in all things, including loving and honoring His Mother the way He did. No one was closer to Jesus than Mary was: no one knows Jesus better than she, no one loves Jesus more than she, and no one served Jesus more perfectly than she. And our Blessed Mother wants to share with us all her secrets to knowing Jesus intimately, loving Him ardently, and serving Him faithfully.

The Holy Spirit wants us to honor His Spouse, who is His most perfect temple. The Holy Spirit is free to live and act in and through Mary as He pleases, without any resistance. Mary cooperates flawlessly with the Holy Spirit. The Holy Spirit wants us to look to Mary as the epitome of what it means to be His temple. Mary wants to teach us how to let the Holy Spirit take over our lives and transform us into His works of art. Our Mother wants to help her children know the Person and workings of the Holy Spirit, to be completely docile to His inspirations, and to surrender entirely to His actions.

Mary loves and wants to help us—she takes her responsibilities as our Mother seriously. Mary fulfilled her role as the Mother of Jesus flawlessly, and she wants to fulfill her role as our Mother as well. Mary naturally cares for her children and wants what is best for them. The wedding feast at Cana (John 2:1–11) shows that Mary is attentive to our needs and intercedes on our behalf with Jesus, who never refuses His Mother. Therefore, Mary wants to have a relationship with each of us, so that she can more readily guide and help us.

Mary leads us to the Holy Trinity. She wants to bring all her children to the Father, Son, and Holy Spirit. She wants our greatest happiness, which is to fulfill God's will for us and become holy and perfect in His sight. Mary does not want anything for herself. She uses our relationship with and love for her to lead us to God and to perfection. Mary wants us to know her and imitate her in loving, pleasing, and glorifying God in all things. There is no competition between Mary and God; there is no contradiction between devotion to our Blessed Mother and faithfulness to the Lord. The Lord wants us to honor Mary, and she in turn wants us to love and serve the Lord.

Mary can act as a bridge to Jesus, the Father, and the Holy Spirit. At the beginning of my conversion, I was very drawn to Mary. I loved looking at images of her and reading about her, and I felt her closeness. Soon enough, she led me more fully to her Son, then to the Father, and finally to the Holy Spirit. Mary can act as a conduit to the Persons of the Holy Trinity. She does not simply want to lead us to herself but to the source of all goodness, beauty, and truth—the Most Holy Trinity.

Thanks to Mary's Assumption, we have a Mother who goes before us to heaven to intercede for and guide her children to follow her. Mary's Assumption gives us hope, direction, and confidence. As our Mother, the Blessed Virgin loves us and wants us to be with her and with God for all eternity. Having shown us the way to eternal bliss by her own life, and now being in heaven with the Lord, Mary is able to do more to help her children achieve the beatific vision.

By being in heaven, Mary has the ability to be with us all, even now. In fact, Mary reveals that she is always with us. For example, Mary told St. Juan Diego: "Do not be troubled or weighed down with grief. Do not fear any illness or vexation, anxiety or pain. Am I not here who am your Mother? Are you not under my shadow of my protection? Am I not the fountain of life? Are you not in the folds of my mantle? In the crossing of my arms?"[169] Mary is truly with us to protect us and give us strength and encouragement to do God's will.

In the movie *The Passion of the Christ*, there is a scene where Jesus is carrying His Cross to Calvary, and St. John and Mary are nearby. St. John asks Mary if she wants to see Jesus, and then leads her to a place where she sees Jesus carrying His Cross and falling

[169] Mirabai Starr, ed., *Our Lady of Guadalupe: Devotions, Prayers and Living Wisdom* (Boulder, CO: Sounds True, 2008), 52.

to the ground. The scene flashes back to a memory that Mary has of Jesus as a child. He is playing and running, but then He trips and falls. Mary immediately drops everything and runs to her Son, picks Him up, and tells Him, "I am here." Jesus is comforted and consoled by His Mother's presence. The scene then switches back to the present, and Mary decides to run to Jesus, who is on the ground beneath the Cross. When she reaches Him, she says, "I am here." Jesus looks up at His Mother, regains His strength, and says to her, "See, Mother, I make all things new." Jesus then gets up, shoulders His Cross, and continues to make His way to Calvary. Mary's maternal presence gave Jesus comfort and encouragement in fulfilling God's plan; likewise, Mary's presence can give us the comfort and support we need to persevere in carrying out God's will in our lives.

As weak, vulnerable, inadequate, and fallen human beings, we need all the help we can get. Jesus knows that we need Mary; therefore, He has given her to us to be our Mother and to help lead us to heaven. As I was going through my conversion and vocational discernment, I felt that Mary was very close to me. I had never had a devotion to Our Lady before. But then, I was reintroduced to the Rosary, and I felt an overwhelming attraction to our Blessed Mother.

During this time, I attended a Cursillo weekend retreat where Mary's presence and influence were especially strong. I remember admiring an image of Our Lady of Guadalupe and being drawn to Mary's *fiat*—"Behold, I am the handmaid of the Lord; let it be to me according to your word"—which was printed out and taped on the wall along with many other passages from Scripture. I felt that our Mother was telling me to make her *fiat* my own and to say yes to the Lord as she did. To this day, I know that Mary is always with me, guiding and helping me to be faithful to Jesus.

Being so close to God in every way, our Mother is a powerful intercessor with the Holy Trinity. As the most perfect daughter of the Father, the Spouse of the Holy Spirit, and the Mother of Jesus, Mary has a lot of influence with God. She is in the "inner circle," if you will. Mary's will is always in perfect harmony with God's will. The Persons of the Holy Trinity will give her whatever she asks for. We all ask people to pray for us, which is good. But why not ask the one who is most pleasing to and connected with the Persons of the Holy Trinity?

All the saints were devoted to our Blessed Mother. Like Mary, the saints show us the way to God. When we examine the lives and writings of the saints, we see that none of them rejected Mary; on the contrary, all the saints, in one way or another, had a strong devotion and love for Our Lady. St. Faustina encourages us, "Nothing is too much when it comes to honoring the Immaculate Virgin."[170] Similarly, St. Thérèse of Lisieux writes: "Do not be afraid of loving the Blessed Virgin too much. You can never love her enough. And Jesus will be very happy, because the Blessed Virgin is His Mother."[171] We can learn much from the saints' understanding of and relationship with our Blessed Mother.

Some people have difficulty growing close to Mary because they did not have a good mother figure. The idea of a mother does not bring them comfort and strength but pain, distrust, or fear. But Mary is different from the mother figures in our lives. Earthly mothers are wounded and imperfect by definition. In Mary, God wants us to have a Mother we can trust, look up to, and rely on—one who is perfect, loves us, wants our greatest happiness, and knows how to lead us there.

[170] *Diary*, no. 1413.

[171] Thérèse of Lisieux, quoted in Donald H. Calloway, MIC, *Under the Mantle: Marian Thoughts from a 21st Century Priest* (Stockbridge, MA: Marian Press, 2013), 20.

The Imitation of Mary

The following are some suggestions on how to cultivate a devotion to our Blessed Mother:

1. Find your favorite images of Mary and display them in prominent places in your home and place of work. Seeing beautiful images of Mary throughout the day will remind you of our Blessed Mother, God's precious gift who loves and helps us.
2. Learn to pray the Rosary, through which we pray with Mary as we reflect on her life, the life of her Son, and the events of the New Testament. The Rosary is biblical; the mysteries on which we meditate are found in Scripture, as well as Tradition. St. John Paul II says that the Rosary is Christocentric, or Christ-centered: not only do we meditate on the life of Jesus but also, at the center of every Hail Mary, we pray the name of Jesus. We can pray the Rosary anywhere and at any time: while driving, on a walk, or in bed.
3. Read books on our Blessed Mother. There are many good books written about Our Lady. The more we read and learn about Mary, the more we will fall in love with her. Also, read the lives of the saints and reflect on their devotion to the Blessed Virgin.
4. Make a consecration to Jesus through Mary. There are numerous guides we can use to consecrate ourselves and all that we have to Jesus through our Blessed Mother. By doing so, we entrust ourselves and all that we have to Mary—knowing that she will intercede for us and guide us to Jesus.
5. Explore the different Marian devotions, such as the Miraculous Medal, the Brown Scapular, and Our Lady of Perpetual Help.

6. Learn and pray the different prayers to Mary, such as the Angelus, the Hail Holy Queen, and the Memorare.
7. Make a pilgrimage to Marian shrines, such as Fatima, Lourdes, and Tepeyac.

Run as to Win

I thank you for having read this book, and I hope and pray that it has helped you to have a better understanding of what holiness looks like and how to apply it to your life. This includes developing or increasing your awareness of and appreciation for supernatural realities, especially grace; having a better understanding of, appreciation for, and devotion to our Blessed Mother; reprioritizing and confirming the values that are most important to you; and seeing the unity between Sacred Scripture, the words of the saints, and the teachings of the Church when it comes to the virtues and practices that are essential to the spiritual life.

Remember that this is not just about us—by becoming holy, we contribute to the goodness of the Body of Christ and build up God's kingdom on earth. St. Catherine of Siena remarked, "If you are what you should be, you will set the whole world ablaze!"[172] Remember, your life is not your own; it has been purchased by the blood of the Lamb. We owe it not only to ourselves but to God and all of creation to be holy and to set the world ablaze. Our life is short, and we do not know when it will end; therefore, make a difference now. Do not put off holiness, because you do not know when your time will come.

[172] St. Catherine of Siena, Letter 368 to Stefano Maconi, quoted in Pope John Paul II, Homily for the Closing of World Youth Day, August 20, 2000, http://w2.vatican.va/content/john-paul-ii/en/homilies/2000/documents/hf_jp-ii_hom_20000820_gmg.html.

Holiness is not a choice but a command: "Be holy, for I your God am holy" (see Lev. 19:2; 1 Pet. 1:16). Mother Teresa explains: "Holiness is not the luxury of the few. It is a simple duty for you and me."[173] When sports teams compete in the playoffs or in the championship game, the players tell themselves to "leave it all on the field," meaning that they intend to go all out and try their best, holding nothing back. If they lose, they know that they gave it their all, and they have no regrets. I would propose the same mindset for us—knowing that this life is the one shot we have, and there are no second chances. Let us, then, do our best, holding nothing back but leaving it all on the field of life. At the end of our pilgrimage, we will know that we gave it our all and will have no regrets. St. Paul, who loves athletic analogies, reminds us to strive for the prize (Phil. 3:14), fight the good fight (1 Tim. 6:12), and run so as to win (1 Cor. 9:24).

Jesus, Mary, and the saints lived this way. As He was about to die, Jesus said, "It is finished" (John 19:30), meaning "it is accomplished." Jesus came to fulfill His mission, and He did so perfectly—giving everything that He had out of love for the Father and for us. At the end of his life, St. Paul expressed the same sentiment: "For I am already on the point of being sacrificed; the time for my departure has come. I have fought the good fight, I have finished the race, I have kept the faith. From now on there is laid up for me the crown of righteousness, which the Lord, the righteous judge, will award to me on that Day, and not only to me but also to all who have loved his appearing" (2 Tim. 4:6–8). St. Paul leaves us an example and encourages us likewise to fight the good fight, finish the race, and keep the faith.

Let us pray with Mary to the Holy Spirit to pour out His graces upon us, our families and friends, the whole Church, and the world,

[173] Mother Teresa, *Where There Is Love, There Is God*, 293.

so that our hearts may be set aflame with the fire of God's love as we strive to imitate the qualities of our Blessed Mother; and so that we may be transformed into Christ for the glory of the Father and the salvation of souls.

Practical Suggestions

1. Keep with you a list of the twelve qualities of Mary to help you reflect on and implement them in your daily life.
2. Imagine that you are on your deathbed. What changes do you wish you would have made? Make them now.
3. Pray the Fullness of Grace prayer daily: "We give you thanks and praise, eternal Father, for all your goodness, especially for giving us Mary as our Mother and model. Help us to imitate her qualities so as to grow in the fullness of grace. Lord Jesus Christ, be with us always and help us to conform ourselves to you and be one with you at all times. Come, Holy Spirit, enkindle in us the fire of your love, and transform us into your instruments of grace. O Mary, our Queen and Mother, help us to become more like you and fulfill our vocation perfectly according to God's holy will. We ask all this through Christ Our Lord. Amen. All angels and saints, pray for us."
4. Visit Fullness of Grace online at www.fullnessofgrace.org and on social media at https://youtube.com/c/fullnessofgrace, https://www.facebook.com/fullofgrace, and https://www.instagram.com/fullnessofgrace/.
5. Listen to the Fullness of Grace podcast at https://www.fullnessofgrace.org/podcasts.
6. Start a Fullness of Grace prayer group to pray about and discuss this book.

Bibliography

Alighieri, Dante. *Paradiso*. In *The Divine Comedy: Inferno, Purgatorio, Paradiso*. Translated by Allen Mandelbaum. New York: Alfred A. Knopf, 1995.

Alphonsus Maria de Liguori. *The Glories of Mary: A New Translation from the Italian*. Liguori, MO: Liguori Publications, 2000.

"Americans check their phones 80 times a day: study." *New York Post*, November 8, 2017. https://nypost.com/2017/11/08/americans-check-their-phones-80-times-a-day-study.

Aquinas, Thomas. *Summa Theologica*. 5 vols. Translated by the Fathers of the English Dominican Province. Grand Rapids, MI: Christian Classics, 1981.

Augustine. *Confessions of Saint Augustine*. Uhrichsville, OH: Barbour Publishing, 2013.

———. *The Works of Saint Augustine: A Translation for the 21st Century, Part II—Letters*. Edited by Boniface Ramsey. Translated with notes by Roland Teske, S.J. Vol. 7, *Letters 100–155*. Hyde Park, NY: New City Press, 2003.

———. *The Works of Saint Augustine: A Translation for the 21st Century, Part III—Sermons*. Edited by John E. Rotelle, O.S.A. Translated with notes by Edmund Hill, O.P. Vol. 5, *Sermons 151–183*. Hyde Park, NY: New City Press, 2018.

Bacovcin, Helen, trans. *The Way of the Pilgrim and the Pilgrim Continues His Way*. New York: Doubleday, 2003.

Baker, Kenneth. *The Will of God: Finding and Fulfilling Your Purpose in Life*. San Francisco: Ignatius Press, 2012.

Benedict XVI, Pope. Encyclical Letter on Christian Love *Deus Caritas Est* (December 25, 2005).

———. Homily for the Easter Vigil, April 7, 2012. http://www.vatican.va/content/benedict-xvi/en/homilies/2012/documents/hf_ben-xvi_hom_20120407_veglia-pasquale.html.

Benedictine Monk. *In Sinu Jesu: When Heart Speaks to Heart—The Journal of a Priest at Prayer*. Kettering, OH: Angelico Press, 2016.

Bloy, Leon. *The Pilgrim of the Absolute: A Selection of His Writings*. With an introduction by Jacques Maritain. Edited by Raissa Maritain. Translated by John Coleman and Harry Lorin Binsse. Tacoma, WA: Cluny Media, 2017.

Bossis, Gabrielle. *He and I*. Translated and condensed by Evelyn M. Brown. Sherbrooke, QC: Médiaspaul, 1985.

Brother Lawrence. *The Practice of the Presence of God*. New Kensington, PA: Whitaker House, 1982.

Brown, Raphael, comp. *The Life of Mary as Seen by the Mystics*. 1951. Reprint, Charlotte, NC: TAN Books, 2012.

Buttrick, George, ed. *The Interpreter's Dictionary of the Bible*. Vol. 2, *E–J*. Nashville: Abingdon Press, 1962.

Calloway, Donald H., MIC. *Purest of All Lilies: The Virgin Mary in the Spirituality of St. Faustina*. Stockbridge, MA: Marian Press, 2015.

———. *Under the Mantle: Marian Thoughts from a 21st Century Priest*. Stockbridge, MA: Marian Press, 2013.

Caso-Rosendi, Carlos. *Guadalupe: A River of Light: The Story of Our Lady of Guadalupe from the First Century to Our Days*. Edited by Patricia Stafford. Front Royal, VA: First Light Press, 2017.

Catechism of the Catholic Church. 2nd ed. Washington, DC: Libreria Editrice Vaticana–United States Conference of Catholic Bishops, 2000.

Catherine of Siena. *The Dialogue*. Translated with an introduction by Suzanne Noffke, O.P. The Classics of Western Spirituality. Mahwah, NJ: Paulist Press, 1980.

———. *The Letters of St. Catherine of Siena*. Vol. 1. Edited and translated by Suzanne Noffke, O.P. Tempe, AZ: ACMRS Press, 2001.

Chautard, Jean-Baptiste, O.C.S.O. *The Soul of the Apostolate*. Translated by a Monk of Our Lady of Gethsemani. Trappist, KY: Abbey of Gethsemani, 1946.

Chesterton, G. K. *Orthodoxy*. 1908. Converted to digital format by Digireads.com Publishing, 2018.

de Caussade, Jean-Pierre, S.J. *Self-Abandonment to Divine Providence*. Rockford, IL: TAN Books and Publishers, 1987.

de Marchi, John, I.M.C. *Fatima: From the Beginning*. Translated by I. M. Kingsbury. Fatima, Portugal: Missões Consolata, 2008.

de Sales, Francis. *Finding God's Will for You*. Manchester, NH: Sophia Institute Press, 1998.

———. *Introduction to the Devout Life*. New York: Vintage Books, 2002.

Dolan, Timothy Cardinal. *Priests for the Third Millennium*. Huntington, IN: Our Sunday Visitor, 2000.

Driscoll, Jeremy, OSB. *What Happens at Mass*. Chicago: Liturgy Training Publications, 2005.

Elizabeth of the Trinity. *Always Believe in Love*. Edited by Marian T. Murphy, O.C.D. Hyde Park, NY: New City Press, 2009.

Faber, Frederick. *The Little Book of Holy Gratitude: Compiled from the Works of Fr. Frederick Faber*. Manchester, NH: Sophia Institute Press, 2016.

Francis, Pope. Apostolic Exhortation on the Proclamation of the Gospel in Today's World *Evangelii Gaudium* (November 24, 2013).

———. Encyclical Letter on Care for our Common Home *Laudato Si'* (May 24, 2015).

Freeman, David, ed. *The Anchor Bible*. Vol. 6, *Si–Z*. New York: Doubleday, 1992.

Gadenz, Pablo. *The Gospel of Luke*. Catholic Commentary on Sacred Scripture. Grand Rapids, MI: Baker Academic, 2018.

Gallagher, Timothy, OMV. *Discerning the Will of God: The Ignatian Guide to Christian Decision Making*. Chestnut Ridge, NY: Crossroad Publishing, 2018.

———. *The Discernment of Spirits: An Ignatian Guide for Everyday Living*. Chestnut Ridge, NY: Crossroad Publishing, 2005.

Garrigou-Lagrange, Reginald, O.P. *Christian Perfection and Contemplation: According to St. Thomas Aquinas and St. John of the Cross*. Translated by Sr. M. Timothea Doyle, O.P. Charlotte, NC: TAN Books, 2010.

———. *The Three Ages of the Interior Life: Prelude of Eternal Life*. 2 vols. Translated by Sr. M. Timothea Doyle, O.P. Rockford, IL: TAN Books and Publishers, 1989.

Hahn, Scott. *The Lamb's Supper: The Mass as Heaven on Earth*. New York: Doubleday, 2017.

Healy, Mary. *Healing: Bringing the Gift of God's Mercy to the World*. Huntington, IN: Our Sunday Visitor, 2015.

———. *The Gospel of Mark*. Catholic Commentary on Sacred Scripture. Grand Rapids, MI: Baker Academic, 2008.

Hesemann, Michael. *Mary of Nazareth: History, Archeology, Legends*. Translated by Michael Miller. San Francisco: Ignatius Press, 2016.

John of the Cross. *Ascent of Mount Carmel*. Edited and modernized by Henry L. Carrigan Jr. Brewster, MA: Paraclete Press, 2002.

———. *The Collected Works of St. John of the Cross*. Translated by Kieran Kavanaugh, O.C.D., and Otilio Rodriguez, O.C.D. Washington, DC: ICS Publications, 2017.

John Paul II, Pope. Angelus, Apostolic Journey to the Far East and Oceania, November 30, 1986. http://www.vatican.va/content/john-paul-ii/en/angelus/1986/documents/hf_jp-ii_ang_19861130.html.

———. *Crossing the Threshold of Hope*. Edited by Vittorio Messori. New York: Alfred A. Knopf, 1994.

———. *In My Own Words*. Compiled and edited by Anthony F. Chiffolo. Liguori, MO: Liguori Publications, 2005.

Kowalska, Maria Faustina. *Diary: Divine Mercy in My Soul*. 3rd rev. ed. Stockbridge, MA: Marian Press, 2014.

Kreeft, Peter. *Fundamentals of the Faith: Essays in Christian Apologetics*. San Francisco: Ignatius Press, 1988.

———. *How to be Holy: First Steps in Becoming a Saint—A Festooning of Abandonment to Divine Providence*. San Francisco: Ignatius Press, 2016.

Leamy, Katy. *The Holy Trinity: Hans Urs von Balthasar and His Sources*. Eugene, OR: Pickwick Publications, 2015.

Lewis, C. S. *The Weight of Glory and Other Addresses*. New York: HarperCollins, 2001.

Marmion, Columba. *Union with God: Letters of Spiritual Direction*. Selected and annotated by Dom Raymond Thibaut. Translated by Mary St. Thomas. Bethesda, MD: Zaccheus Press, 2006.

Martin, Francis, and William Wright IV. *The Gospel of John*. Catholic Commentary on Sacred Scripture. Grand Rapids, MI: Baker Academic, 2015.

Martinez, Luis. *True Devotion to the Holy Spirit*. Manchester, NH: Sophia Institute Press, 2000.

Mary Day by Day: Marian Meditations for Every Day Taken from the Holy Bible and the Writings of the Saints. With an introduction by Rev. Charles G. Fehrenbach, C.Ss.R. Totowa, NJ: Catholic Book Publishing, 1987.

Mitch, Curtis, and Edward Sri. *The Gospel of Matthew*. Catholic Commentary on Sacred Scripture. Grand Rapids, MI: Baker Academic, 2010.

Montague, George T., SM. *First Corinthians*. Catholic Commentary on Sacred Scripture. Grand Rapids, MI: Baker Academic, 2011.

———. *Mary's Life in the Spirit: Meditations on a Holy Duet*. Frederick, MD: Word Among Us Press, 2011.

Mother Teresa. *Mother Teresa: Her Essential Wisdom*. Edited by Carol Kelly-Gangi. New York: Fall River Press, 2006.

———. *No Greater Love*. Edited by Becky Benenate and Joseph Durepos. Novato, CA: New World Library, 1989.

———. *Thirsting for God: A Yearbook of Prayers, Meditations and Anecdotes*. Cincinnati, OH: St. Anthony Messenger Press, 2000.

———. *Where There Is Love, There Is God*. Edited by Brian Kolodiejchuk, M.C. New York: Doubleday Religion, 2010.

Murray, Paul, O.P. *I Loved Jesus in the Night: Teresa of Calcutta—A Secret Revealed*. Brewster, MA: Paraclete Press, 2008.

Nouwen, Henri J. M. *Finding My Way Home: Pathways to Life and the Spirit*. Chestnut Ridge, NY: Crossroad Publishing, 2018.

———. *The Return of the Prodigal Son*. New York: Doubleday, 1992.

Orti, Vicente Carcel. "Pope John Paul II's teaching on the martyrs of our century." *Tertium Millennium*, March 1997. http://www.vatican.va/jubilee_2000/magazine/documents/ju_mag_01031997_p-56_en.html.

Pascal, Blaise. *Pensées*. Translated by W. F. Trotter. Dover Philosophical Classics. Mineola, NY: Dover Publications, 2003.

Paul VI, Pope. Apostolic Exhortation on Christian Joy *Gaudete in Domino* (May 9, 1975).

Philipon, M. M., O.P., ed. *Conchita: A Mother's Spiritual Diary*. Translated by Aloysius J. Owen, S.J. New York: Alba House, 2009.

Philippe, Jacques. *Searching for and Maintaining Peace: A Small Treatise on Peace of the Heart*. Translated by George and Jannic Driscoll. Staten Island, NY: Alba House, 2002.

Pius XI, Pope. Encyclical Letter on Christian Marriage *Casti Connubii* (December 31, 1930).

Preiss, John C. *The Miracle and the Message: 100 Years of Fatima*. Huntington, IN: Our Sunday Visitor, 2017.

Puhl, Louis J., S.J., trans. *The Spiritual Exercises of St. Ignatius: Based on Studies in the Language of the Autograph*. Chicago: Loyola Press, 1951.

Ratzinger, Joseph Cardinal. *Called to Communion: Understanding the Church Today*. Translated by Adrian Walker. San Francisco: Ignatius Press, 1996.

———. *Fundamental Speeches from Five Decades*. Edited by Florian Schuller and translated by Adrian Walker. San Francisco: Ignatius Press, 2012.

———. *The God of Jesus Christ: Meditations on the Triune God*. Translated by Brian McNeil. San Francisco: Ignatius Press, 2008.

———. *The Spirit of the Liturgy*. Translated by John Saward. San Francisco: Ignatius Press, 2000.

Raymond of Capua. *The Life of St. Catherine of Siena: The Classic on Her Life and Accomplishments as Recorded by Her Spiritual Director*. Translated by George Lamb. Charlotte, NC: TAN Books, 2003.

Roman Missal: English Translation According to the Third Typical Edition. Totowa, NJ: Catholic Book Publishing, 2011.

Scanlan, Michael, T.O.R., with James Manney. *What Does God Want?* Huntington, IN: Our Sunday Visitor, 1996.

Spitzer, Robert. *Finding True Happiness: Satisfying Our Restless Hearts*. San Francisco: Ignatius Press, 2015.

———. *God So Loved the World: Clues to Our Transcendent Destiny from the Revelation of Jesus*. San Francisco: Ignatius Press, 2016.

———. *The Light Shines On in the Darkness: Transforming Suffering through Faith*. San Francisco: Ignatius Press, 2017.

Starr, Mirabai, ed. *Our Lady of Guadalupe: Devotions, Prayers and Living Wisdom*. Boulder, CO: Sounds True, 2008.

Stuhlmueller, Carroll, ed. *The Collegeville Pastoral Dictionary of Biblical Theology*. Collegeville, MN: Liturgical Press, 1996.

Teresa of Ávila. *Interior Castle*. Translated and edited by E. Allison Peers. Mineola, NY: Dover Publications, 2007.

———. *The Way of Perfection*. Translated and edited by E. Allison Peers. New York: Random House, 2004.

Therese of Lisieux. *St. Thérèse of Lisieux: Her Last Conversations*. Translated by John Clarke, O.C.D. Washington DC: ICS Publications, 1977.

———. *The Prayers of Saint Therese of Lisieux: The Act of Oblation*. Translated by Aletheia Kane, O.C.D. Washington, DC: ICS Publications, 1997.

———. *The Story of a Soul: The Autobiography of St. Thérèse of Lisieux*. Translated by John Clarke, O.C.D. Washington, DC: ICS Publications, 1996.

Tugwell, Simon, O.P. *Prayer in Practice*. Springfield, IL: Templegate Publishers, 1974.

———. *Prayer: Living with God*. Springfield, IL: Templegate Publishers, 1975.

Vatican Council II. Constitution on the Sacred Liturgy *Sacrosanctum Concilium* (December 4, 1963).

———. Dogmatic Constitution on the Church *Lumen Gentium* (November 21, 1964).

———. Pastoral Constitution on the Church *Gaudium et Spes* (December 7, 1965).

Visions of Purgatory: A Private Revelation. New Rochelle, NY: Scepter Publishers, 2014.

Vonier, Abbot. *The Human Soul*. Bethesda, MD: Zaccheus Press, 2010.

About the Author

Fr. Quan Tran is a priest in the Diocese of Orange in California and is currently assigned to St. Bonaventure Church in Huntington Beach. Prior to entering the seminary, he worked as a deputy district attorney for Orange County for ten years and a deputy public defender for Kern County for two years. After receiving his bachelor of business administration from Baruch College (part of the City University of New York system), he graduated from Pepperdine University School of Law with a juris doctor.

For his seminary training, Fr. Tran attended the Pontifical North American College in Rome, while earning a bachelor of sacred theology and a licentiate in sacred theology from the Pontifical University of St. Thomas Aquinas, also known as the Angelicum.

In 2017, Father started his Fullness of Grace ministry to help Christians grow in their faith by forming a deep spiritual life in which they live out their vocations to holiness, intimacy with God, and bearing witness to Christ. You can learn more at www.fullnessofgrace.org.

Besides offering talks, retreats, and spiritual direction, Father enjoys going for walks, exploring different cuisines, and contemplating the beauty of nature.

Sophia Institute

Sophia Institute is a nonprofit institution that seeks to nurture the spiritual, moral, and cultural life of souls and to spread the Gospel of Christ in conformity with the authentic teachings of the Roman Catholic Church.

Sophia Institute Press fulfills this mission by offering translations, reprints, and new publications that afford readers a rich source of the enduring wisdom of mankind.

Sophia Institute also operates the popular online resource CatholicExchange.com. *Catholic Exchange* provides world news from a Catholic perspective as well as daily devotionals and articles that will help readers to grow in holiness and live a life consistent with the teachings of the Church.

In 2013, Sophia Institute launched Sophia Institute for Teachers to renew and rebuild Catholic culture through service to Catholic education. With the goal of nurturing the spiritual, moral, and cultural life of souls, and an abiding respect for the role and work of teachers, we strive to provide materials and programs that are at once enlightening to the mind and ennobling to the heart; faithful and complete, as well as useful and practical.

Sophia Institute gratefully recognizes the Solidarity Association for preserving and encouraging the growth of our apostolate over the course of many years. Without their generous and timely support, this book would not be in your hands.

www.SophiaInstitute.com
www.CatholicExchange.com
www.SophiaInstituteforTeachers.org